S0-BBY-621

CHILD-CENTERED GROUP GUIDANCE
OF PARENTS

CHILD-CENTERED GROUP GUIDANCE OF PARENTS

S. R. SLAVSON

International Universities Press, Inc.

NEW YORK

Copyright 1958, by International Universities Press, Inc.

Library of Congress Catalog Card Number: 58:11380

Manufactured in the United States of America

Contents

Contents

Introduction

It has been my privilege in the past decades to till the soil in many fields of our social scene some of which included engineering, business, childhood education, research, group work, labor organization and education, journalism, university teaching and lecturing, politics, social service, community organization and finally group psychotherapy. None of these, however, seems to me as valuable and as promising for human welfare and happiness as the enterprise with which the present volume deals. While the actual process is, admittedly, not as stirring to the imagination or exciting to the intellect as some of the others had been, its value to the enhancement of human happiness amply compensates for the lower poignancy and excitement. For, after all is said and done, the most worth-while of all efforts is that which directs itself toward the prevention and reduction of human suffering. And what better way is there, short of social and economic change, to achieve this aim than providing *children* with a healthy childhood? And how can one be assured of success in this without creating for children tension-free homes, understanding and security, and opportunities for full growth and unfoldment?

The natural life-urge, the *élan vital,* can flourish or be stifled; it can reach full bloom or be impoverished and forever remain dormant and even die. Despite our prevalent constriction of the personality and deplorably limited vision, some among us still appreciate the rich potentials of the average human. That which is achieved by the outstanding few are beacon lights to show the way for all of us, and remind us of the possibilities that lie hidden in everyone far beyond his actual accomplishments. In many instances these may be quite different from talents and works bearing the high assessment in current values. The fact that so few have trodden the path toward the fullest self-realization and self-fulfillment has to be laid at the door of our false cultural values and rigidities, which are themselves the result of social conditions under which we live; the restricted educational procedures by means of which parents and teachers impose their limitations upon children, and the overpowering fears and anxiety to which most are subject. The influences of parents, however, at a time when children are most vulnerable and impressionable rank the highest. The prime craving of contemporary man is to be reasonably happy and to have the ability and disposition to create a favorable climate for himself and for others. In this the family is pre-eminently important.

This volume deals with a technique of helping parents through their own intellectual and emotional effort to do this to the extent that other reality factors would permit it. This is not a technique of therapy or of teaching or education or of imparting information. Rather, parents who have faced the inevitable difficulties of child rearing and parent-child tensions are helped to understand *feelingly* the plight of being a child, as well as their own as parents. They are encouraged and helped to evolve *attitudes* and take steps that decrease the unhealthy elements in the child-parent relations and to free their children toward wholesome growth and personality integration, at the same time making their own lot less fraught with hardships and guilt.

This method of parents' group discussions, while in itself in consonance with the most enlightened educational practices, is specifically characterized by the fact that emphasis is laid *exclusively* on the child, his reactions and behavior, and the meaning of these in terms of his Augian task in his strivings toward self-fulfillment. Parents are helped by special strategies as well as content of the discussions not only to "understand" but also to empathize with the childishness of children and to have faith in the ultimate outcome of the natural but guided sequences in their development.

We have made known to the profession the principles and techniques of Child-Centered Group Guidance of Parents long before the publication of this book, and I am happy to say that it has been adopted by a number of influential agencies and individuals in full or with some modifications. Among these are the Brooklyn (N.Y.) Bureau of Social Service, where it had been introduced by one of my trainees, and the Jewish Family Service of New York, after a number of conferences with me. Mr. A. D. Buckmueller has told me at the First International Congress on Group Psychotherapy held in Toronto in the summer of 1953 that he and his co-workers have modeled their work with parents in St. Louis, Missouri, on our plan.

Child-Centered Group Guidance was also presented by me at the 1951 National Conference of Parent Educators called by the Child Study Association of America, and the contents of Chapter V and the Appendix that describe how these groups can alleviate family tensions were presented at the 1953 Conference of the American Group Psychotherapy Association.

Some time after my work with groups that met in the various homes was in operation, the Child Guidance League was launched in Brooklyn, N.Y., which follows a similar plan. They conduct a number of groups that meet in the homes of the various members under the leadership of psychologists. It is with genuine pleasure that we record the change of the procedure in the training for parenthood by the influential Child Study Association of America from didactic teaching to group discussions and full participation in them by the members of its many parents' groups.

I am greatly indebted to the Jewish Board of Guardians for the opportunity to test my notions in this new field and to my colleagues Leslie Rosenthal, Etta Kolodny and Irving Mintz who, with others, have collaborated with me on this project and have cheerfully accepted supervision and training and, as a result, helped clarify the thinking on the subject at many points.

Child-Centered Group Guidance of Parents had its origin in the general community[1] and was developed and elaborated in a clinical setting but its full value and significance, in my opinion, will be realized when it is applied in the general community where it first originated. This point I elaborate somewhat in the last chapter of the book. Such a development is in a sense a reversal in the history of

[1] See Chapter I, Historic Background.

medical and mental health sciences. Communal measures for maintaining health usually stemmed from the clinic, but the practice under consideration here originated in the community, applied in a clinic, and should be returned to its service where it can be of greatest effectiveness in creating a healthy life milieu for children and adults alike.

S. R. Slavson

Croton-on-Hudson,
New York,
1958

CHILD-CENTERED GROUP GUIDANCE OF PARENTS

Historic Background

As in the case of activity group therapy, which was an accidental discovery resulting from a recreational project with maladjusted pubertal girls, Child-Centered Group Guidance of Parents also emerged from another project.

About nine years ago, three young mothers presented themselves at my office seeking advice for a group of fathers and mothers, ten couples, who had been meeting for about a year without outside leadership to discuss some of the "problems" they had all encountered in rearing their babies. The children of this group of young people were around 18 months old. They were all, except in one family, the only and first born. Since the families lived in the same housing project, the mothers met each other daily on the community playground where their babies played together. They had been guided in their discussions by a handbook on child care which was greatly in vogue at the time and had found this book helpful. As time passed, however, they discovered that many of the situations with which their offspring confronted them could not be handled in a stereotyped and "logical" manner. They also found that lacking perceptiveness in the field of child development, they were frustrated in their efforts and, in their words, "went around in circles." With a single exception, the parents were all college graduates and sufficiently influenced by the contemporary psychologic climate to recognize that they needed professional guidance and sound information. One of the distinctive features of this group was that nearly all of the fathers took a keen interest in the group and attended its meetings whenever they could free themselves from evening business engagements and a baby sitter was available. The group met in the different homes, each couple successively serving as hosts and providing soft beverages at the end of the session.

In casting around for the help and guidance they felt they needed, they were referred to me as one who could advise them where they could secure a discussion leader. As they unfolded their ideas and enumerated their needs in the interview, I was impressed with the eagerness of the very attractive and intelligent young women and the genuineness of their desire to avoid pitfalls in the rearing of their children. I told them that I would like to visit their group before recommending a suitable leader. Accordingly, I sat in at one of the sessions to observe the membership, the sincerity of their interest (for I was afraid that this may have been a socially motivated group), the level of their intellectual functioning and emotional health.

The group was in many important respects ideally suited for the project they had undertaken. Its members were young, of upper-middle social and income status, and all the men but one were in a profession. The one exception was a businessman, but he had a strong predilection for the arts, one of which he pursued as an avocation with great success. He was personally and culturally well matched with the others in the group. It was evident from the start that the participants had intellectually exhausted a great variety of topics relating to their children's behavior, but even when they agreed in theory, there was hesitancy and confusion as to what to do and how to deal with specific situations. Though a variety of suggestions and opinions were offered on every topic, helpful conclusiveness was lacking. It was clear that these young people must have been frustrated and fatigued as a result of their evenings together. They were truly "going around in circles."

The constitution of the group, their seriousness and eagerness were sufficiently enticing for me to undertake its leadership rather than turning it over to one of my associates. It was to be a new experience for me, since up to that time the bulk of my work with parents had been either in therapeutic groups or in individual therapy, or along strictly educational lines, i.e., imparting general theoretic information. In this group I saw the needs of the parents to understand and deal with *specific* situations with their babies as being paramount. They were aware of their need for information as to *how* to conduct themselves in specific and definite ways in meeting the demands and needs of their children, rather than relying on general principles. What they needed was to implement their information by appropriate performance. They were all eager not only to carry on adequately at the moment, but through their studies at college and the influence of the current "psychologic climate," they were aware of the permanent effect their treatment of the children may have on their future. This obviously frightened them a little, for while the courses they had attended at college, the books they had read and the discussions in the group had alerted them to the importance of childhood mental health, they had not acquired the techniques with which to achieve the results they sought with such eagerness.

One of the decisions I therefore made at that first contact with the group was that all talk would have to be practical: they would have to be directed away from abstractions and toward *actual situations* in their daily lives. Another decision was that the members would have to find their own solutions to "problems" and ways of dealing with them, once they understood the elements involved. Each parent's or couple's way of dealing with their child would probably be different from the others, even in the same type of situation. It became clear to me that the differences in the backgrounds and personalities of the parents and the cumulative interpersonal attitudes on the part of each couple and their child would have to be taken into account; there could be no blanket answers or standard ways of meeting even simple situations in all families. I also made up my mind that I would have to convey to the group my conviction that each could solve what he considered difficulties in his own way, with as little direction from me as possible.

What my own role was to be was not clear, but in view of my experience in education with children built on psychoanalytic understanding of personality and extensive teaching on the graduate university level through the discussion method as well as in non-academic discussion leadership with adult groups, I anticipated that this role would largely be a passive one or one of a "participant observer." This anticipation was fully realized partially due to my own disposition, my convictions as to what the educational process is and, even more important, it met with the needs of these young people.

From the very outset I turned the discussion from "bookish" subjects and generalities to actual occurrences in the homes usually during the very day of the evening on which the meetings were held. There soon was a deluge of questions relating to the members' experiences in dressing a child, feeding, sleeping schedules, use and sharing of toys and playthings, conflicts among children on the playgrounds, introduction of a baby sitter, dealing with grandparents, resistance in children to cutting hair, fears of fitting new shoes, toilet training, scheduling of the mother's time, the father's role with a small baby, and the innumerable elements and functions that seem to baffle the young inexperienced parent in the narrow confines of a city apartment and all the inherent difficulties that result from it. All questions were translated into some actual experience rather than permitting them to remain in abstract form. I would ask the parent why he asked the particular question. This would call forth a narration of the occurrence or a series of them that brought the "problem" to attention. Once a situation was described, the group was asked how they thought it could best be dealt with or what they thought the proper answer was. After this I would withdraw from the discussion. This I did by what I later termed the "dozing method." (Dozing in this instance referred to light sleep and not administering a dose of medicine.)

Since the meetings were held in a home, the members of the group sat around in a circle in the living room, which contained comfortable chairs and divans, though because of the large attendance less luxurious seating arrangements such as folding chairs were provided for some. The most comfortable upholstered armchair was always reserved for me by the hosts. It was in these relaxing circumstances that I would rest my head on my hand, shut my eyes and give every semblance of being either asleep or resting. This position was not only welcome as being restful after a strenuous day's work but was adopted to indicate to the group that they were on their own; that they could not look to me for solutions of their quandaries, or expect me to give them ready-made answers which they expected me to do. They soon became accustomed to the role I assumed and, as a result, had to make every effort to clarify by themselves, their thoughts on all questions raised by the different men and women before they would turn to me.

From time to time I would open my eyes and ask a question or make a comment at points where I felt the discussants were becoming confused, diverged from the central theme, or the participants began to show signs of frustration. After asking the question or making the statement, I would "doze off" again. After some months the group evidenced their awareness of my strategy and sometimes would pass humorous remarks about it. In fact, in the second year of the group's existence, a new member who joined it to replace one that had left the city turned to me with a question. One of the original group members told her smilingly: "Don't ask him anything. He will not answer you. You have to learn the hard way here."

At the very first session when I visited the group, one of the women stood out as the most informed on matters of child psychology and development, quoting voluminous textbook information on the subjects. In later sessions it became clear that she possessed vast information and was an avid reader in these fields. She still continued to attend numerous lectures while a member of our group. In the discussions this good woman, who had been a teacher in a private school before her marriage, dominated the scene. She had ready answers to all questions expostulating theories at great length. These were usually correct, but of little value to the now even more confused young people since theories did not help them in dealing with the situations they faced with their children. She proved a rather difficult stumbling block to the realization of my plan to help the parents toward self-direction, judgment and independence. But we had to deal with her tactfully since she was the prime mover in the group. In fact, the organization of the original group was her idea and the result of her effort. It was evident to me from her attitude that she resented, perhaps unconsciously, having to relinquish her position of leadership to me, but it was also evident that she could not be antagonized if the group was to continue.

We, therefore, at first treated her informational contributions with deference, but tactfully showed their irrelevance to the matter under discussion, and how little help they offered in dealing with children. This was accomplished through a series of questions directed at her rather than straightforward disagreement. It was months later, when I thought the group accepted me and had been convinced of my ability to help them, that I made the flat statement to the effect that parents are better off not to go to lectures on child rearing since general principles do not always apply to a specific child or a specific family and, turning to this mother, advised her not to go to lectures any more. This was done after she had taken up much of the group's time in several preceding sessions with reports of lectures she had attended. Later on, while she no longer regaled the group with the content of lectures, which I firmly believe she had quit attending, she still resorted to an enormous amount of reading, the learnings from which she narrated to the group.

At one point I stated calmly that "nothing of real significance to our lives can be learned from books."

"Nothing?" exclaimed one of the fathers, a young lawyer.

Just as calmly and with an even voice, I corrected him. "No, not nothing; but nothing of real significance. One can acquire from books much information and many interesting facts, but nothing that truly and deeply affects our lives can be learned from books. This we must acquire from experience and our own feelings and reflection." This statement seemed acceptable to all for no demurral was registered from either the men or the women present. From that time on our erudite mother never quoted a line from her reading, if she continued to indulge in it, but once she turned to the group and asked, "What is Mr. Slavson's function here if he does not answer our questions?" I smilingly said: "I am having a good time here and what's more I get paid for it."[1] Having been put in her place and forced into the appropriate role, we had no difficulty with the woman after that and she stayed on throughout the two and one half years of the group's existence and never absented herself from a session. It was this question that confirmed my earlier suspicion that she was envious of my leadership position.

---

[1] This approach is not recommended as a blanket technique, but seemed suitable in this situation.

Perhaps it would be pertinent to record that despite, or maybe because of, this woman's extensive reading, attendance at lectures and the mass of factual information on the subject of child psychology and development she had accumulated, her baby was a serious sleeping problem. The little girl presented difficulties in falling asleep and would wake up eight to ten times during the night crying. The fact that the mother was pregnant at the time and required more rest than usual created special difficulties for this family. That we were able to correct the little girl's sleeping problem may have been instrumental in her accepting our guidance relative to the limited efficacy of abstract information and theory.

It was not until some months had elapsed that she could bring herself to seek help with her difficulty. We asked her to describe details such as how the child was put to bed, in whose presence this was done, the time of the evening, the relation of bathing and retiring for the night, the child's behavior and reactions to the bathing, the father's participation, if any, the presence of fears and anxieties, and other such facts. We were unable to glean the reason for the child's restlessness from these details, however. We then asked the mother when the sleeping difficulty had originated and she said it began when the family had been in the country the preceding summer. Where had they been? She then told us they had spent the summer at her mother's country home. What were the sleeping arrangements? Well, she said, the three slept in the same room, whereas at home the child had a room of her own. In addition, the grandparents had a large family and it was often necessary for them to sleep in different rooms.

It became clear from this narration that the frequent change of rooms was the cause of the difficulty since the waking in the mornings in repeatedly unfamiliar surroundings caused anxiety in this fifteen-month-old baby. It was this anxiety that prevented her from relaxing upon going to bed and caused the fear, and her wakefulness. Despite her professional training and voluminous reading, this mother was not aware of the importance of the *security of place* to a baby and a small child.

When this became clear to the group, the question was asked what one could do to allay the already existing fear. The conclusion we arrived at was that nothing could be done directly; that the baby would finally settle down as the summer experience receded in her memory, but as the mother bedded the child down she should reassure her by saying in a soothing voice that she would wake up in her room and that her chair and teddy bear would be there and mummy and daddy would be there and they would all have breakfast. It was understood by all that severity, punishment or threat would only increase the child's anxiety. She was by now about twenty months old and could *perceive*, if not comprehend, the meaning and intent of the mother's words.

During one of our discussions, the question of crying came up for consideration and how to deal with it in a small child. We explained the naturalness of crying as a form of expressing and communicating emotions, but emphasized the harm that could result from the tension that *excessive* crying generates. At the same time the point was made that if a mother listened carefully to their quality and pitch, she could distinguish the cries of pain, fear, vocal exercise and self-indulgence and that the mother then could respond accordingly. A few months later our pedantic mother, who was now quite big with child, reported with an air of triumph and satisfaction that her little Janet, who was now about two years old, had slept through the night for more than a week. "How did this come about?" the others in the group inquired. Well, said this mother, now that she understood the reason for her Janet's reaction and that she had to wait until her daughter had forgotten her summer experience, she just waited for a chance to act. One evening when she put the child to bed and walked out of the room, the little girl began to cry, but the mother observed the weeping did not have the shrill, panicky quality of the past; her crying now was more of the "self-indulgent" kind, she said. She then returned to the girl's bedroom and told her very firmly: "Now, Janet, you go right to sleep. Mummy will not come in again if you cry. You sleep and I'll see you in the morning." Thereupon she walked out of the room, closed the door, and she had not heard from the child all that night and for ten nights thereafter.

Insight and proper training have done the trick. It was repeated occurrences such as this one that engendered confidence in us on the part of our group members and in our method.[2]

Only one other member of the group presented us with a difficulty. This was one of the fathers, who had never missed a session in the group's two and one half years' existence. The trouble he gave us was through his use of technical and psychoanalytic terminology and concepts as a result of the personal analysis he had had. Not only were these alien and in part, at least, incomprehensible to many of the participants, but his remarks had the effect of removing the discussion out of the intended orbit. This difficulty was treated by the simple device of my pretending that I did not understand what he meant or asking him to elaborate on his statements. He soon recognized my disapproval of his use of the terminology and the group very clearly saw through my strategy. Their relief at not being confused by ponderous terms was very evident and they appreciated my having checked this member's use of them.

It was at the end of the second group season and in the third that almost half of the membership was replaced by newcomers. Members terminated attendance largely because they moved to the suburbs, to other cities and one could not continue because of changes of jobs and working hours. Only one dropped out because she claimed the discussions were "confusing" her. She was one of the original three women who had come to consult me and she proved resistive in later sessions because of the group's general disapproval of her leaving her baby in the grandmother's home to excess while she "socialized." Our discussions seemed to create too much guilt in this young mother, but she was unwilling to give up the pleasure she derived from her social activities. She resolved her conflict by quitting the group in its second season, but not before she had achieved a considerable degree of understanding of her child's needs.

The shift in membership of the group had a salutary effect for us since through it we discovered that some parents could not respond to our technique. The original ten couples with whom we

---

[2] There were three other children that presented sleeping problems, each for a different reason. In all cases the parents were able to correct the difficulties after they had traced the causes through the help of the group.

For other illustrative situations from the group see pp. 37, 77-80.

started had apparently passed through a process of self-selection and elimination before so that those who remained responded favorably to the objective type of discussion we have pursued. The new members did not go through this selection process and some of them responded differently. Some insisted on having ready answers to their questions and importuned me to give instruction and advice; others seemed to have too many personality problems to assimilate the insights that were offered them in regard to their children. It was obvious that the difficulties the children presented had been in response to the parents' own neurotic needs. One of these newcomers was particularly contradictory in her attitude.

Her two-year-old boy was very hyperactive and aggressive and she kept regaling the group with his numerous antics. While she appeared to seek help with her "problems," she actually enjoyed the child's capacities to create difficulties. She saw them as "cute" and hidden behind her complaints was admiration for his cleverness and prowess. I once spent part of a day and an evening in observing the boy in his home setting, as I did in the homes of several other members of the group.[3] My suspicions were confirmed. It seemed to me that both parents, especially the mother, did everything they could to activate the boy toward the very behavior of which they complained. Both parents attended the group regularly, though for a comparatively short period, and both came to me seeking individual psychotherapy some years later.

As I gained experience with this type of group, I organized others at the Child Guidance Clinic of the Jewish Board of Guardians. Here the groups were single-sexed to prevent conflict and enmity among the couples as they discussed the daily treatment of their children. Since the caseworkers who conducted the groups had had no experience with the technique, there was always the danger of activating enmity among husbands and wives that might prove deleterious to the couple's relation. In addition, the cultural level of the clinic's clientelle and their controls were much lower than among the members of the original group. A still further deterrant to mixed groups was our awareness that the parents at the clinic were of necessity more disturbed and faced more serious prob-

3 See also p. 79.

lems since their children were older and already sufficiently maladjusted to need psychotherapy. While the work of the original group was a prophylactic effort, the clinic groups had a therapeutic aim for the children. We, therefore, decided to place fathers and mothers apart from each other.

The experiences and observations I made in the original group were translated into clinical and diagnostic terms. Special and meticulous attention was given to the selection of parents suitable for this method to which, for obvious reasons, I have given the label "Child-Centered Group Guidance of Parents." The phrase "Child-Centered" distinguishes it from guidance and counseling in which the total life situation and relations of the participants are considered. In the technique with which we are dealing here, attention is focused on the child and the child alone—his nature, his fears, his needs, his strivings, his behavior and its meaning, and the most efficacious way of dealing with him and his acts in the interest of his, the family's and the community's mental health.

Another essential element in this practice that stemmed from a fortuitous circumstance in our original group was the spacing of the group meetings. Although the group had met weekly before they consulted me, I was unable to allot them more than one evening a fortnight because of other commitments. The question arose whether they could meet without me to continue discussions on the alternate weeks. This plan I rather arbitrarily rejected since I felt they would become confused by the many different and conflicting viewpoints and opinions that would inevitably arise. Without leadership and direction these might undo our work. The meetings on alternate weeks proved a great boon. It so transpired that this prevented the parents from becoming dependent on the group as they had to rely more upon themselves than they would otherwise. An additional element was that parents had two weeks to experiment with methods of dealing with situations rather than the shorter period of one week which in certain circumstances would not have been sufficient to obtain results or test out new plans of action with the children. It is advisable, however, to meet weekly at the outset of the group for four or five weeks so as to mobilize the members' interest and establish a routine. This is especially helpful in a clinical setting.

Some Aspects of Parent-Child Relations

Before we proceed with our thesis of the nature and process of Child-Centered Group Guidance of Parents, it may be helpful to define it and perhaps also to draw the contrasts between guidance and psychotherapy. This is important because the lines of demarcation between the two are not always clear; they are frequently confused, even though by definition they should be quite different as to dynamics and processes.

Basically, one can say that in psychotherapy we seek to change the psychic organization of the personality by altering the constitution and quantum of the various psychic forces and to balance them in a manner that the individual can function more effectively and more efficiently than he had heretofore. This requires decathecting certain areas within and outside the personality, re-evaluating some past experiences, memories, situations and relations that arouse undesirable or irrational responses. The process by which this is accomplished consists of free catharsis in a transference relation through which the patient regresses to earlier traumatic situations and recalls memories of events that had caused anxiety, fear, guilt and tensions. The resulting insights and the new perceptions and understandings of past events are perceived in new meanings and relations, fixations are dissolved, the libido is redistributed and the cathected areas (foci) within the personality are diminished in their intensity and importance.

Another major outcome of the therapeutic process is establishment of adequate ego boundaries, and strengthening of the ego so that the individual can deal with problems, tensions and anxieties more adequately and face them or repress them sufficiently so that they do not cause him further difficulty. Still another is correcting the structure and function of the superego, by lessening its demands in those whose superego is too strict, and to render it more restrictive in individuals where it has not been sufficiently developed. Thus the individual can be more discriminating as to what is permitted and prohibited and what is moral and unmoral.

Because of the resulting feelings of adequacy and the decrease of inner tensions, better functioning in reality and improved self-image arise. This is made possible in part by the state of inner relaxation and in part because the patient becomes aware of inner strengths and a capacity to deal with reality more adequately. These results are achieved predominantly through the dynamics of transference, catharsis, ego strengthening, reality testing and acquiring sublimation patterns for expressing primary drives and needs.

It is evident from even this brief outline of dynamic psychotherapy that the procedure requires an intensive transference relation with a therapist, by self-confrontation and regression permitted by the therapist and by the patient's own ego and by acting out in a manner that ordinarily creates guilt and anxiety. This is of necessity a prolonged process. When a psychoneurotic constellation is integrated in the psyche, has its roots in early childhood and is charged with painful memories and infantile fears, it requires intensive and lengthy treatment. In practice, however, one comes across persons who need help in adaptation and adjustment without requiring so profound an alteration in psychic organization. This is particularly true of parents who need to change their relation with their children. With them we have employed another process which, though stemming from the same psychiatric source, is vastly less intense, and which we describe as *guidance*.

In guidance the aim is to affect specific attitudes which do not proceed from strong neurotic conflicts and compelling needs to behave in a particular manner; rather the behavior is a result of misconceptions of what the function of parenthood is, what the parent's role is in the development of the child, and of the rather universal lack of knowledge or misunderstanding of the needs of young children.

A predominant number of parents who have not been exposed to this knowledge view the child as an object with almost inanimate characteristics and devoid of sensitivities and a personality of his own whom they can bend to their will. Parents by and large do not recognize the fact that memories, in many important instances of an organic and emotional nature, are stored up in the child and are structured in his personality which determine his future character, values, attitudes, and life pattern. Experience reveals that parents either do not believe or are shocked when these ideas are presented to them. Adults who would never allow themselves to be arbitrary, domineering or abrupt with another adult do not hesitate to act violently toward children. They demand implicit obedience, assuming that children have no individuality and do not, or ought not, have any autonomy; they must submit to the authority of the parents. Nor do parents realize the permanent effect of their arbitrary and sometimes even cruel treatment upon the future of their children.

Persons with clinical experience recognize that whenever the behavior described here is part and parcel of the parents' structured neurotic need, that is, of a compulsive or compelling nature, change in this behavior can be affected only by a change in the psyche of the parent. It would be necessary first to eliminate the conflictual areas and defensive patterns of anxiety-denying behavior of which the child is a part before a change in their conduct can occur. When a child is a part of the syndrome of the parents' character or neurosis, only a change in character or a resolution of the neurosis can bring about an alteration in behavior and attitude. However, the majority of parents who treat their children badly do not do so because of such intensive urges, but rather because they are victims of culturally determined and habitually set attitudes and values. They are subject to the propensity to relive with their children the patterns of their own childhood. This continuum is both common and understandable.

By and large parents who come from a family where they were treated with consideration, respect and sensitivity will treat their children similarly. Conversely, when one was treated gruffly and his sensibilities were not respected, he will tend to deal with his children in a similar manner. This imitation and repetition trend in the education of children is perpetuated not only because of one's own childhood background, but also through the cultural and community attitudes to which one is exposed.

Mothers and fathers living in the same culture usually speak of their children in the same vein and support one another in their methods of dealing with them. Attitudes are further buttressed by existing educational instrumentalities and the cultural emphasis which they reflect. Adults are constantly encouraged in our culture to be strict and "make children behave" and "obey." It is therefore not surprising that some psychologically unsound patterns in dealing with children are so universal.

Common observation shows that when a father and mother fully accept the child and their role as parents, even if their manner of treating him is faulty, he can absorb such treatment with less harm than where such favorable family preconditions do not exist. However, where in addition to the lack of knowledge as to the child's needs and ways of meeting them, there is also present a rejection or only a half-hearted acceptance of the parental role, the child is almost certain to react with some behavior difficulties or worse.

In our efforts to guide parents toward more adequate functioning, we rely upon the natural tendency of people to follow the pleasure principle. We assume that unless there is present a psychologic distortion or a blocking to the operation of this principle, the majority of parents prefer to live in a harmonious family milieu if only they knew how to create one. I hold that there is an instinctual desire on the part of the average man and woman to avoid difficulties and conflicts that beset them, their children, the family atmosphere and society itself. Parents, therefore, need to be guided and shown how to prevent stress and strain. The trend toward health has to be, and is utilized in psychotherapy, not only in guidance. We know that when a patient resists improvement and has no wish to rid himself of suffering and discomfort, little can be done for him. In skillful hands resistance can be overcome and healthy trends induced, because latent in everyone is the wish for a life free of suffering. In some this positive striving may be less strong than in others; this is usually the case with seriously disturbed persons. The average parent, however, can be reached by new learnings he can understand, especially when he is helped to *arrive at them through his own effort and reflection.*

It has been our experience that properly selected parents respond quickly to learnings which they feel would ameliorate their problems and improve their relations with their children. We found that despite their earlier rigid and authoritarian values, if suitable procedures are employed, they quickly perceive the fact that children are highly sensitive, that they are fundamentally afraid, and that they need support and security from parents. These results cannot be achieved, however, through mere conceptualization, such as is employed in lectures, didactic classes, or abstract teaching and discussions. Parents make these new attitudes and values their own only if they are helped to arrive at understanding and conclusions through *their own efforts,* and are aided in evolving techniques most suitable to themselves in accordance with each one's particular situation, personality and family setting. The lack of resourcefulness among parents in dealing with family situations and children is very striking. We were surprised how little the average parent understood the nature of childhood, and as we shall presently see, how they welcomed and effectively integrated into their daily living the knowledge they had acquired.

One of the more destructive concepts parents acquire through the cultural emphasis is that they are remiss in their responsibilities if they are nonpunitive. What seems like cruelty toward children is not always but most often a result of ignorance, a feeling of helplessness and frustration in relation to the child whose personality, being primitive, is necessarily stronger than that of the parent. Another error derived from the value system in our culture, and rooted in fear, is the belief that a child's attitude and behavior will persist forever. Adults fail to accept the transitory nature of a child's reactions which constantly change during the maturational process. The prevalent fatalistic conviction that a child will not change without the parents' pressure is a source of much tension and friction. Infantile behavior that persists into adolescence or adulthood is, of course, undesirable, but this does not necessarily occur. To remain infantile, conditions abetting it must exist. The child inevitably grows both physically and mentally. Hence, the assumption that a child will not change psychologically with his progressive organic development and as a result of cultural demands from his peers and adults, parents included, has no basis in fact. Parents must be impressed with these facts because the opposite attitudes are strongly ingrained in them. These and other misconceptions and anxieties are more common among parents with first children, for almost any parent learns from his experience with the first child that much of his anxiety had been unfounded.

The frame of reference by which adults view current events is predominantly oriented toward the future. This is in opposition to that of children, who live in the present and cannot perceive the relation their behavior has to the future. Being dominated by the primitive pleasure principle, they cannot but see the act only in the present with no reference to the dimension of time. The act, to a child, is sufficient unto itself. To the adult, on the other hand, each act and event is seen as a precursor and progenitor of future events; and if one is undesirable, a whole train of developments of like nature is envisaged. Thus a child's act, incidental or phasial though it may be, is a source of anxiety to the adult lest it become permanent or the beginnings of a series of like nature. As we have already indicated, this is not only not necessarily so but occurs only when it is directly or indirectly encouraged by parents and educators. Behavior appropriate to age and maturation automatically appears as a result of readiness and social and educational influences to which a child is exposed.

Among the many sources of adult-child conflicts is the former's not always justifiable expectation of consequences of behavior and acts that the child cannot possibly anticipate. Because of his lack of experience with life and people his concepts of the relation of cause and effect is as limited as that of the dimension of time. To the child, the act is both the aim, the end and the satisfaction; to the adult, the end or consequence is detached from the act, and satisfactions are most often derived not from the act itself, but follow from it in more or less practical results. The adult's inability to identify or at least empathize with the child's inability to envisage the social aspects of his behavior and the absence of reflective thought in him is a major source of the adult's impatience and irritability. This lack on his own part gives rise to his punitive and retributional treatment of the younger generation generally, and of his children specifically. The inability to understand and accept the childishness of children and their fundamental hedonism is a source of much tragedy in our society. Parents must accept the fact that the child is by his very nature egocentric and hedonistic, as they themselves had once been. All these incompatible trends and acts tend to be modified and disappear in the normal course of development if aided by the educative conditions of the child's total life and his relationships with his parents. The hedonistic urges of a child need to be regulated, controlled, and in time prohibited; but to be effective, such educative influences and restraints have to be dosed by slowly progressive measures consistent with the child's readiness and evolving capacities to withstand deprivation and control and applied by persons whom he loves or at least accepts.

The conflict between the instinct of children and the "reasoning" of adults is still another source of their eternal disharmony. The child is dominated by his instinctual urges which he must *progressively* modify and curb; but this takes, what seems to parents, an interminable time. Most often parents believe that the child will never reach that stage. In their terror of this eventuality they set out with unrelenting persistence to suppress and inhibit the child's natural and wholesome centripetal flow of *élan vital* lest the coveted "controls" are not acquired by the time the child grows older. They fear that the instinctual (what they consider selfish and wayward) behavior will become a permanent feature of his character and personality. It is, therefore, necessary that this be "knocked out" of them, which the parents proceed to do with frightening constancy and persistency. Actually, because of his identification with (internalization of) the parents' self-controls, the demands of peers, also the consequences of organic, psychological and social maturation, and through the demands upon him by the life situation, the child inevitably evolves most of the controls of his impulses.

The reasonable and reasoning orientation of adults in regard to their children's behavior is effective only when it is *graded* to the child's capacities to benefit from them. When they have accumulated the experience through action to recognize the significance of the "logic" presented to them and are old enough to comprehend the relations of cause and effect and perceive events in the dimension of time and of consequences, the "reasonable" approach can be effective. Parents and teachers must, therefore, sharpen their own perceptiveness to recognize when a *specific* child has reached that stage in relation to a specific phenomenon. They must also learn to recognize the significance each act has to the child as well as employ appropriate language and manner of presentation to reach him and to enlist his cooperation.

Another culturally ingrained idea is that parents must be in authority, and the child submit. The domination-submission motif is predominant in nearly all. While the foundation of this notion is sound, the manner in which it is carried out—the peremptoriness and authoritarianism and the denial of individuality to the child— undermines the parent's position as a model of identification, which is essential to his child's maturity. Almost instinctively parents correctly feel that to fit in as acceptable members of society children must make their own adult attitudes and develop inner controls. They also vaguely recognize that the obedience to one's superego has its roots in obedience to parents, who are during the child's formative years the external representatives of what will later become his internalized superego.

However, what parents do not adequately recognize is that internalization occurs only when the child *accepts* the parents as persons and as safe protectors. Only then will he internalize their superego and ego. When the child is antagonized, he partially or entirely rejects them and will not model himself after them. In order to survive and avoid pain, he may submit to the parent and even give up his autonomy, but his personality will, as a result, forever remain impoverished, which is a source of chagrin and suffering to all concerned later on. Parents, therefore, have to recognize that while their original intent is sound, the manner in which it is carried out may negate their aim and work against them rather than with them. We shall see in other parts of this volume that unless they are motivated by uncontrollable destructive drives or impelled by neurotic needs and urges, they can readily recognize this, for the truth of it is quickly confirmed in their own experience. Parents soon discover that while the first steps are difficult and require self-control and tact, the outcome is one of greater inner peace and family harmony.

A major handicap to constructive parenthood is the almost universal lack of knowledge that a child's needs for security and love are as definite and imperative as are his needs for physical sustenance. Parents who without question follow dietary requirements and health measures are in most instances unaware of psychological needs of the child, which are not infrequently more important than are his physical needs. It has been demonstrated time and again that a child cannot assimilate food, nor can he develop physical health unless he is sustained also psychologically. The child does not eat with his mouth alone: he eats with his entire body and psyche. This fact is easily demonstrable by the failure of the best physical care where children are denied adequate affection, and is particularly true during the early years of life. Children, for example, brought up in institutions that provide the highest nutritional requirements and physical care remain physically (as well as emotionally and intellectually) retarded because of insufficient love and security.

A dramatic illustration of this was provided by a foundling home in Prussia during the reign of Frederick the Great. Frederick, who was the founder of the Prussian military system and psychology, desired to develop a hardy, unemotional type of person for his armies. One of the measures was to supply to the orphans and foundlings the best medical care and nutrition, but withdraw from them all affection and close personal relations. The result was that *all* of the children had died within a comparatively brief time. That man does not live by bread alone is poignantly true of children. The recent studies of Dr. René Spitz on hospitalism and on emotional neglect of children confirm the Prussian experience.

No one who appreciates the complex dynamics in the development of personality will recommend relying on the instinctive resources of parents in bringing up their children. The urge to parenthood is instinctive, especially in females of all species since it fulfills organic functions, but in *homo sapiens* psychologic care cannot be entrusted to instinct. Nature provided for the survival of the species as physical entities, neglecting entirely the psychological aspects of the infant's and child's life. One can speculate on this enigma but with little practical results. It may be helpful to say that the complexity of human emotions beyond the primary ones necessary for biologic survival—fear, love, and hate—is outside nature's scheme. One cannot escape the suspicion that the bewildering complexity of the human psyche and the profundity of man's intellect is an inexplicable accident in nature. Perhaps because of this accident, the "missing link" has not yet been found, nor will it ever be.

The need for knowledge in the psychologic care of infants and children is becoming increasingly and more poignantly apparent as man is divorced ever more from his natural habitat and is thrown into a complex society. Adaptations are conditioned by the demands of environment, and the more complex they are, the more complex must be the responses of the organism and psyche. Similarly, the more restrictive and repressive a culture and the more the psychologic and social forces grow in their complex interweaving, the more numerous and more complicated must the adaptive patterns become—and the more distressing.

A civilization that divorces man from his natural habitat—a simple physical environment with space, color and physical freedom and comparative quiet, devoid of excess conflict and competition—makes safeguarding the individual, and particularly the child, against excessive emotional stress imperative. The child's world is a world of space, freedom, locomotion, experience with simple objects in a simple environment such as a farm provides, with its green grass, colorful flowers, enticing birds, friendly domestic animals, and simple objects to play with and assemble. These provide experiences that evoke latent interest and the capacity to deal effectively with environment and control it. In a condition full of complexities beyond his understanding and scope, with restrictions against exploration and free movement, the child's psychological development must of necessity be impeded and distorted. This condition is even more compounded when pressure and demands from adults are added to those that frustrate autonomous biological drives.

While in the economically more favored group, nurseries and "rumpus rooms" are provided for children's play, in most homes no such advantages are to be found and the crawler and toddler unavoidably disturbs the adults as soon as he emerges from the limits of his own room. Because homes and furnishings are designed for adults only, the child cannot but become a "nuisance." Thus, from his earliest days, he feels hemmed in, restricted, frustrated, and what is worst of all, rejected.

Schools are even worse as regards the vasomotor requirements that are the foundation of both physical and mental health. Confinement in seats in a state of immobility impedes growth of tissue, function of nerves and muscles, intellectual expansion, and prevents proper coordination and integration of the personality as a whole. General metabolism is greatly interfered with in some respects, and overstimulated in others. While there is constriction of instinctual drives through limitation of physical movement, there is excess of intellectual activity. The eyes particularly are subject to serious damage, as are muscles of arms and fingers as they are involved in writing and drawing. Excessive use of small muscles and inadequate exercise of the large muscles, which can be provided only in free activity and play, is the cause of serious psycho-organic imbalance. In view of the fact that animals are so constituted that frustration to and imbalance in the organism is transformed into emotional tensions and neurotic reactions, the damage assumes an alarming nature. In man, as well as in some mammals, these neurotic reactions are generalized, that is, they affect all reactions and not only those involved in a specific area. They are transferred to and affect all other situations and relations and permeate the total psycho-organic responses of the individual.

In addition to the damage a child sustains from inappropriate physical function, damage to his personality accrues also from the emotional tensions that may exist in the home. Western society has freed man from many primitive fears, such as destruction by wild animals, warring tribes, the failure of crops, drought, and inadequate food supplies. Even to a greater extent was he freed from fear of early and sudden death, from recurring climatic catastrophes and epidemics. With the elimination of fears of biological survival, however, new fears of psychological origin have emerged. Though part and parcel of the former, they proceed from man's sociopsychological matrix and are different in character and content. Fear and anxiety are not caused by exigencies and dangers emanating from unbridled natural occurrences, as was characteristic of primitive man. They are rather anxieties emanating from interpersonal relations and society's demands in order that one may survive both as a biological entity and as a social atom. Many of these anxieties stem from necessary taboos, ethics, morals, and mores, which, though necessary, are in conflict with, or are a negation of, primary biological urges.

Man is the battleground between these impelling urges on the one hand, and social taboos and group disapproval, on the other, which create for him tension and conflict. The requirements for survival in a society are too frequently in opposition to his biological nature, but in the struggle social survival takes precedence over individual survival. The individual, therefore, finds himself, if not submerged which is frequently the case, certainly merged with the group, for otherwise neither he nor society—as it is now constituted —could survive. Because of their interdependence, one cannot survive without the other.

These limitations, inevitable as they are, are hard on adults; they are infinitely more so on children. Restrictions play greater havoc with children because of their organically propelling dynamic drives, their self-centeredness and narcissism which have to be diminished and overcome with progressive maturity. The parent is here placed in the anomalous role of one who though loving, sustaining and supporting the child, faces the need to restrict, deny and limit him so as to lay the foundation for a socialized personality. This duality of functions in which the parent is caught up creates a serious dilemma for him. His intentions in limiting and frustrating the child are to help the latter grow into an emotionally healthy adult, but the child lacks the understanding to discern its intent. He interprets it as unfriendly and hostile, and the parent as cruel, who because of his physical strength subjugates him and forces him into a submissive status. This results in permanent antagonism toward parents, an antagonism that is never fully obliterated even when the child later in life grows to understand intellectually the parent's aim.

Unfortunately, this is not a one-way antagonism. The parents, too, react with hostility toward the child. His resistance and disobedience as he grows older set up undercurrents of mutual antagonism which springs forth with varying frequency in open quarrels and recrimination. A major contributing factor to this never-ending battle is the parents' traditional or compelling need to dominate their children, even after they are grown and independent. The resulting tension undermines the child's much needed feeling of security and distorts his conception of himself—his worth and self-esteem. It renders some children asocial and even antisocial because in rejecting the parent, they also reject the social values and mores that he represents, while others become excessively conforming, personally impoverished and socially unproductive.

There is still another source of anxiety in a child. This is the tensions that frequently exist among the individuals that constitute his immediate environment, namely, his parents and siblings. Antagonisms on the part of parents toward each other and among siblings create an atmosphere which empathically a child, and even a young baby, registers and absorbs to make it a part of his life. The *quality* of his emotional constitution, like the quality of the body which is determined by the quality of the food he ingests, is conditioned by these relationships. The feelings of relaxation or tension, friendship or hostility are of all human situations most telling in the family. Just as the constitution of the physical organism is conditioned by the quality of the food, so are the feelings and attitudes determined by the type of feelings to which the child is exposed, for he responds to these both psychologically and organically.

Modern life, both because of its numerous insecurities and demands, creates many tensions in the family which can be designated as *socially induced tensions*. One cannot overlook the tensions that originate in economic insecurity—poverty, job uncertainty, inadequate incomes, unsuitable occupations. Particularly destructive is the uncertainty on the job and the destructive relations that exist in nearly all factories and offices among superiors and their subordinates. Tensions that originate here are carried over to the home and displaced on members of the family. Devoid of any sense of social responsibility and having no democratic or social frame of reference, foremen, managers, and employers are not aware of the effect of their acts upon the total social atmosphere. Antagonism, hostility and fear inspired by superiors in their subordinates is one of the major causes for drinking, for example, and in some cases, even for heavy drinking. Much of the tension exists in families of persons employed under unfavorable conditions or engaged in fluctuating or insecure businesses.

A surprising number of men, as well as an increasing number of women, feel the need for drink after a day's work to gain relief from tensions accumulated during the day. These are partly the result of monotony and overexertion. Overstrain of the intellect and physical inactivity characteristic of so many jobs of necessity produce organic imbalance, and every imbalance creates tension, requiring some means to re-establish equilibrium. Narcosis through alcohol (and more recently through tranquilizers) is one way out in these circumstances. Control of aggression is reduced through such narcosis and, therefore, is acted out on members of one's family. Persons with better ego strengths may not discharge their feelings through overt acts, but instead become depressed and unhappy. They withdraw from the family circle.

Sexual maladjustment among marital partners is another source of tension that in subtle ways affects the child since nothing that relates to his parents escapes his attention. Other areas of incompatibility may be divergence of interest and psychological differences generally. In some instances these problems require intensive treatment on the one hand, and evolving a plan of life that would reduce tensions, on the other. Whatever the circumstances, whether they are favorable or not, parental functions cannot be left to chance and instinct; they must be learned as are all other skills and trades. To allow individuals to undertake parenthood with all its complexities and responsibilities with no knowledge of child nature and needs and the many pitfalls one is subject to is a commentary on our so-called civilization. While it is unthinkable that anyone would enter a trade or profession without adequate preparation, no one has seriously suggested that preparation for parenthood be incorporated as a part of the education of young people. The knowledge, skills, duties and responsibilities here are by far greater and more complex, requiring in addition to understanding the child also a degree of self-understanding and a great deal of self-control.

No mechanic would be permitted to work with materials the nature of which he does not know. He is taught how to deal with the raw materials of his trade, their nature and quality, and the techniques of working with them so as to transform them into the desired finished product. Preparation for white-collar occupations, as well, is required of all who plan to undertake them. Cookery and homemaking receive some attention in the education of young people. Either parents or schools offer or impose training in these essential functions. While an increasing number of high schools train in these and allied occupations and trades, nowhere are young people prepared for parenthood. This function they enter completely unprepared. They have no knowledge of the nature and psychologic needs of childhood or the skills to deal with the enigmatic and not too easily understandable behavior of infants and children. Parents who *understand,* not just know, the nature and needs of children could greatly reduce the pathogenic conditions in the home, even under unfavorable socioeconomic circumstances. It is to this end that the present volume is directed. Our aim is to demonstrate that even parents who have already made serious mistakes with their children can, through their own effort, find ways of correcting past errors, eliminate tensions, reduce antagonisms and hostilities, establish favorable relations with their children and mates, and create a relaxed climate in the home.

Among the chief errors of "parent education" is the assumption that information is necessarily transformed into practice. John Dewey emphasized that ideas cannot be transformed into experience; only experience can be transformed into experience. Education, even in allied fields, does not necessarily help a parent to deal better with his children. One is surprised to observe men and women trained in the fields of education, psychology, psychiatry, and child development, unable to deal with their own children appropriately.

Transfer of training was proven to be chimerical, though there is some measure of such transfer, in my opinion, through general development and increased perceptivity. Skills, however, can be developed by practice only. It is therefore necessary that skills of parent-

hood be directly imparted, rather than assume that once a person
has studied child psychology he will know how to deal with a child.
In work with hundreds of parents, I found that many of them,
though intelligent, trained in their professions, with a good understanding of child psychology, transgressed the most essential elements
of mental health. Perhaps some illustrations will make this point
clear.

I was once visiting the home of a couple, both of whom had
been trained and who had practiced in the fields of mental health
with children. There were two children in the family, whom I had
never seen before, a girl of about six or seven, and a boy of about
three or four. While the father, his wife and I had our drinks in the
living room, the children were having their supper in another room
and were out of our sight. They were, however, able to hear us
chatting. When the children finished their supper, they were permitted to come in to be briefly introduced to the visitor. After intro-
ductions, we continued with our conversation giving no heed to the
children. After some time the girl picked up a book and asked the
father: "Can I write in this book?" The father, very sternly and ad-
monishingly barked: "You know you were told many times that you
cannot write in books. Books are to read and not to write in!" The
girl's inquiry had a different meaning than her manifest question.
She wanted attention that was removed from her and turned to the
visitor. She wanted to be included in the group. She was especially
concerned with the fact that we were about to repair to the dining
room, leaving her behind. Her choice of a particularly objectionable
inquiry was one way to get attention, to delay being abandoned, and
was part of her resentment against being ignored. Sensing the disappointment in the child, I picked up a piece of plain paper and
asked the girl to bring me a pair of scissors, which she did with
alacrity. I then cut out a piece the size of the book, inserted it in the
book and told her she could now write in it. She appeared pleased
and did not demur our leaving the room as we proceeded to the
dining room. However, during the course of our dinner, the children
appeared at the dining room door several times and were repeatedly
told, in a stern and peremptory voice, to go back to the nursery to
play.

It does not require much insight to discern a whole series of errors and lack of empathy with their daughter on the part of these professionally trained parents. The children's curiosity about the visitor and their natural desire not to be left out were completely unrecognized. The fact that they were isolated during their supper where they could hear voices, especially one of a stranger, undoubtedly interfered with their giving the necessary attention to their food. Their meal, therefore, could not have been very satisfactory. The father did not perceive the significance of the child's asking for permission to do what she well knew would be denied her, namely writing in a book, and responded in a manner full of anger and irritation. The children were further denied the company of the parents and the visitor during the latters' dinner, as they had been during their own repast before. Thus they had been rejected during the entire period.

Instead of making themselves and their guest accessible to the children by including them in the "party" and having them eat with the adults (something that should be the practice in all families), they were sequestered and excluded, which unquestionably caused them distress. We shall not attempt to examine this situation in terms of deep-seated attitudes on the part of the parents and the possible recrimination between them in which syndrome the children have been caught. What interests us is their lack of understanding and empathy. While emotional undercurrents were undoubtedly present, nonetheless, had these parents, trained as they were in professions so closely allied to parental functions, applied some of their "knowledge," their management of the situation would have been different. They did not appreciate the importance to the children of being part of the circle, feeling accepted, and the guest accessible to them. Instead, their inferior status was unnecessarily emphasized.

As evidence of the absence of skill, we should record the father's reaction to my cutting out a piece of paper the size of the book, inserting it and handing it to the girl with the suggestion that she could now write in the book. Observing his daughter's eager acceptance of it and her obvious satisfaction, he exclaimed *in the children's presence,* with evident surprise and some sarcasm in his voice: "You really have technique!"

A more disturbing episode occurred in the home of a similarly trained professional of considerable prominence, which illustrates even more poignantly to what extent parents do not utilize acquired information where their own children are concerned. The daughter of this man, whose wife was a member of the same profession as himself, was allowed to have sex play with the son of a next-door neighbor until four years of age. In fact, the parents had a "scientific interest" in the play and kept record of the form it took at various stages. However, when she reached the age of about four, the sexual play between the two children began to assume a more realistic form and the parents peremptorily forbade her henceforth to see the boy. As a result, the girl went into a depression.

Here are parents who certainly must have known intellectually at least what the implications of such guilt-producing sexual activity were and should have anticipated developments. They could have prevented the trauma which their girl later experienced, the results of which will cause her much difficulty later in life.

Still another illustration of the point we are endeavoring to make that general information is not applied in actual practice is supplied, again, by another practitioner in a similar field whose wife was an artist. I once met them during a walk as they were wheeling a baby carriage in which their eight-month-old boy was strapped down. He was tied down prone on his abdomen in such a way that all he could see was the inside of the carriage. To see the sky, or anything else around him, he had to twist his head and crane his neck to such an extent that his face would turn crimson. He was unable to move his body, not even his arms. The only organs which were movable were his neck and legs. As we stood and talked the boy in order to see me strained himself so that his face turned crimson with the exertion. Certainly the father if questioned would have known the harm of such physical restriction and its emotional concomitants. Nevertheless, he did not apply this knowledge to his own child.

Such breaches against both common sense and knowledge, however, are not limited to any one profession. In one family where I was called in to unravel rather serious complications, I found the father, an intellectual man who had had a prolonged psychoanalysis, had permitted himself to take over the major part of the physical care of his two children relegating the mother, a college graduate, to a subordinate position. This caused serious confusion in the minds of the two-year-olds, to which they responded with extreme aggression and hyperactivity. In fact, the situation grew so serious that actual physical danger to the children became imminent. The problem of this family was readily remedied when each parent and the maid were helped to assume his proper role and the atmosphere was quickly cleared. Here again we have a demonstration of the fact that though intelligent, college trained and analyzed, the parents did not apply their theoretic knowledge to their situation. However, because of these factors they were able quickly to assimilate and apply the guidance offered them.

In another family of devoted, well-educated parents with a high level of intelligence, there was a little girl of three years of age who was very impetuous, given to temper tantrums, and still not toilet trained. The parents have obviously overinfantilized the child and watched her throughout her wakeful hours. Either one or both parents would sit and keep their eyes focused on the child as she was playing or moving about the apartment or playground. When I was called in for consultation and called it to their attention, the mother told me that the child actually screamed at them and her grandmother not to look at her, but they did not take her seriously; they rather thought it was cute. Actually, the child was frightened by the adults' staring at her.

We see from the foregoing episodes how otherwise well-meaning persons, with good theoretic knowledge of child psychology and child development, had not been able to perceive the subtler needs of their children. They did not understand them, nor had they the skills to deal with them appropriately. Numerous situations arise in the course of a day that require sensitive handling. Many of these, though insignificant in themselves—in fact, so insignificant that even enlightened adults are surprised that they should be important and influence the child and his relation to the parents—actually determine the family climate and the eventual development of the child's personality.

Parents are not alone in unfeeling treatment of their children. Many professionally trained persons to whom they turn for help and guidance lack the psychological insight to prevent traumatic reactions in children which frequently leave a permanent stamp on their personalities. In my work with some four or five thousand families, I have encountered innumerable instances of unbelievable callousness on the part of professionally trained persons whose specialties should have disposed them toward understanding mental health measures. Only two instances related by two mothers in one group session will suffice to illustrate this point.

One mother described how her boy at the age of three years was rushed to the doctor's office where he was "immediately grabbed by the nurse" so that she did not even have a chance to say good-by to him. Though the boy knew he was to have his tonsils removed, the way he was rushed in and was put under an anesthetic shocked him so that after the operation he lost all desire for food, became dehydrated and was ill for weeks. To this very day, the boy, now eleven years old, refuses to go into a barber shop or a store for new shoes or "do anything like that." If things are brought home, he accepts them, but he will not go out toward new experiences. The mother tries to "reason with him," she said, but she understands that he probably still bears in mind the fear of being grabbed and hurt.

Another mother in a therapy group told of her boy turning blue with rage. When asked how this started, the mother said that her pediatrician told her to let the child, as a baby, yell. "He's just mean," the doctor said, "and if he has an impulse to yell, let him yell it out." She did that and had since believed that when a child of hers yells beyond a certain point, he was just out to hurt her. She was not told that crying is the only way a child has to convey his needs.

A child's life consists almost entirely of minutiae, and it is with these that parents must deal properly. This they can learn only through direct preparation for parenthood and equally direct re-education of those parents who have had a bad start with their children. But education for an empirical function as a parent cannot be theoretic and conceptual for, as already indicated, concepts are too far removed from practice. However, it is obviously impossible to supply an actual situation in which practice in parenthood can be acquired. A method of education and re-education needs to be devised that will supply parents with *vicarious* experiences in dealing with situations as they arise in everyday relations in the home. This is found in the case method presentation in psychiatry, in social work and in *free discussion* techniques of progressive adult education. Basically, this consists of meetings of groups of parents who have children of the same sex and nearly the same ages where they can exchange experiences, describe their way of dealing with situations in the home and then evaluate their effectiveness in free discussion. The aim here is to help each participant learn or evolve ways of dealing with *specific situations most suitable for them* and for their children. Separate groups for fathers and mothers are usually less risky, though mixed groups can also be conducted.

In our society mothers are more involved with their children than are fathers, since the responsibility of carrying the day-to-day chores of the family falls on them. As our society is now constituted, pressures and daily demands of management of relations in the home are less felt by fathers since they are out of the home most of the day. In recent years reduction of hours of work, long week ends and smaller living quarters throw the man into greater and more prolonged proximity with his family which devolves upon him duties that hitherto fell to the mother. Despite these new and comparatively recent developments, mothers still carry the bulk of the burden of the home and children. Further, because of the mother's biologic constitution and function, she is necessarily more attached psychologically to the child than is the father. This attachment which has its origin in the organic unity of mother and child in prenatal stages continues after birth and creates stress for both. The mother has to resolve her ambivalence toward the child in seeing him as an extension of herself on the one hand, and her need to free herself from him, on the other. This struggle sets up intense emotional currents that many cannot resolve without help.

On the basis of observation, we can posit that *the basic emotion of children is fear, and that of parents is guilt.* The guilt of parents stems from several sources. One of these is the different roles a mother is forced to assume during the transition from nurture to discipline.[1] The nurture period is usually much easier on both parent and infant. She can accept without conflict the parasitic dependence of the

---

[1] Slavson, S. R.: *Child Psychotherapy.* New York: Columbia University Press, 1952.

child on her due to his helplessness and fragility. At this stage, most mothers can give of themselves unreservedly. This attitude changes when the infant becomes ready for spoon feeding and toilet training. Here resentment arises in both parent and child. The baby now asserts himself, resists change and challenges the mother. The aggressive feelings of the mother toward the child that were held in abeyance now come to the fore, which in turn generate in her guilt feelings. However, despite these, most mothers express anger, reprimand and scold the baby and even punish him. Since the maternal and protective instincts are outraged by this, guilt is further intensified.

Another source of guilt in parents is their unconscious feeling that they are responsible for the child's illnesses, stresses and suffering which are inevitable in the course of growth and development. A child's illness always makes a parent feel guilty because deep down he feels he should have prevented it and the ensuing suffering to his offspring. The guilt is even more intense where some form of permanent damage occurs. Feelings of guilt stem also from the parent's resentment against the child when his ego grows stronger and he becomes self-assertive, and challenges the parent's authority. This resentment is usually acted out directly but is sometimes disguised. Whatever the form it takes, parents feel guilty because of it, since the moral demands in our society are that parents must be kind to their children, must harbor no negative feelings and their harshness must remain within certain limits.

A less recognizable source of guilt, but an ever present one, are the inherent destructive urges parents feel toward their children that in their extreme take the form of death wishes and in primitive societies took the form of infanticide. This startling and incongruous attitude is amply confirmed in clinical work with parents. A surprising number reveal deeply guarded and repressed wishes that their children die. Some even reveal a desire to kill them. Basing the deduction on the well-accepted fact that neurotic content is not unique with the neurotic, that it is only exaggerated in him but present in less intense degrees in all, we are justified in concluding that infanticidal urges are not as rare as our own guilt would lead us to suspect.

I recall sitting many years ago with a judge in a children's court when a girl of about thirteen years of age was brought before the bench. Both father and mother appeared at the trial. The girl's infraction was a rather minor one and the judge, who was a woman, was inclined to dismiss the case. The father pleaded that this be done. The mother, however, with crimson face and anger flashing from her eyes insisted that her daughter be "sent away." She kept repeating her demand despite the fact that the social worker involved, the father, and the judge did not concur. The judge, a kind and gracious elderly woman, herself a mother and grandmother, turned to me in a state of confusion and asked: "Why does this mother insist on getting rid of her child?" Without adequate consideration as to the effect my answer would have on this admirable lady, I said: "This is a case of vicarious infanticide." The expression of shock and surprise on the judge's face instantly sobered me as she explained: "What? That is not possible!" I realized my mistake too late, but I was right, nonetheless.

Occasionally, and these occasions have been growing more frequent in recent years, readers of newspapers are shocked by the reports of killings of children by their parents, both mothers and fathers.[2] While some of these homicides are committed in fits of anger, anguish or insanity, many are the acts of hitherto "normal" persons with no evidence of mental derangement. Many of these acts are motivated by revenge against the mate, others are results of what seem to be temporary aberrations, while a small number are committed in cold blood when the burden of the family overstrains the parent's capacity to bear up under it. In some instances, and for more or less the same reasons, parents abandon their children as a less violent means of getting rid of them.

The very fact that a child is a product of the mother's body makes her desire to reincorporate him, which spells destruction to the child. The fact that the child adds to the father's and mother's responsibilities makes them wish, perhaps unconsciously, that this responsibility and burden be removed. Death wishes are manifested unmistakenly in very disturbed parents, and many children of such

---

[2] Patricide and matricide cases are reported as frequently, thus revealing that the fundamental antagonism is mutual.

mothers refuse to eat food that had been prepared or even handled by them. Some vomit the food while others refuse to swallow it. In some instances children verbalize their fear that their mothers want to poison them. The children, through their frequently uncanny perceptiveness, register the hidden motivations of parents.

The remarkable perceptiveness of children as regards attitudes of adults and especially their parents is demonstrated by the following episodes:

In one of my parent guidance groups the question of kissing children was discussed during which it was pointed out that kissing is a substitute cannibalistic act, symbolic of devouring, and that little children are afraid of being kissed, especially by strangers, because they perceive the unconscious source of the act. This intent is revealed by the phrase in common usage, "He is so cute, I could eat him." Since the participants, though college graduates, were not versed in anthropological lore, they accepted this reasoning, but with a grain of salt, as it were. A month or two later one of the mothers in the group told us the following: "When we discussed the question of kissing, I must confess that I was not convinced by the parallel drawn between kissing and cannibalism, but something happened since that seems to make it right. The other day I gave Susie [three-year-old] a bath and after the bath, I said to her 'Now give Mummie a hug and Mummie will kiss you.' 'No,' answered Susie, 'You'll eat me up.'"

The reaction by a five-year-old girl also buttresses our contention that hostility is present in parents and that children are not unaware of it. The girl's mother was in treatment for a psychoneurotic disturbance and one of her problems was her intense dislike of her child. Once, when the mother, as a result of treatment, attempted to be affectionate to her daughter, the latter said: "I know Mummie, you're trying hard to love me, but you can't."

Whatever the method employed and whatever reason there may be for committing violent acts, the motive behind them is actual or vicarious infanticide. Again drawing upon the hypothesis that whatever is resident in the psyche of one human, even if he is psychotic, is common to all and that the difference lies only in the degree and intensity as a result of different degrees of sublimation and repression, we must arrive at the conclusion that these trends are inherent to parenthood. This strips parenthood of much of its idealized aura. When parents can accept without fear and guilt their unconscious trends, rather than overidealize themselves, they will be able to function more constructively and lay a sounder foundation for the mental health of their children.

It does not mean that parents need actually recognize all their impulses. It would be expecting too much of them; and its value is very doubtful. Parents can, however, recognize, as is shown in their conversations recorded elsewhere in this volume, that there is more or less universal disregard for the person of the child, his autonomy and his self-assertive, independent trends. The parents' awareness of their hostile feelings toward their children cannot but create guilt in them since these feelings counter the ethical requirements of our society which demand that parents "love" their offspring, that they protect and cherish him, and that they do not harbor antagonism against him. It also outrages the parents' internalized, socially conditioned superego that is in conformity with these demands. Failure in this causes narcissistic injury to the parent for his self-image is depreciated and his self-esteem suffers. It is, therefore, understandable from our knowledge of the operation of ego defenses, that parents would project the blame for their failures upon the child so as to whitewash themselves in their own estimation. One outlet is punishment. The act of punishing, though having even deeper significance than we need to consider here, serves parents in a number of ways.

Punishment relieves tension accumulated from anger and resentment; it releases anxiety and allays guilt. The annoyance that all adults feel toward children (because of the irreconcilable difference in the operation of the pleasure principle in children and the reality principle in adults and their vast difference in ego functioning and superego restraints) creates a reserve of tensions that has to be periodically discharged. Guilt feelings as a result of the conscious and unconscious attitudes and acts are also transformed into tension, both of which are discharged through punishment because the act of punishment transfers the seat of guilt upon the one who is punished. Thus guilt is allayed by the simple act of displacing responsibility from the parent upon the child. This process is well demonstrated by a scene which one can see duplicated numerous times during even a brief walk on any city street. A small child, three or four years old, walking unattended, falls and either because of shock or actual hurt begins to scream. Eight of ten mothers, by actual count, pick up the child and slap him for falling down. This is a very transparent way of the mother's working off upon the child her guilt feelings aroused by her lack of vigilance and failure to guide and protect him. There are, however, innumerable less apparent manifestations of this process.

Of interest is the fact that social mores evolved by adults buttress their cruel and primitive behavior. On the one hand, these demand love and tenderness, while on the other punishment is approved and encouraged. By this dichotomy, society accomplishes several purposes. It allays superego demands and simultaneously yields protection against children and their anarchic impulses. It also supplies adults, among whom teachers are included, with targets of hostility that serve to reduce their own discontent with society and its demands. I have always been convinced that the more cruel parents are toward their children, the more guilty they feel; that the former is related to and is an outcome of the latter. Parents in conflict and burdened by guilt resolve them through punishment; thus punishment has an organic relation to guilt.

Because of the inevitable difference in roles assigned to fathers and mothers in the family constellation in our society and the difference in their day-to-day responsibilities and functions, it is understandable that there would be a concomitant difference in their attitudes. The annoyances and anxieties of mothers who continually carry the responsibilities of children for prolonged periods and in an intimate, direct way, set up in them feelings which are alien to the father, a good part of whose time is spent away from the home during the many critical events in the child's life. The struggles between parent and child during the various phases of his growth, the accommodations the mother has to make to his unbridled egotism, and the self-control she has to exercise are beyond the father's ken. To these must be added the anxieties and fears resulting from illness, injuries, and accidents and the feelings of failure and despair as the child makes his way into his peer culture in its various phases.

We can add to these the physical drudgery of maintaining a home and the numerous chores that a baby and child add to the already overworked and harrassed woman. Many of these are not altogether pleasant or aesthetically satisfying and though some mothers in some nations are being freed from some of them by modern home technology, the burdens are only reduced, not eliminated, while the proponderant majority still carry on in the old ways. It has always seemed to me that no mother can entirely forgive a child for the excruciating pain of childbirth, which was recently shown by tests to be the greatest pain to which the human organism can be subjected. There is no doubt that while the many pleasures and even delights in discharging the instinctive maternal functions compensate a mother for this pain, it is difficult to imagine that the memory of it is entirely obliterated.

As we view the father's place in the total scheme of child bearing and rearing, we see quite a different perspective. The father does not have the same intimate and direct contact with the baby and child. Though in present-day families fathers discharge some functions that had been the province of mothers in the past, they do so by delegation. They do not bear the full brunt of the responsibility, exigencies and anxieties. Even the disciplining of children, which was in the remote past the province of fathers, is no longer so; mothers now do the bulk of disciplining and punishing, which creates irreparable confusion in the child's mind as to her role in his life.

Fathers serve more as ego supports now and are the distant and enigmatic persons with no defined place in the small child's life and imagery. That he is a source of strength and security is brought home clearly to him since he is the source of material and psychologic support. He is usually the person who manages the matter of weekly money allowances, although here, too, modern mothers do not remain neutral of quiescent. Fathers are persons who want their home quiet after the day's work and while they thus frustrate children, they do it less than mothers. All this does not mean that they are not a source of pleasure on occasion. Fathers do take their children out, especially boys, on their free days and, like the mothers, get into difficulties with their offspring whenever they attempt to use their authority.

We, therefore, see that, by and large, the meaning of parents in the life of the child is different; one is charged with greater significance than the other and therefore each impresses himself upon the child's personality differently, not only quantitatively, but qualitatively as well. We can, therefore, expect that the attitudes of the two parents would be also at variance, which we have found to be the case as revealed in the group discussions of fathers and mothers, some of which are recorded in this volume. If one were to characterize these attitudes in a single term for the sake of simplification, one could say that *mothers' basic attitudes is one of resentment and that of the fathers' is guilt.* The former resent the rather heavy physical and emotional load they are compelled to carry, while their husbands feel guilty for not providing better conditions for their families so that a more gratifying life would be possible. There are also other factors that favor the emergence of guilt in the man which I have described elsewhere.[3]

The fact that the child has a biologic and organic tie to his mother, which is not the case with the father, is undoubtedly a major source of the differential significance of the two parents. The organic unity of the child and mother and later the intimate physical contact of the two create at once strong empathy as well as laying the foundation for strong antagonism because of the unavoidable symbiotic relation between them against which both rebel. These needs are the forerunners of submission and compliance to the mother from which the child has to free himself as he grows older which is achieved by throwing off the subtle or overt domination of the parent. This again begets guilt and hostility in the child and disappointment, resentment and guilt in the latter. Because the inherences and content of father-child relation are not as deeply affecting and involved, the father's influence upon the child is considerably less charged with affect. This does not mean that his part in the child's development is negligible. He is of utmost importance as an object of identification for the boy, if he is to assume the male role adequately later in life, and a pattern for love and attachment for the girl, if she is to assume a feminine role and function as a woman in our family-centered culture. Where fathers are strict, overbearing

3 *Child Psychotherapy, loc. cit.*

and overassertive, they become the cathected objects to a degree that may partially overshadow the mother in the psychic organization of the child with consequent undesirable results.

The child is begotten endogenetically and is actually the product of the parents' bodies, especially the mother; therefore he may be considered by them, as is often the case, an extension of the mother's (and sometimes the father's) ego and personality. As already stated, much of the domination of the child and the constriction of his individuation and independence trends by parents, and more so by the mother, stems from her unconscious feeling that the child is actually a part or an extension of herself. This is more clearly and more intensively manifested by neurotic parents and is even more striking where the parents are psychotic. In the latter it may assume a parasitic or a symbiotic relation of very destructive proportions.

But the parasitic and symbiotic urges are not confined to the pathologic alone. They are present in all parent-child relations, but where the ego boundaries and strengths are adequate in the parents the child is not overwhelmed by them and can achieve a workable individuality. These trends do not always express themselves as authoritarian domination. The feeling that the child is part and parcel of the parent can take the form of infantilization and over-protection. This too denies him his rightful opportunity to become an independent, self-directive entity. We found it in practice that these parents are less responsive to guidance and even therapy than are their opposites who tend to reject and dominate their children. This may be due to the fact that the pampering parent's feelings proceeds more often from neurotic sources with strong erotic components than is the case with the former. Neurotic symbioses and emotional parasitism have their roots in intense unconscious needs for erotic gratification and oral dependence which is not always the case in the domineering parent.[4] Usually, though not always, the pattern of behavior of the latter stems from their particular type of ego functioning, which is more readily accessible to the less intensive therapies and guidance.

An additional factor that may operate in this greater accessibility

---

[4] Parental domination, however, may be a reaction formation to oral dependence and stem from it.

of the punitive parent is that the social mores and value system in our culture disapprove of his way of treating children. Kindly and indulgent approaches are more acceptable and more approved. Thus the intrapsychic needs are buttressed by social approval making them more yielding to less intensive influences than in the case of the doting parent.

III

Principles and Practice in Child-Centered
Group Guidance

Despite the deeper implications of parenthood men and women have discharged their role as parents with varying degrees of adequacy without having the awareness of any or many of the dynamics, only a few of which were enumerated in the preceding chapter. Men and women who had the good fortune of being themselves nurtured in a comparatively constructive family atmosphere by parents with reasonable tolerance and tact discharge their parental role without creating too many difficulties. There are also men and women who because of external conditions or their subjective states, such as physical health and psychic organization, are able to carry on without excessive strain and negative effects. Parenthood is not an excessive burden to them and as a result they do not react with glaring anger, irritation, resentment, neglect or overprotection. This is sometimes described as "readiness for parenthood." While this apt phrase strikes at the core of the situation, it is rather unclear because it does not tell us what constitutes such "readiness." We shall not enter into the complex concept lest we stray too far afield from our central aim, but everyone can recognize interferences with parental functions which stem from infantile characteristics, anachronous cravings and other personality problems. While these cannot be always corrected, certainly not in the vast numbers of adults, methods for preparing them for positive parenthood must be evolved so as at least to reduce the strain upon succeeding generations.[1]

1 This topic is discussed in some detail in Chapter XI.

As already indicated, such techniques can be helpful only in the absence of serious intrapsychic distortions and where an urge toward health and equilibrium is waiting, so to speak, to be guided toward realization. We must assume that the majority of parents fall into the category who can be helped to correct their misconceptions as to the function and role of parents and give up their past habits and traditional practices. It is with these that we deal in Child-Centered Group Guidance.

The groups consist of eight mothers or fathers who are assigned to separate groups and meet on alternate weeks for 90 minutes to two hours. They are most effective when the children of the parents are of nearly the same age and of the same sex. This is necessary so that the experiences of the participants are as nearly alike as possible. Similar experiences and like situations aid mutual identification, facilitate sharing and mutual help, enhance the significance of communications and render the discussions more practical and meaningful. When points of commonality are lacking, the discussions are apt to become theoretical, which is less likely to occur when all concerned are at one in their preoccupations. We shall see presently that discussions and conversations must at all times concern themselves with *actual* situations as they occur in the lives of the parents and *only those that relate to their children.* It is for this reason that the factor of commonality is so important. The report on or presentation of a situation[2] by one parent mirrors in varying degrees those of the other participants. Reactions to and reflections of a situation therefore take of necessity a practical turn since they touch each one in an intimate and realistic fashion. The choice of participants here, as in all types of effective group work, group counseling, group guidance, and group psychotherapy is the main pivot of success and we are devoting an entire chapter to this important topic (see Chapter VIII).

To illustrate the nature of these discussions we reproduce below a condensed record of one session of a group of fathers of boys eleven to twelve years old. This is the eighth session of a guidance group in

2 Note that the terms "problem" or "difficulty" are not used in these groups and are not referred to as such. The terms "situation," "occurrence," "development," "event," are used instead.

which all but two parents are new. Mr. Cross, a very punitive father, attended about twenty sessions in a former group from which the other fathers had been discharged. He was carried over because of his stubborn insistence on dealing with his son harshly. (The subsequent improvement in Mr. Cross is detailed in Chapter V.) Mr. Black had attended six or seven sessions in another group before it was interrupted by the summer recess, and he was included in the present group. All the others were new to the guidance group.

After an initial pause, Mr. Kent said that if no one else would start the discussion, he would. He then described how his boy was not doing so well at the afternoon parochial school so that now he was receiving private instruction. This seemed to work out better. Mr. Cross remarked that his boy's religious education was a waste of time. Sol was not getting "a damn thing out of it, nor did others." Both Mr. Stein and Mr. Kent questioned it, Mr. Stein stating that it depended on the child. Mr. Kent remarked that his boy had done better than he, the father, ever did. In reply to this Mr. Cross remarked that in his boy's case, it was the fault of the teachers since they did not know how to teach. In addition, he felt that it cut into children's playtime a lot and there were probably many other things that a child would rather do, especially if the teacher was like Sol's and did not make learning interesting. He then related an anecdote about his son. The boy was studying Spanish rather than geometry and when Mr. Cross questioned him about this, Sol remarked he was afraid of the Spanish teacher but that he could beat up the math teacher by himself.

Mr. Kent then recalled that about a month before, the leader had given an interesting example of the keen imagination of children and remarked that "children of this generation seem to be smarter." Some discussion on this ensued during which Mr. Day and Mr. Stein brought out that this generation of children were being given greater advantages. Mr. Cross in a resentful tone remarked that there was a book entitled *Parents Can Be People*. He asked the leader directly: "Did you hear about a return to the old school of handling children —stepping on them?" and added with a smile that sometimes he felt like jumping on them with both feet, further commenting that he and his wife could rarely get to see any of their favorite programs on television because the children insisted on viewing their programs. To this, Mr. Day replied that he gave his children an allotted time for television and he stuck to it. Mr. Kent laughed and told Mr. Cross that he should get himself a second and cheaper television set than the one the children have. Mr. Cross said his solution was to throw out the set they now had. Mr. Kent recalled how one time he had pulled a tube and then told his son that the set did not work.

Mr. Black arrived at this point, about twenty minutes late, and again seated himself somewhat on the periphery of the group. Mr. Day continued the discussion around television by stating that sometimes he had used the device of tossing a coin to settle arguments between the children. Mr. Cross remarked that this did not work for him because Sol was a sore loser. He then described with approval in his voice how Sol had been "kidding" his little sister, who is very thin, and had told her that if she stood "sideways" in school, she would be marked absent. There was laughter from the group and Mr. Kent asked with some surprise how old Sol was and Mr. Cross remarked, "His Highness is twelve." Mr. Kent registered the sarcasm in Mr. Cross's tone and remarked: "You're rough on him." The latter replied: "Yes, and he knows it—maybe that's the trouble." Mr. Cross added that sometimes he made a special effort to get along with his son and later wondered if the child did not think the father was trying to "handshake with him."

Mr. Kent brought up a situation in which he felt that there had been some deceit on the part of his son who had said he was going to take a bath, but instead just sat in the bathroom and then gave the father "a flimsy excuse." Mr. Kent felt the boy had attempted to put something over on him and insisted upon the boy's taking a bath. The leader asked how this had worked out. Mr. Kent hesitated a moment and said, "Well, he was mad, but the next morning, he was friends." Questioning by the other fathers brought out that Mr. Kent's apartment was in the process of being painted and that there was a lot of paint all over the house which smelled strongly, especially in the bathroom. Here Mr. Cross remarked wryly that perhaps Mr. Kent should have bathed his son in paint.

Mr. Black participated for the first time in the session by noting his son's refusal to take a bath in winter and also remarked that the boy hated to lose time out from his reading. Mr. Cross humorously suggested to Mr. Black a device developed in veterans' hospitals which projects reading matter on to the wall so that a person lying on his back could read it. Mr. Day remarked tolerantly that his son liked to take toys into the bath with him.

Mr. Klinger arrived at this point, one half hour late.

A rather lengthy pause ensued. In view of the fact that four of the members present were fathers of enuretic children, the leader cited an instance which had occurred previously that day when a father had reported in reference to his son's bed wetting that he, the father, had told his son that something must be bothering him to make him wet and had suggested that the boy could tell it to the father. The leader asked the group what they thought of such an approach. Mr. Kent said that on one occasion his son had been tense about something and he had suggested that the boy tell him what was troubling him and it had helped. When no other opinions were forthcoming, the leader remarked that in the case he had just cited, the father had used the wrong approach because the child would not know why he wet and talking to him about it would just make him more anxious and focus more attention on something which should be ignored.

Here Mr. Cross emphatically pointed out that there could be one type of tension one day and a different one on another which might contribute to wetting and so the father would not really be able to do much by talking about it. Mr. Kent recalled that his son had once wet after a disturbing dream and the parents had offered him the opportunity to talk about the dream, but he told them that he was trying to forget it, and they let it go at that.

Mr. Klinger attempted to involve the leader in a general theoretical discussion about fears by asking if fears were the basic reason for children coming to the clinic. The leader did not respond to this. Mr. Klinger then asked how parents could avoid fear and build up confidence in children. Mr. Cross, addressing Mr. Klinger, stated that he was not sure about fears, but he did know that Sol's bed wetting continued because initially the parents made the mistake of "creating a terrific uproar" about it, thus frightening the child and also making him resentful. He then brought up his problems with his younger son. The boy is at the stage where he is continually shouting even to say the most ordinary things and that "the yelling shakes the walls." Mr. Kent asked Mr. Cross if he himself yelled in the house and Mr. Cross responded that at times he did, but not enough for the child to yell that much. When Mr. Cross asked the leader directly about this, the latter suggested that it would pass, provided that the parents did not make a fuss about it and make it important. Mr. Cross then recalled that once as an infant his older son, Sol, had screamed terribly and would not let the parents out of the room for a whole day. He wondered if that had something to do with the boy's subsequent bed wetting. He noted that his wife had not pressed the two younger children in toilet training and that they had been trained easily. Mr. Stein stated that his five-year-old offered no trouble in this area and that there had been an improvement in his older son, Peter, who now wet only about once in two weeks and recently went three whole weeks dry. Mr. Klinger then asked Mr. Cross how the younger boy reacted to Sol's wetting and Mr. Cross remarked that there was no particular reaction. Mr. Black smiled and wondered if the younger boy called the older names.

A pause followed and the leader asked Mr. Black how things were working out in the mornings in relation to Sam. (Mr. Black had once brought to the group's attention a daily and bitter conflict situation with Sam in which Mr. Black ran around to find the boy's clothes and books for him, tried to get him to eat in time, kept nagging the boy in order to get him to leave for school on time.) Mr. Black seemed pleased at this evidence of interest on the part of the leader and remarked with satisfaction that they had moved and were now living in a larger apartment. He now leaves Sam alone in the mornings and the boy takes his own breakfast. "If he is late, he is late, and there are no more fights in the morning," he added. Mr. Black felt that there was also an improvement in that the child now had to take a bus to school and rode with other children. He said with pride that he no longer ran to gather the boy's books and if the boy asked where his books were, Mr. Black replied he did not know. He keeps out of the situation. He recalled that before he came to the group, he used to worry more about Sam's books than the boy did himself.

Mr. Cross then related that Sol's confirmation was approaching and the boy wanted a "thank you" card with his picture on it because one of his cousins had it, but that Mrs. Cross had "tabled this idea." Somewhat resentfully Mr. Cross remarked that the boy had very definite ideas about what he wanted and did not want. Mr. Black reported here that he had promised Sam a hamster if he would not bite his nails altogether or would do so less during the Christmas vacation. (In a recent follow-up interview with Mr. Black, he reported that the boy had been asking for a pet. This was discussed with the father and it was recommended that a pet be obtained for the child.) Mr. Black continued that the other day there were visitors in the house who told a story about the Gestapo. Mr. Black noted that during the telling of the story, which was a somewhat tense one, Sam started to bite his nails. Mr. Black recognized on his own that the nail biting was a result of tension and fear. At this point, Mr. Klinger in a very friendly manner offered Mr. Black the use of a hamster cage which his children no longer needed. Mr. Black thanked him and explained that Sam was making a cage for the hamster in the club (activity therapy group). Mr. Klinger readily said that he understood. Mr. Klinger also suggested that Mr. Black might get a parakeet which he described as a very good pet.

A very reticent and silent man, Mr. Black now appeared really to open up and began to talk eagerly about his relationship to Sam. As he did so, he brought his chair right close to the table so that he now was for the first time within the circle. He indicated that he no longer worried about Sam's fish but let it alone and the boy now took care of it himself. Mr. Cross remarked that recently Sol did not want to have a haircut even though he needed one badly, and Mr. Cross and his wife decided to let "social pressure work instead of harping on it" themselves and see what happened. A week later the boy went by himself and got a haircut. Mr. Cross still did not know why he went, but perhaps it was due to pressure from his friends. Mr. Black somewhat eagerly described that he had had a similar problem for a while, until Sam copied another boy whom he admired and had a haircut.

At this point Mr. Klinger addressed the leader. "Do you feel that the group has been helpful and is achieving its purpose?" he asked.

The leader nodded in the direction of the other men, but did not reply himself. Mr. Cross in a semihumorous manner remarked to Mr. Klinger: "Well, Sol would not be alive today if it were not for this group. We would have killed him by now." Mr. Black remarked to Mr. Klinger: "I used to beat hell out of my boy but now I count to ten and twenty and sometimes even fifty before doing anything rash." Mr. Kent said: "There certainly is improvement. I have less fights with my boy now. I hit him less and there is less brutality." He then pointed out to Mr. Black that he himself had made progress being able to leave the boy alone in the mornings.

Mr. Black confirmed this by saying: "Sam has improved 25 per cent in less than a year." Mr. Cross remarked to Mr. Black: "You should have no complaints at all. That's good." Mr. Black admitted he was quite pleased although his boy "still has a long way to go, for instance, he still leaves his room like a stable." Mr. Black continued that he knew they could leave it to the boy to clean up, but they just could not do it. To this Mr. Kent responded by pointing out that if the boy could make his own breakfast and go to school by himself, he could clean up his own room, too. Mr. Black appeared somewhat doubtful about this. He then spoke about the larger apartment as being a big help in that Sam and his sister now had separate rooms whereas previously they had shared a room and fought with each other; also, at the present time, when his wife came home with a headache, she could lie down in her own room and have some rest.

Thereupon, Mr. Klinger remarked that if Mr. Black carried that to its logical conclusion, the solution would be for the children to live in one house and the parents in another and added: "Like this, you just don't see them as much as you used to." Mr. Black half admitted and half denied this. He then indicated that there was still difficulty in Sam's social adjustment. He was still an "outcast" and still did not go out. Here Mr. Kent recalled that Mr. Black had told him that Sam had met a friend at the seashore. Mr. Black confirmed this but then recalled two summers ago that the child had not even left the house at all. Mr. Black indicated that the teacher had told them that on a recent school trip the children were told to double up and Sam did not double up with anyone but walked by himself.

Mr. Cross made the last statement of the session by describing something Sol had said. There are a pair of twins in Sol's class whose mother goes everywhere with them even on school trips. Sol told his parents: "I used to think you two babied me, but you're nothing like that mother of the twins."

The leader's impression: This session was marked by (1) Mr. Black's active participation in the group. (2) Mr. Cross for the second consecutive time reported Sol's recognition of his parents as different and the realization that they compare favorably with parents of his peers. (3) Mr. Cross exhibited a continuing trend to discuss difficulties of other children, rather than concentrating solely on Sol as the black shee which he had done exclusively in the past. (4) The evaluation of the effect of the group on the fathers stimulated by Mr. Klinger's question showed that three fathers described the benefits of the group: curbing readiness toward physical punishment of children and more patience toward children's behavior.

Discussion. As one could expect, the fathers start off with resentment against their children and with their annoying behavior which in this instance is centered around television. They are also jealous of their children who have advantages that they themselves did not have. Being aware of the leader's convictions on child rearing, Mr. Cross taunts him when he speaks of the "new ways" of dealing with children, namely "stepping on them." By this Mr. Cross acts out his hostility toward his own father, which is one of his central difficulties, as we learned later. He discharges his resentment against the leader who, by his acceptance and gracious manner, brings into relief Mr. Cross' irascibility and cruelty to his son (see Chapter V). Behind his sarcasm is guilt. However, the value of this conversation lies in the fact that the fathers in the group go beyond mere complaints. They seek ways of dealing with situations. Though the suggestions are not practical or appropriate, their value lies in the fact that the men explore possibilities *on their own.* The solutions will eventually come from their *attitudes* and not from the information as to how to deal with a specific situation. This is suggested later by Mr. Black in relation to school and his son, but the leader does not draw this out or point it up to the group. He waits until the men arrive at this in the future through *cumulative perceptiveness* and their increased sensitivity to children's needs. If they fail to do this within a reasonable period, he may have to formulate it for them later, but by that time a *state of readiness* would have been achieved in the participants and his formulations would therefore be meaningful to them. At this point a peroration on "attitudes" would be only a conceptualization that would fall flat. Waiting and timing are essential, here as it is also in psychotherapy.

In the next situation, bathing by Mr. Kent's son, the leader asks how the father's "insistence" worked out. This is done in order to condition parents to try to examine their own acts and to counteract their tendency to place the blame for all difficulties on children. This is brought home to him by the leader's question, for Mr. Kent hesitates for a moment, and under the pressure of the other men admits that there were extenuating circumstances, namely, the odor of paint in the bathroom, which Mr. Kent seemed to have ignored while he was pressing his son. Here the group mates and not the leader make a father stop and examine the relation of cause and effect, which is only too rarely done by parents. He now sees more justification for his son's resistance to bathing; it was not entirely disobedience. One of our aims is to condition parents to reflect on their responses and acts before putting them into operation. This is brought out very clearly and touchingly in many of the discussions to be quoted later.

The leader now notes a hesitancy in the group to continue— whether it was Mr. Klinger's arrival that interrupted the trend or not we cannot say—and he utilizes a common element in the father's situation, their boys' enuresis. He does not lecture at them, however, but rather submits for their examination an *attitude* of another parent. By using an extraneous case rather than directly relating it to the men present, he avoids activating anxiety and guilt. He makes the matter rather impersonal. This tact "pays off," as it were, for all the fathers, including Mr. Cross, speak freely of this problem with their children and, by identifying with or emulating the leader, display rather remarkable tolerance and a genuine effort to understand and empathize with their children in this malady. Mr. Cross actually admits that a mistake was made in his household in raising a "terrific uproar."

Although Mr. and Mrs. Cross applied for treatment for Sol, who is here under discussion, Mr. Cross transfers the focus of his preoccupation from him to his younger son. This is, as pointed out by the leader in his report, a salutary development. He seeks the leader's help—quite a change from his previous arrogant attitude. He then makes an effort to trace and understand the events leading to the boy's bed wetting. No longer does the father blame the boy for this, but is beginning to see impersonal, but unavoidable external circumstances. This cumulative awareness and the transfer of the onus of guilt from the child prepare the ground for a more effective dealing with his difficulty. This unquestionably occurs in the case of the Cross family, as is amply demonstrated by future developments (see Chapter V). The fact that the Stein boy has improved, because of a changed attitude in the parents resulting from the group discussions with both parents, encourages the other fathers in the group. It also demonstrates how "transfer of training" occurs through *change in attitudes*. The Steins apparently applied to the younger child what they have learned in their groups about the older. Thus the total family atmosphere is affected through the growing understanding of one of the children.

Another pause follows, but the leader does not interpret it as resistance as he would in a psychotherapy group, nor does he evoke from the members reactions to or explanation of the silence. Rather he again focuses attention upon a child, in this case that of Mr. Black. He chooses Mr. Black because he is a shy, seclusive person who seldom participates in group discussions. The latter seemed pleased when the leader turned his attention to him. This attention was a way of encouraging him to be more active in the group and to reassure him of the leader's acceptance and of his equal status in the group with the others. Parenthetically, Mr. Black's boy was a member of an activity therapy group, as were Mr. Cross's, Mr. Friedman's, Mr. Black's, Mr. Klinger's, Mr. Jasper's, Mr. Schaeffer's and Mr. Sands' boys. Mr. Klinger's son received individual treatment as well as being a member of a therapy group. Mrs. Cross, Mrs. Day, and Mrs. Friedman were in mothers' groups and Mrs. Black in individual treatment. Mr. Black's son, like his father, was found to be shy and withdrawn in his group and at first kept very much to himself.

Mr. Black was a professional man and the only one with a college education, the others being small businessmen, salesmen and factory workers. The striking characteristic in Mr. Black's relation with his son was that the latter continually sought to stump his father with questions on obtruse, highly scientific and esoteric subjects, the knowledge of which the boy acquired through voracious reading. He had a very high intelligence quotient and a retentive mind and took delight in exposing his father's real or fancied intellectual inadequacy, a delight that he communicated to his mother, as though attempting to appear more worthy than was his father. While the core of this pattern is in the oedipal struggle between the father and son, who was, by the way an only child, the father's laying himself open to the tyranny of his son as exemplified by the anxiety of getting the boy to school, sharpened this struggle and gave the boy an upper hand over his father. Following a number of discussions in the group of this situation, Mr. Black acquired sufficient self-confidence and detachment to withdraw and to leave to the boy the responsibility of getting to school on time. This had the effect of not only helping the boy mature, but decreased the tension between the two.

The leader's technique in asking Mr. Black about his son's behavior in a situation that had been discussed in previous sessions is that of *recalling*. It served several ends in this case, in addition to the one already pointed out, namely encouraging Mr. Black. The recalling method helps all to keep abreast of developments; to evaluate the effectiveness of the technique of dealing with specific situations. If successful, it encourages other parents to adopt the same approach in a similar situation; it helps to bring new understandings and learnings upon a specific problem; it gives the group members gratifying feelings of success, actual and vicarious, and above all, by focusing again and again on children's behavior and its meaning. By this the leader also emphasizes the *primary group code*.

Striking empathy and understanding is clearly displayed in the next paragraph where Mr. Black promises his formerly very much hated son a hamster that reduced the latter's nail biting, and his growing sensitiveness to his son's difficulties reflected in his observation that tension and fear increase nail biting. The growing feeling of mutuality among the group members is reflected in Mr. Kent's offer to give Mr. Black a cage. We shall describe in more detail (Chapter X) the effect upon the personalities of parents of being part of an intimate group in which they share with little restraint their thoughts, feelings and confusions and where reigns an atmosphere of good will and an honest desire to help one another. Presided over by a calm, uncritical and unpunitive leader, such a group incorporates all the best features of a good home and ideal parent-child and sibling relations. We are, therefore, suggesting that there is every possibility that a guidance group conducted on this plan offers to the participants emotional re-education in human relationships through a substitute ideal family. In this respect, these groups affect adults as activity therapy groups do children.[3]

"At this point Mr. Black appeared really to open up," is the leader's cryptic description of the effect of having been accepted by the group and being so successful with his son. In fact, so enthusiastic is he, that he forgets his shyness and moves his chair closer to the table where the others sat. His success infects Mr. Cross who now admits of having allowed his son to make his own decision in the matter of a haircut, which is a far cry from his original conduct.

Again Mr. Klinger attempts to enveigle the leader into a theoretic discussion, but the leader instead of falling into the trap refers the question to the group where it rightfully belongs. He does this by a gesture, rather than verbally. There is a significant difference here. If the leader were to formulate the question for the group in such words as, "Well, what do the rest of you think?" he would (1) put the members under obligation to answer him, and (2) he would tacitly approve irrelevant and abstract discussions abrogating the primary group code, which is to consider only practical matters not abstractions. Mr. Klinger's question is nonetheless answered by all the participating fathers, which should have pleased the leader greatly.

The technique employed here by the leader can be described as that of *active avoidance* as differentiated from *passive avoidance* in which silence is the sole tool. In active avoidance the leader responds with a gesture, grimace or verbal reaction which does not involve

[3] See my *Introduction to Group Therapy*. New York: International Universities Press, 1954, pp. 201-206.

him, but rather turns the situation over to the group. A question like "What do you think?" is an example of active avoidance. The usual result of passive avoidance is that the subject is dropped. Active avoidance may have the same effect but most often encourages the continuation of the discussion, as was the case in the present instance.

In addition to a number of striking features in this brief report of a 90-minute session, it illustrates the skill of the leader, who is a trained psychotherapist, to avoid being drawn into a theoretic discussion. This he does on a number of occasions, notably when Mr. Cross asks him about the new techniques of dealing with children and Mr. Kent attempts to involve him in a general discussion of fears. This the leader avoids, because it helps the parents to continue in their interchange concerning their children's overt behavior and reactions and their own part in dealing with them. The technique he employed here is that of *passivity* and is only one of such techniques. Others are *deflection, retracing, recalling,* and *diversion,* which will be described at the appropriate time later.

The significant feature of this session is that the participants confine themselves to a discussion of their children and a frank admission of their own behavior, which some of them are beginning to recognize as having been inappropriate. This concentration on the central topic is a result of the *primary group code.* By this is meant that, though not conceptualized, formulated or codified, groups arrive at a basic perception or recognition of the aim of the group and its procedure. Here the primary group code consists of three elements: (1) the subjects for discussion are the children and the way parents deal with them; (2) free participation by all without formality, routines or organization of the discussion; and (3) the leader is not a pedagogue, an authority or a sole source of information to whom the members have to turn.

What is of utmost importance to practitioners of this method is that these "codes" are not laid before the group; nor are they formulated. They are rather unverbalized practices which emerge through the *selective responses* by the leader. The fact that he repeatedly avoids, and therefore discourages, certain topics and responds to others, impresses itself upon the participants and they, too, soon adopt a *self-selective* pattern. This requires a considerable amount of restraint and judgment which is in most instances preconceptual and nonverbal. We shall point out (Chapter VIII) later the value of this technique as an *anxiety avoidance* device which is not under consideration at this point.

The facilities for conducting these groups in a manner illustrated here are hard to come by. A great deal of experience and persistent and rigorous training is necessary before one develops the vigilance, perceptiveness, *anticipatory judgment* and an ability to react appropriately to remarks by members of the group. This is amply illustrated in Chapter VIII on "Pitfalls." To bring home the degree of training and self-control required, the following record of a group discussion of about a year before by the same leader is reproduced here. This is the ninth session of another group. Three fathers are absent, five are present.

Mr. Friedman began by discussing with Mr. Jasper their children coming to the "club" (therapy group). Mr. Friedman described that his wife had stealthily watched Morris from behind a building[4] to see how he crossed the street so that he would not be injured. He did cross carefully and he would now be allowed to come to the group alone. Mr. Jasper stated that he did not know when his boy would be able to travel alone and added that perhaps the fault was with his wife as well as with the boy. Mr. Friedman recalled how nervous his son was when he first took the train alone and yet the boy was greatly satisfied and proud at having done it correctly.

At this point, Mr. Schaeffer entered and the leader introduced him and Mr. Friedman. Mr. Jasper turned to Mr. Schaeffer and with a smile said that he had been wondering whether all of Mr. Schaeffer's child's problems had been solved or whether Mr. Schaeffer just could not come to the meetings. Mr. Schaeffer smiled and said that all the problems certainly had not been solved yet, though there had been improvement.

As he had done at previous sessions, Mr. Friedman commented upon his son's unevenness in school marks and Mr. Jasper said that his son, Eric, used to "drop in his marks," but in the past year

4 See also pp. 120-121.

(since he was a member of an activity therapy group) they have become higher and have remained more consistently so. Mr. Friedman then remarked upon the uneven quality in his son's handwriting: sometimes it is very good and sometimes it looks just like the writing of a two-year-old.

Mr. Daws addressed a question to the leader at this point saying that he would like an answer to his "problem." He went on to describe somewhat vaguely the fact that his older daughter bossed his son, refused to "play school" with him and in general alternated between ordering the child around and withdrawing from him in certain ways. Mr. Friedman asked how long this had been going on. Mr. Daws was again vague, implying that it had been going on for quite a while. He then stated that he thought that the girl was showing a need to act superior to her brother. She probably liked to boss him around. Mr. Friedman laughingly interjected: "She's just like a woman. She wants to be boss." Mr. Daws recognized that his daughter saw her brother as a rival, "as an enemy," and that it dated back to the time when his son returned from a foster home (a temporary placement), about three years before. He indicated that she probably was afraid of being replaced by the boy in the parents' affections. The leader said that Mr. Daws had analyzed well some of the underlying factors and then asked how Mr. Daws and his wife could help the girl to feel that she would not be replaced by the boy. Mr. Daws appeared somewhat surprised at this question, smiled and indicated that recently he and his wife had attempted to give her more attention and affection.

At this point, Mr. Sands entered the room and there was an exchange of greetings around the table. (Mr. Sands appeared first to seek the leader's attention before turning to the others.)

Mr. Jasper brought up the question of why there seemed to be more boys in treatment than girls and referred to an article he had read in which it was stated that a greater percentage of boys than girls were in need of treatment. There was no response from the others to this and the leader commented that in our culture there appeared to be more pressure on boys as they were growing up and perhaps more tension between the boy and his mother. Mr. Jasper wondered whether there was not more of "some kind of sexual problem between mothers and their sons." Mr. Friedman's reaction to this was that his son Morris had never asked him about sex and yet he had asked his mother about it when she was pregnant. Later he got the information from the boys on the street and Mr. Friedman smiled as he said the boy came back and rather jokingly described that he and his mother had called things by different names and she had explained things differently although the facts seemed to be the same.

Mr. Daws then remarked that as a girl grows older, she "feels more affinity with the mother." Mr. Friedman questioned this but did not give any specific reasons. Mr. Sands then entered the discussion by expressing the opinion that a girl in her teens had more in common with her mother and added that, for instance, she certainly could not discuss her "periods" with her father.

Prefacing his remark that he only had one child, Mr. Jasper said he would be interested in the opinions of those present who had more than one: did they find strong attraction between the mothers and boys and was this any different in cases where there was more than one child? Mr. Schaeffer brought out rather humorously that he only had one child and suggested with a smile that Mr. Jasper ask Mr. Daws. Mr. Daws smiled broadly and said he had five and he had not noticed this. Here Mr. Friedman gestured toward Mr. Daws and apparently referring to the latter's five children, exclaimed, "He's a good man!" Mr. Schaeffer repeated with a certain questioning, derisive quality in his intonation: "good man?"

Mr. Daws now began to stutter rather markedly. In fact, he stuttered more than he had had in any of the previous sessions. He said that he found that his son right now was seeking out the mother but expressed the conviction that as the boy grew up, he would seek out his father. Mr. Jasper asked Mr. Daws if Mr. Daws' son played with the other children in the family and in the brief discussion that ensued, it came out that the age range among Mr. Daws' children was rather small. Mr. Friedman laughed and said that Mr. Daws "doesn't waste time."

Mr. Daws described the differences between his son and his older daughter in that the girl was much more friendly and outgoing whereas his son would rather keep to himself and was more quiet.

Mr. Friedman said that his little girl, age two, had high fever recently and since then has expressed much more fear of her brother Morris. Morris had teased her in the past, but for some reason the girl seemed quite frightened of him now. Morris, being "nervous" himself, probably made the little girl nervous, too. Mr. Daws advised Mr. Friedman to let the son dress and feed the little girl and take care of her and in that way he would feel closer to her. Mr. Daws remarked that his boy did that for his little brother and then added; "We make him."

Mr. Sands, with humor and yet with obvious criticism, said: "You have to put him to work some time. You can't have him become a bum; after all, he's ten years old!"

More openly critical, Mr. Schaeffer asked Mr. Daws point-blank: "Did it ever occur to you that your son might resent this?" The latter, speaking rather generally, maintained that dressing and feeding and doing other chores for the smaller children was in some way beneficial for the relationship.

Addressing the group, the leader asked specifically how dressing and feeding of a younger child by an older one helped improve their relationship. Mr. Schaeffer quickly remarked that that was what he was asking also and appeared to be challenging Mr. Daws again. Mr. Schaeffer continued that Mr. Daws should pay the boy for doing these things and he wondered if Mr. Daws had ever thought of that, adding that two cents would go a long way. Mr. Friedman described how he once gave his boy twenty-five cents to do some-thing and after that the boy wanted to be paid for everything. Mr. Schaeffer stated that Mr. Friedman had made a mistake by giving the boy too much money. Mr. Friedman admitted that he had real-ized it.

Mr. Daws was then asked about his son's reaction to carrying out the responsibilities for the younger children. Mr. Daws became somewhat defensive and claimed that it only happened once in a while, at the same time implying that the older child did not care for these tasks. Then Mr. Schaeffer, challengingly, asked Mr. Daws if he, himself, ever did the dishes. Mr. Schaeffer appeared mollified when Mr. Daws said that he not only did the dishes but also washed clothes. Mr. Jasper again remarked that he had only one child but that he himself was one of six and everybody helped each other in his family. Mr. Schaeffer, as if brushing the thought aside, said that was "the old days"; nowadays an only child resented doing things like this.

Mr. Friedman recalled that he was one of three children and that they had lived in a cold flat on the East Side and he used to bring the coal up every day whereas his brother had somehow got away with it, and he did remember being resentful against his brother. Mr. Schaeffer appeared to brush this aside by saying quickly, "So what?"

Mr. Daws then asked the leader if it was good for a child to have responsibilities around the house. The latter said that it would depend on the total situation and illustrated that one child might work very hard and very proudly to build something with his father in the backyard and that the same boy might be very angry and fretful about being told to do some other task in the house, such as washing dishes or something like that. Mr. Sands stated he felt that it depended on the relationship in the house and he illustrated it by saying: "It is the same thing as working for a boss; if you like him, you will work overtime and do everything for him, and if you don't, you will do only what you actually have to." Mr. Friedman concurred in this; he felt Mr. Sands was perfectly right.

At one point during the discussion, the leader suggested to Mr. Daws that perhaps in his home some of these small jobs could be divided into those more suited for boys and those more suitable for girls. Mr. Daws thought about this for a while and then recalled that his son Morton did like to use the vacuum cleaner and that this was probably a more masculine occupation because it involved strength to pull the cleaner around; he indicated that he saw that this might be more suited to Morton than feeding the baby or doing dishes.

Mr. Sands then addressed Mr. Daws and recalled that at the very first session, Mr. Daws had spoken about punishing his boy for not taking good care of one of the little children who had fallen off a chair when Morton, Mr. Daws' son, was supposed to be watching her. Mr. Sands added that he thought his memory of it was correct, but asked Mr. Daws to correct him if he is wrong. Mr. Daws hesitated for a moment and then seemed to recall the situation. He told Mr. Sands that he had a good memory. A little defensively he described that, after all, the boy had been set to watch the little girl and he let her fall. He added that, after all, boys "are really little men" and implied that responsibility, therefore, could be assigned them. He further added that actually he administered only light punishment.

Mr. Schaeffer asked what the difference between light and heavy punishment was. Mr. Daws considered it light punishment when he struck the child's hand or his "behind" with a ruler. Mr. Schaeffer, in apparent surprise, exclaimed, "What!" Mr. Jasper, too, expressed surprise, remarking he thought that "all that went out of fashion long ago." Mr. Jasper turned to Mr. Schaeffer and asked what he did to punish his child. Mr. Schaeffer said that he never hit his child; then turning toward Mr. Daws with much feeling, he demanded to know why Mr. Daws' son should have to watch "your kid; he's a human being."

Mr. Daws replied that his son was able to watch the younger child because he "is not a machine; he thinks." Here Mr. Schaeffer somewhat hotly retorted, "That was just the point." When the discussion led back to punishment, the leader asked if any of the men had found that punishment really worked; and he explained that by "working" he meant accomplishing an end without causing all sorts of angry feelings in the home that were carried over into other situations.

There was a brief silence. Mr. Schaeffer then explained that he did not hit his child but that he took away the television and that the boy seemed to remember it. Mr. Friedman commented that on the occasions when he had hit his boy, he found the latter got so disturbed that it actually was not worth it. He was surprised that Mr. Schaeffer's son obeyed his father. Mr. Schaeffer, smiling and with some pride, exclaimed: "What do you mean? After all, I am the father!" He stated that whenever he punished his child, he always explained to him the reason why.

Mr. Friedman remarked at this point that his son was "nervous" and resented anything he said. In reference to doing dishes, Mr. Schaeffer remarked that sometimes he and his son did them together and had a lot of fun in the process. He emphasized that a boy liked to imitate his father and when he saw the father help in the house, the boy would want to do the same. He said he would like to ask the group something, and described how the other night his son, John, had awakened at 3 A.M. and told him that he had had a "bad" dream and asked to go into his father's bed.

He and his wife have twin beds and he did not ask any questions, but simply told the boy that he could get into bed with him. At the same time he was trying to figure out why the boy should want to do this. Mr. Friedman guessed that the boy had been frightened by something and repeated the fact he had narrated in a previous session that Morris looked under his bed every night because he was afraid that someone might be there. Mr. Schaeffer explained the boy's wanting to get into the father's bed on the basis that the parents recently had their beds redone with foam rubber mattresses and that the boy heard the parents saying how comfortable it was to sleep on them. Here Mr. Schaeffer remarked somewhat humorously that probably the boy was jealous and wanted to try out what he had heard was so wonderful.

Several of the men told Mr. Schaeffer that if his son continued to get into the parents' beds, they should get him a foam rubber mattress of his own. Mr. Schaeffer agreed that he would if the boy continued to do it. There was some laughter at this. Mr. Friedman expressed some doubt as to whether the foam rubber was the real reason and implied that he felt the boy was frightened of something. Mr. Schaeffer denied this.

Mr. Daws tried to return to the leader's question about punishment, but Mr. Schaeffer interrupted him to ask if he had ever wrestled with his son. He advised Mr. Daws to let his son "smack you around; he'll love it." Mr. Daws said that he did not approve of it. Mr. Schaeffer, speaking heartily, told him to try it and to see how well it would work and "see how close you'll get to him after that," adding that he did it "all the time" with his son and rather humorously imitated how his son hit him and probably thought that he was striking a boy on the street that he did not like. The boy did not hurt him, he said and added, gesturing toward Mr. Daws, that this would bring more results than striking the child with a ruler which was Mr. Daws' practice. It was not so much the hitting as the fact that a child tried out wrestling grips which he has seen on television.

The leader asked how long Mr. Schaeffer would continue to let the child discharge his feelings in physical contact with the father. Mr. Schaeffer smiled at first, stating that the boy was almost as big as he was now and he would probably have to stop soon for his own "self-protection," but added more seriously that it would taper off as the boy grew older.

There was some humorous interplay when Mr. Sands commented that after all Mr. Daws had five children and if he wrestled with them all it would probably be too much for him. Mr. Daws smiled at this with obvious pleasure. He then returned again to the question of punishment and he seemed somewhat anxious about the group's reaction to his statement that he hit his son with a ruler. He attempted to prove that this was not really as serious as the group seemed to think, stating that the boy cried for about five minutes but then was all right again. The boy "must become interested in doing things," he concluded.

Mr. Schaeffer brought out that his father never actually used to hit them but that he would hold up a strap and would threaten them. Humorously Mr. Schaeffer said that that was enough for them; the children behaved. There was some laughter at this remark. The leader asked how hitting a child helped him become interested in doing something. Mr. Daws smiled, appeared somewhat embarrassed, and said that was not actually what he meant and then made rather vague and very general remarks. Mr. Sands insisted that the leader asked a question, but he certainly knew the answer and added emphatically that hitting a child was just a way of relieving the parents own feelings.

Mr. Friedman concurred with this statement, relating that once he had struck his son and felt better himself. There was laughter in response to this which appeared to release the mounting tension in the group activated largely by Mr. Daws.

Mr. Daws now tried to shift the responsibility for punishing the children onto his wife, stating that he has to punish them because when he comes home from work his wife tells him how the children misbehaved and urges him to beat them. Mr. Schaeffer questioned Mr. Daws as to whether the latter really had to do it, and Mr. Daws indicated that if he did not, he would have trouble with his wife.

Mr. Friedman said that he had really learned his lesson and then brought out that once when he attempted to hit his son, the boy pulled a knife on him. Since then he had not attempted to touch the boy. He had learned his lesson, he repeated. Silence ensued. It was the leader's feeling that Mr. Friedman's statement shocked the men. Mr. Jasper remarked how casually Mr. Friedman described the violence. The latter said that he might be casual now, but he certainly had not been when the incident occurred.

Mr. Schaeffer reverted to a general criticism of Mr. Daws for hitting his children. Mr. Sands said he knew that the book said that one sometimes could strike a child, "But you have to do it when you are calm and rational." Mr. Daws somewhat eagerly asserted that he was calm when he hit the children. Mr. Schaeffer smilingly said: "O.K., now you have our permission to hit them." The men smiled at this. (Again trying to allay anxiety.)

Mr. Sands said he admitted he did not know how to punish his son, but that he did know how to punish his little girl. He just has to tell her that he will not talk to her or else he threatens not to bring her the drawing book on Fridays and she immediately becomes amenable to whatever he wants her to do. Mr. Friedman, with feeling, addressed Mr. Sands: "She must have a great love for you." (There seemed to be jealousy and longing in Mr. Friedman's tone as he said this.) Mr. Sands replied that he did not know what it was between him and the little girl. There was something that enabled him to influence her, but not the boy. Mr. Friedman then asked if he had brought up both children the same way and Mr. Sands indicated that he had. Mr. Jasper doubted this, pointing out that the two children were of different sex and were considerably apart in age and wondered if they actually could have been brought up in exactly the same way. Mr. Sands acknowledged that there probably had been a difference.

When Mr. Sands brought the discussion around to describing his son John's unfriendliness and undemonstrativeness, the leader asked if the boy had ever been demonstrative or affectionate. The father recalled that even as a small child John used to slide off his knee. The leader wondered why a child should do this and Mr. Sands admitted that the child did not react like that to everyone, that he trusted some people, like his aunt. Mr. Sands also mentioned that the boy had spoken warmly about a counselor at camp. He apparently worshiped the counselor.

Mr. Sands then criticized John's lack of imagination, describing how much more imaginative the little girl was. Though she was younger, she beat children at cards, and "even cheats me." She was able to tell good stories, etc. He then added that perhaps she got these skills from her father. He does not know why John did not learn these things from him. Mr. Sands described John's habit of rocking his head from side to side at night as a way of putting himself to sleep, at the same time also talking to himself about the day's happenings. Mr. Sands thought that when the boy talked like that "he also probably makes up some things and builds himself up," and added that the boy probably made of himself a hero. He was strongly opposed to allowing the boy to rock and talk, but his wife thought that it should be permitted. His wife goes out two nights a week and he is left home with the boy. On those nights he walks into the boy's bedroom and tells him: "There will be none of that monkey business tonight," and threatens to keep the door open, which John does not like because it is "like being spied on." Mr. Sands asked the leader whether this approach was right or wrong.

Mr. Jasper wanted to know whether Mr. Sands had ever asked his son why he rocked. The latter shook his head negatively. The leader asked Mr. Jasper whether he thought that the boy could answer that question. Mr. Sands stated that he did not think so. However, Mr. Jasper repeated his question and suggested that Mr. Sands might ask the boy. The leader then asked if an eleven- or twelve-year-old boy would be able to talk about a very deep memory of being gently rocked to sleep in the cradle. There was some discussion about this in which it was pointed out to Mr. Sands that his disapproval and his wife's approval showed the child that the parents had different opinions. This could be confusing to the boy. Mr.

Sands recognized this fact. None of the group actually criticized him for disapproving of the child's bedtime activity.

The leader asked Mr. Sands if he thought that he could go into the boy's room and suggest to him that he tell him about what happened during the day, allowing the boy to embellish or garnish the stories if he felt a need. Perhaps father and son could even make a game of it. The leader further pointed out that it would be a more maturing experience for the boy if he shared his thoughts with another person, especially his father. Mr. Schaeffer expressed approbation of this and told Mr. Sands: "It will bring you closer to him." Mr. Sands expressed interest in this and said that he would certainly try it and added that this sort of specific advice was what he had come to get.

When the leader said that he was not¯sure how it would work but that it might be worth trying, Mr. Sands said laughingly (in reference to the child's rocking to sleep and talking to himself): "I might even end up doing it myself." (This last appears to have been a crucial remark for Mr. Sands who himself was an infantile character and who resented seeing the same problem in his son.)

Discussion. This session begins with complaints against the children which brings the men close to one another and puts them at ease through the dynamic of universalization.[5] When Mr. Daws complains about his daughter, the leader confronts him rather directly with his responsibility. This embarrasses Mr. Daws which the leader wrongly describes as "surprise." The latter assumes here the role of the aggressor and taskmaster, instead of accepting Mr. Daws and attempting to help him find his own solution. The proper technique here would have been to ask for a specific instance of the girl's domination and rejection of her brother and the situations that activate them. We found that as parents dwell on a situation and describe it in detail, and the more detail the better, it is clarified in their minds and they are able to find solutions by themselves. Even if suggestions from others, including the leader, become necessary, they assume greater significance and more pertinent meaning when preceded by such verbal (and thought) rumination. The mind

5 See my *Analytic Group Psychotherapy.* New York: Columbia University Press, 1952.

holds on what it has worked; that which is given it without such antecedent effort is deflected and easily forgotten. The leader should, therefore, have encouraged Mr. Daws to elaborate by a series of questions so designed that the father could recognize the elements or dynamics involved in the relation of his two children. As it was, the therapist made Mr. Daws feel guilty for he implied that the parents had not done enough to meliorate the family situation.

Mr. Jasper traps the leader into a comparatively irrelevant discussion of the incidence of treatment for boys and girls. In addition, the explanation is incorrect. The probable reason is that boys act out during latency and puberty, while girls present problems to their parents and the community at adolescence. Their acting out is, by and large, not along the lines of aggression and destruction, but rather along the lines of sex. The proper technique is not to respond to such a question or evade it.

The leader's mention of "tension" between boys and girls and their mothers set off a chain reaction of sexual interest. This involves not only parents vis-à-vis children, but also their own sexual activity and latent homosexuality. They refer, for example, to Mr. Daws as a "good (potent) man" and not "wasting time," a reference to the frequency of sexual intercourse (potency). Indeed, so anxiety-producing is this interchange that Mr. Daws' stuttering is reactivated.

Mr. Daws' panic arouses sadistic trends in the other fathers as shown by Mr. Sands' sarcasm and Mr. Schaeffer's more open attack. Mr. Daws attempts to defend himself, but the leader only adds to his distress by asking the group how caring for a younger child by an older can benefit their relation. This is a not-too-well-disguised criticism of Mr. Daws, releasing further the group's antagonism toward him. Mr. Schaeffer is particularly vehement. (One wonders whether the hostility toward Mr. Daws is not at least partly fanned by jealousy of the fact that the latter has a larger family than any of the others; that is, he is sexually more potent.)

This peroration leads Mr. Friedman to recall his childhood, the relations in his family, and his resentment toward his brother. Luckily, he is stopped short in this by Mr. Schaeffer. The free-associative catharsis that is suitable for psychotherapy was peremptorily interrupted and one can assume that Mr. Friedman was frustrated and disturbed. But Mr. Daws still feels crushed and now seeks to re-establish himself with the group and leader and to allay his guilt and anxiety. This he attempt to do by asking the leader whether it was wrong for (his) children "to have responsibilities around the house." The latter gives him an entirely inappropriate answer and Mr. Sands hits the "bull's eye," as it were, by bringing in the analogy of the relation of a boss and employee, to which Mr. Friedman accedes. However, the discussion is still abstract; it is not focused on the matter at hand; namely, the meaning of children's behavior and how one deals with it.

Instead of deflecting the discussion from Mr. Daws, who is hard put to it, the leader directs it again toward him by the suggestion of division of labor for boys, activating Mr. Sands and the others to take Mr. Daws to task rather severely. Mr. Daws, now in the throes of attack, tries in every way to defend himself on many fronts.

Again the leader puts before the group an abstract question as to the effectiveness of punishment, thus activating guilt in the fathers (they fall silent), making it necessary for Mr. Schaeffer and Mr. Friedman to defend themselves. The anxiety leads Mr. Friedman to speak of his son's "nervousness" that sets off Mr. Schaeffer to reveal his homosexual involvement with his son when he speaks of the latter's getting in bed with him. (The central difficulty between Mr. Schaeffer and his son was of a sexual nature.) By synchrony of the unconscious, Mr. Friedman associates this with his own son's sexual (castration) fears (he looks under the bed every night) and is practically on the threshold of interpreting Mr. Schaeffer's homosexual trends when he rejects the suggestion of a foam rubber mattress for the boy, saying that the boy "was afraid of *something.*" Naturally, Mr. Schaeffer would deny this, though he is undoubtedly by now quite anxious.

But Mr. Daws still broods about punishment. (It was known that he, of Near-East origin, was a strict disciplinarian and punished his children frequently and very severely.) In line with his own need for physical contact with his boy, Mr. Schaeffer gives Mr. Daws misleading advice to wrestle with his children. The leader here is treading on thin ice when he refers to Mr. Schaeffer's "physical contact" with his son. This was rather risky, to say the least. Mr. Daws' pre-occupation with punishment as he returns to that subject reveals again his feelings of guilt and anxiety. Even the leader now notes his "anxiety about the group's reaction to his statement that he hits his son with a ruler." Mr. Daws continues to justify himself and seeks to re-establish himself in the group's grace.

Again the leader asks an abstract question, namely, "How does hitting a child make him want to do things?" instead of directing the question to a specific child or a specific situation so that the members of the group could probe it in practical and operational terms. It is rather significant and interesting that, though Mr. Daws is again embarrassed, Mr. Sands and Mr. Friedman—one objectively and the other subjectively—recognize that striking a child is only a way of discharging feelings on the part of the parent (see Chapter I).

Now, because of loss of face in the group, Mr. Daws shifts the blame on his wife, and Mr. Friedman makes the rather startling disclosure that shocks the group into silence that his son "had pulled a knife on him."

Mr. Sands then piles one accusation after another against his son and wife. He "works off his spleen" as it were, unaffected by the leader's and some of his group fellows' efforts to throw some light on his feeling and to help him deal with the situation. The leader's suggestion that Mr. Sands should review the day's events with his son is a good one but may be inappropriate, for obviously the relation as it then existed between them was not conducive for such confidences.

Apart from the specific errors, anxiety and aggression against a scapegoat (Mr. Daws) in this session, the members' and leader's unclarity as to the focus, aim, objective and direction, stands out uppermost. There is a conglomerate, an ebb and flow, an inconsistency and confusion as to what they seek to accomplish. The discussion is diffuse; one topic is taken up before another is clarified. While such disjointedness is often found in these groups at early sessions, there should be some focus and concreteness in the ninth session. We observe in addition the emergence of a great deal of anxiety-producing disclosures: activation of hostility in some members; fear and anxiety in others without working them through;

sexual material comes up, which is counterindicated; even homo-sexuality is touched on.

These are all the results of an unclear primary group code, an undefined aim, uncertainty as to what direction the discussion should take and a misconception of his role by the leader. As a result, the group members raise deeply affecting issues that remain unresolved and unanswered and therefore result in generalized dissatisfaction.

The reader will not be surprised that Mr. Daws dropped out of the group. Mr. Schaeffer had to be removed, because his inner (homosexual) difficulty could not have been reached by this type of guidance.

It is evident even from a cursory reading of the two records of the sessions one year apart that the atmosphere in one is quite different from that in the other. In the earlier (in point of time) session the participants are full of anxiety and guilt and the content hovers between psychotherapy and guidance. The participants are left hanging in the air, as it were. Although they are made aware of their intra- and interpersonal problems and are made anxious and guilty, they receive no clarification, thereby increasing their anxiety further. One of the important reasons for maintaining the discussions in guidance groups on the operational or functional level is to prevent inducing anxiety, for once it is so activated, one automatically seeks relief from it by continuing to explore the anxiety-provoking idea, memory or relation. This takes one into psychotherapy. By the law of homeostasis, every state of anxiety sets up mechanisms for eliminating it (as is also the case in the physical organism) through re-establishing of equilibrium. This may be achieved by calling forth one's ego defenses, by release through acting out or talking, or through mastering the situation through "understanding."

From the point of view of mental health, whenever anxiety is aroused, avenues for eliminating it must be provided. The grist of psychotherapy is anxiety. Unless there are clinical indications to the contrary, in psychotherapy anxiety is allowed to run its gamut, for it is the resultant emotional pressure that propels the patient to continue treatment. This is obviously not the intent in Child-Centered Group Guidance of Parents. The aim here is (1) to sensitize parents to the nature and needs of children, (2) to alter attitudes and values, and (3) to evolve appropriate ways of dealing with them. This aim determines (a) the selection of group members, (b) the grouping, (c) the role of the leader, and (d) the content of the discussions. The guidance groups are in every regard different from therapy groups since the basic conditions and goals are different. To allow anxiety to mount without providing relief or insight would serve to intensify tensions in their families rather than relieve them.

In the guidance groups with which we are concerned here, the objectives are to evoke empathy with children and a recognition of their fears, anxieties, feelings of weakness and insecurity inherent in childhood and to eliminate conditions that intensify and magnify them through the climate in the family and other areas of the child's living situations and relationships. This can be conveyed as information by didactic techniques of class and lecture, but information thus acquired has proven ineffective in the vital and dynamic living process requiring responsiveness to the subtle nuances of feelings and emotions. Illustrations of this are known to everyone but are further supplied by only a few incidents recorded on pp. 77-82. Such confirmations can be multiplied *ad infinitum* for only that is retained by the mind on which it actively works. That which is "taught" is evanescent as the morning mist.

The techniques of our type of guidance, therefore, seek to give root to thought, deliberation and reflection by tying them with actual events and experience. This gives them significance. Parents must come to *realize* that their child's acts, whether annoying or not, are manifestations of inner necessities only minimally determined by his nature and that they are predominantly conditioned by past experiences in which parents and others played a determining part. Practitioners of this method are always impressed with, and surprised at, discovering the universal trend on the part of adults to blame children for having specific characteristics and behavior patterns as though they were self-created entities and no one had a hand in shaping them. Parents are, by and large, particularly blind to their influence in these matters.

The grist of the discussions are *actual occurrences* in the home, preferably those that are fresh in the memory of the participating parents. Whether it is disobedience, refusal to eat, dawdling, delay in dressing, an act of violence against a sibling, antipathy to school, withdrawal from play with peers, stubbornness, TV programs, refusal to bathe, hyperactivity in the presence of friends or relatives, general boisterousness or its appearance in special circumstances, shyness— these are the starting points for a group discussion. The circumstances and events that immediately preceded and may have evoked the behavior or act are explored, and their cause is traced to antecedent circumstances and events. These may take place in the immediate or remote past. A child's truculence, disobedience or rebelliousness can be traced to the fact that the father had come home with a present for another child without giving the first adequate recognition. A surprising number of even well-meaning parents are not aware of the effect such a simple act may have upon a child. A thorough recounting of all the minutae of a difficult afternoon or evening can be traced to a parent's unreasonable, sharp and angry response to a child of which the parent may not even be aware. An exploration of a particularly disturbing day in the course of a guidance group session may reveal the school as the understandable source of the difficulties at home. The child's annoying and difficult behavior is found to be a displacement of his anger against a teacher or a playmate.

Uncovering the relation of cause and effect of the child's behavior is one aspect of the work of Child-Centered Group Guidance of Parents. The other is to help the parents evolve ways of correcting the situations in the present, and avoiding them in the future. In one situation peremptoriness may have to be avoided, while justifiable arbitrariness may have to be explained to the child in another instance so as to make it more palatable to him. We can attest to many instances where a child "melted," to use the parents' own words, when they apologized for their untoward or unreasonable behavior because of their having been in an irritable mood or state of ill health.[6] The children in these instances have responded not only with subsequent self-restraint, but with warmth and helpfulness. A parent's occasional, but only occasional, admission to his child of his errors, if it is true and justifiable, is the greatest assurance of a cordial and mutualistic relation. To compensate a child for the thoughtless neglect of him through preference of another is the only corrective for a disturbed relation, and to recognize a child's difficulties at school or with friends in an understanding, not in a chastising or critical manner, brings the child ever so closer to his parent.

Parents must be helped to accept their child's anger with maturity and empathetic feeling. The child has to have a target for discharging his feelings of frustration, his anger and his disappointments and his safest target is his parent who loves him and with whom he feels safe. He has a right to feel that those who love him will accept also his outbursts and in this expectation, they must not disappoint him. When feeling overwhelms the child, he must discharge it. Uncontrollability must not become a rule of life nor is it to be allowed to remain unchallenged, but a child cannot be expected entirely to withhold the negative factors of his biologic nature if we are to establish a basis for mental health. Once his feelings are discharged and emotional equilibrium established, the child is ready to recognize what had transpired and the parent can tactfully help him do so.

Such humane ways of dealing with children are not the rule among the majority of parents. They rather lose patience and in their anger retaliate in kind, thus demonstrating their own emotional inadequacy and immaturity. By lack of sympathy and understanding, they alienate and antagonize their children. Self-control in children and adults is derived from their parents' demonstration of strength and restraint. Parents have to be led to understand and accept the fact that they are the sources of the child's character and strengths, which cannot be achieved through didactic means or by harshness. But such recognitions can emerge only from their own growth and from thoughtfully examining the elements of these and

6 This procedure is obviously not recommended where the child planfully instigates or provokes the parent, when appropriate restraint is essential; nor is it advisable to use explanation or apology as a general pattern for parents' relation to children.

other human relationships.[7] They cannot be taught by rules or rote. Groups more so than individual guidance favor establishment and re-establishment of such wholesome attitudes. The interaction and the interstimulation of a number of minds focused on a given problem or subject activate each participant and elaborate and enhance his thoughts and insights. The group process is one of chain reaction that activates clarity of thinking and feeling of each member in it.

We have already indicated that the leader's role is of no small significance in this process. Persons untrained in perceptive thinking tend to make discussions diffuse, desultory and unfocused. It is the leader's responsibility to make the most of opportunities presented by the group members: to help them separate the chaff from the wheat and to come to some definite conclusions and understandings. Most often the participants accomplish this themselves, especially as the group progresses in its deliberations and experience, but tactful and directed help from the leader has to be forthcoming as the need arises at different stages in the group's development. Above all, the leader must prevent escape into generalities and philosophic disquisitions as well as avoid activating unnecessary anxiety. The latter is accomplished by limiting discussions to actual occurrences; the former, by leading questions directed toward eliciting narration of what actually occurred and of the accompanying and precipitating events. The fullest possible details and elaborations are an utmost necessity in this.

Explorations and analyses usually lead to practical considerations of routines and physical arrangements in the home. As one of the group members describes the procedures and sequences of his or her management of the household and of the children, others offer numerous suggestions for changes. These are examined in as much detail as possible and appropriate replanning is made by the group. According to need or indication, the leader may or may not participate. At all times the group must have its say first and if they solve the situation satisfactorily, all he needs is to agree. When despite all efforts an appropriate solution is not reached, he may put his own in a form of a question for the group's discussion and evaluation, or he

[7] Again the point has to be made that where neurotic blockings exist, our method will not be effective.

can directly suggest the most suitable line of action according to his lights. The method employed will depend upon the state of the group, the therapist's relation to it, and the importance of the topic under discussion. The significance of these discussions reaches beyond the solution of specific situations in the relation between the parent and the child or evolving specific strategies. The very act of participation in a serious effort *feelingly* to *understand* the child's maturation, his relation to the problem situation, and his *feelings,* evolves empathetic insights into and appreciation of the child as a human, feeling, responsive, defensive and sensitive entity, with rights as well as responsibilities. These insights lay the foundation for a genuine respect for children as persons and childhood as a phasial stage leading to progressive maturity with inherent needs for security, love and status.

The father of a thirty-month-old girl, an only child, to whom she was strongly attached, left the family for several months on a business relocation trip. The girl inquired as to his whereabouts several evenings before she seemed to dismiss the subject. Soon after, however, she proceeded to wake up every morning about two o'clock, to go into her parents' bedroom and insist on sitting on a chair by herself and quietly watch her mother sleep. When the latter inquired of little Janet why she did not stay in her own room, the girl would quietly say, "S'eep, mummy, s'eep. I sit here." The mother was greatly disturbed by her child's strange behavior, especially since it occurred regularly for ten consecutive nights, and in a wrought up state she brought the problem to the guidance group of which she was a member.

A protracted discussion ensued with a great many opinions and suggestions, but no one inquired as to the meaning of the girl's behavior. After almost an hour of conversation during which he remained completely noncommunicative, the leader posed the question, "Why does Janet sit and watch her mother? What meaning does it have for her?" Again a flood of explanations poured forth in the course of which the leader again remained silent, but none had hit the mark. He then asked the following: "Is it not possible that Janet, by watching the mother, is trying to make sure that her mother as well will not leave her as did her father?" This was so inherently correct that everyone present seemed to respond with unverbalized acquiescence, except the mother who now quite spontaneously almost exclaimed: "That's right! That's what she once said to me. As I was bathing her, she asked me: 'Mummy, you no go away.' I assured her but apparently that was not enough." The leader then said, "Janet must have said something about her father beyond inquiring about his homecoming." "Yes," reported the mother, "after several days she said: 'Bad, bad daddy. I don't want daddy!'" The leader then asked the group: "Do you think this rejection of the father had something to do with her actions at night?" There was no response forthcoming and the leader explained that having openly rejected her father, the little girl became afraid of losing both of her parents and wanted to make sure that she would not be abandoned by her mother, hence her nocturnal watchfulness.

The question then arose as to how one dealt with such an unusual situation and after a brief discussion, the group concluded that the mother and the girl should sleep in the same room during the father's absence. The leader thought that this was a good solution. The mother then wanted to know whether she should move the child's small bed into her room or move her bed into the child's room. There seemed to be a consensus, quickly arrived at, that the child should be moved into her mother's room. The leader disagreed, explaining that under this plan, the child would have to sustain two changes in sleeping location that might create difficulties later on. It would be better, he averred, to leave the child in her own room without any changes by reversing the plan suggested by the group.

It must be noted that throughout the discussion that took up full two hours no mention was made of the child's fears and anxieties or of her hostilities toward the father and distrust of her mother; nor was the possible effect of this experience upon the child stated or implied. The situation which was very unique with bizarre overtones was treated in a matter-of-fact off-hand fashion so as not to increase further the mother's obvious disturbance and unmistaken fear. In fact, on the evening when the discussion occurred, she appeared drawn, fidgety and worried which was unusual for this rather well set-up woman.

The sequel to this episode is both interesting and puzzling.

When Janet's mother came to the next group session, two weeks later, she looked her usual smiling self. She came rather early when only one other woman was present and did not mention the panic she had felt in the preceding session, nor the outcome of the discussion. The other woman asked: "Well, how did things work out with Janet? Did you move your bed into her room?" "No, I didn't have to," was the surprising reply. "Why not?" asked the other. "Well, Janet stopped coming into my room without my having to do anything," her mother said. "When did it happen?" the other asked. "The very night we discussed the problem. I came home, went to sleep and Janet slept through the night in her own room and never again repeated her visits to mine." "And we wasted a whole evening on you!" the other said with a touch of disgust. "Indeed, you did not!" Janet's mother answered with alacrity, "You relaxed me and I seemed to pass it on to her." How the mother induced relaxation in her little daughter through her own calm is a subject for a metaphysical speculation on which we would hesitate to embark here.[8]

Another couple reported the difficulties they have experienced during the meals of their twin sons about twenty-eight months old. Other group members have, through their questions, uncovered the fact that the children ate in the rather small and crowded kitchen, each sitting in a separate highchair, while the mother was busily occupied in the preparation of the different courses to be served them. The leader pointed out that the hectic movements of the mother and the fact that she was the focus of the boys' attention because of it, distracted them. As a result they threw the food at each other, upset the plates filled with food, banged the spoons and threw them about. In this case he had visited the home, since other serious problems existed there in relation to the children, and

8 Perhaps it should be noted that none of the children of the parents in the group presented unusual difficulties. This was a preventive group for parents of children who started when the latter were about eighteen months old and were attended by both fathers and mothers as a prophylactic measure.

suggested that the children eat in the living-dining room facing the rather large picture window looking out upon a river nearby. To prevent damaging the expensive carpeting, he suggested that an oilcloth be spread under the high chairs to catch the spilled or thrown food. No difficulties were experienced in this area after that.

A mother complained that her three-year-old son threw violent tantrums when he returned home with her and his little brother, four months old, from their daily stroll in the park. When asked to describe sequences of events in great details, she stated that when they entered their home her older boy announced that he was hungry, she would first feed the baby and then him. When this error was called to her attention and she changed the rigid routine she had followed, the tantrums stopped and much difficulty had been prevented. After members of the group helped this mother to rearrange the feeding sequence, the leader elaborated on the fact that not only did hunger make the boy irritable but the only too apparent preference the mother displayed for her younger offspring was an additional cause of the older boy's behavior.

The parents' awareness of current situations is only part of our aim. Though this is a usual and natural outcome of the shared conversations in the group, the leader frequently has to help the participating parents to recall circumstances and events in the past that set the stage for the current difficulties. As parents' interest is directed toward understanding their childrens' behavior and re-actions and as they grow more sensitive to children's feelings, they recall how they have neglected them when they were babies or young children for another younger child, for a sick relative, because of pressure of business or because of some personal preoccupation. They recount the illnesses of the children, the treatment they had received at their hands and those of nurses, doctors, relatives. Out of expanded perceptiveness, they recognize the causal relation be-tween a poorly carried out tonsillectomy and current fears, or resent-ment and anger on the part of their children for the neglect they had sustained at the hands of the parents in the remote past because of an ailing grandparent. Even if the effects are irrevocable, which is sometimes the case, the recognition that the child does not behave as he does out of onerousness or "badness," or that his behavior is within his free choice to take or leave, but is rather a continuation of a pattern that has its roots in understandable causes, renders the parents not only more understanding but more tolerant. The substitution of these newly acquired feelings for their blind intolerance and impatience cannot but result in responses more suitable to the needs of the child and to resolution or diminution of conflict situations. The reader will find the interviews quoted in this volume replete with illustrations how the discovery that their children were involuntarily reacting to earlier unhappiness had wrought complete alteration in the parents' treatment of them.

One mother who had bitterly complained of her eleven-year-old son's intense hostility, spitefulness and disobedience toward her and treated him punitively because of it, changed her attitude when the group helped her to recall some of the circumstances of her son's past. During the exploration of her difficulties with the boy, an only child, she was helped to become aware of the fact, hitherto unrecognized by her as significant, that when he was a baby, she would tie him in a highchair and let him sit for hours while she tended to a small candy store she and her husband conducted on a floor below their residence. She was able to recall his crying and fidgetiness, but felt helpless because of the demands on her time. As she was elaborating on this circumstance, she also recalled that she and her husband would take off an occasional evening from their business leaving the child in his crib and the door to their apartment unlocked so that any of the neighbors who heard him cry could come in and attend to him. A series of various types of neglect of the child were brought out by this mother as she examined the child's past (most of which were unavoidable due to realistic demands on her, such as going to work to support herself, her mother and her son when she separated from her husband). These deprivations and anxieties to which the boy was subjected did not occur to her to have contributed to the current difficulties. She assumed, as many parents do, that a child could and should grow up balanced and cooperative under any conditions. When the new awareness was actuated by her fellow group members with the help of the leader, her punitive and retaliatory dealing with her child was modified for the better.

The leader had an opportunity to call the parents' attention to the importance of consistent, secure relations with adults upon whom a child's biologic survival and emotional health depend; that physical neglect and abandonment, even if they are a result of necessity, as was in the case under discussion, arouse actual instinctive fear such as in lower animals when they are threatened. Brief explanations and formulations on the basis of the group members' discussions and awarenesses are helpful provided the leader does not resort to them too often.

In the case under consideration here, the leader had to be on the alert to prevent excessive guilt on the part of the mother by pointing out that the mother had probably done her best under most unfavorable conditions and that the situation was not irreversible; errors can be corrected and by dealing with her son in the future in a positive and understanding way, the relationship can be corrected, and that psychotherapy for him may be necessary. The point that the leader had made, which is perhaps more important than any other, was that conditions produce unpreventable effects upon people, as they do in the realm of inanimate nature. The relation between cause and effect is universal. This is a rule that parents must use to guide themselves in dealing with their children.

The important outcome of the technique of exploration of the cause is that parents come to recognize that they had some part in the development of their children's conduct, as illustrated by the case just cited. Their proneness to lay the entire blame upon the child is shaken by the revelation of details of which they had honestly not been aware. Out of their own words and memories loom the circumstances of which they had been consciously or unconsciously a part and their anger against the children for current annoyances are as a result abated. This discovery can, of course, produce guilt and have negative effects upon the parents' relation to the child. The risks of these are, however, greatly mitigated by the fact that the parents come to these recognitions through a slow evolutionary process rather than as a sudden or peremptory statement or interpretation. The individual's intellectual *inclination* and emotional readiness prepare him for the discovery which is cushioned by the antecedent and gradually expanding series of recognitions.

However, of even greater mitigating effect is the circumstance that these realities are unfolded through a cooperative effort of a number of persons in similar circumstances and that the impact is shared by more than one person. The awareness and recognition that emerge lose their sting in the fact that one is not alone in the transgressions. All those present have made the same or similar mistakes; all are to blame, if blame is to be meted out, which, of course, is not done. The phrase "I am glad to find that I am not alone in this" and similar sentiments are ever repeated. Through this setting guilt feelings are prevented with the avoidance of consequent emotional disturbance and retaliatory acting out against the children, for when parents are guilty they act out their guilt against their children either by punishment or pampering.

In this the leader also can be helpful. He explains that error and misjudgments in child rearing are inevitable. No one, no matter how well trained and cautious, can ever be free of them. He has to point out that this is partly due to the fact that preparation for parenthood is not part of our educational plan or effort; also, that no one can know exactly what is indicated and right for any given child and a particular stage in his development since each is different from every other, and what is suitable for one may be quite unsuitable for another; and finally, that parents are not superhuman and conditions of health, mood, material considerations and numerous other factors may cause them to act in a manner that would have been quite different were conditions more favorable. This approach dulls the cutting edge of guilt and instead of becoming defensively constricted, parents grow more receptive to new awareness and new lines of action with their children. Each has to find these for himself, with the help of the group and the leader. Thus the parents' perspective is directed toward the future as well as toward the past, and feelings of defeat are turned to hopefulness and optimism.

At the risk of being redundant but with the intent of intensifying the emphasis, we repeat that the unearthing of past events must be the effort of the parents with only suggestive or stimulative questions or remarks from the leader. Questions like, "Why should your child do this?" "Can you see any reason why he should do this?" "Can you see any reason for this?" Or statements like, "You know, nothing ever happens without a cause. Something must have happened that you have forgotten that makes your child do this." As a matter of experience, the leader has little need even for such leading questions and statements once the group gets on the way. The members stimulate each other's memories and reflections and help one another toward clarification and understanding.

Under all circumstances, the leader has to give full sway to free expression on the part of the group members. This permissiveness not only helps the parents toward clarity, but through it he demonstrates the role that a good parent should play. Even when a member enters a prohibited realm such as the relation with his mate, memories of suffering and deprivation in the past, or destructive and delinquent acts that arouse strong feelings of self-pity and hostility, the leader does not check the flow of the productions. He and the group hear him out, but as soon as he comes to a halt, the leader steps in and redirects the discussion to some child's behavior and act. Thus the leader by not responding to the "extraneous" content brings into focus that part of it with which a parents' guidance group can and should deal. He may say, "You said something about Jimmy's being disobedient. When and under what circumstances does he show it most?" When one parent has not offered such a logical inroad, the leader may say, "Mrs. X (another parent) has told us about her girl's being choosy about food. I wonder what foods she does not like."

As this strategy is employed repeatedly and consistently for a number of sessions, the group accepts the limitation and none ever returns to speaking about his feelings, backgrounds or relationships. This we term the "primary group code."

Above all, the leader must have faith, which is always justified by experience that even the lowly and poorly educated can find solutions for themselves that meet their particular needs at their own levels and circumstances through their own efforts, once they have the chance to do it.

IV

Learning to be Parents

When the discussions are held to practical problems and to ways of dealing with them without arousing guilt and anxiety, results can soon be observed as the following episodes show.

Mrs. Bernheim was a widow in her thirties whose husband was killed in the war when their only son, now ten years old, was a baby. Having been left in straitened financial circumstances, she lived with her child for a period in one room and slept with him in the same bed. There was a brief episode of remarriage which she soon dissolved because of the stern and unkind treatment her second husband accorded her son. The man seemed unable to tolerate the close relation between his wife and stepson and urged placement for the boy. The tension having become intolerable to her and seeing the boy rejected, Mrs. Bernheim had to choose between the two. She chose the boy, who because of the unfavorable condition in his environment was brought to a child guidance clinic. For a period after separation from her second husband, Mrs. Bernheim went to work leaving her son with relatives, but later gave up her job to devote herself to the care of her child, living on a widow's pension and her husband's insurance. Part of the latter she had put away regularly in a bank account for the boy.

The male caseworker, who treated the mother and the boy, about seven years old at the time, described Mrs. Bernheim as a "very sweet and very dependent" person. She gave the impression of being always on the verge of tears, even when the situation she was describing was neither serious nor pressing. She became inordinately dependent on the therapist, would frequently become depressed, though there was no pathology present, and would come to him crying about insignificant details in her life. After two years of individual treatment, from which Mrs. Bernheim derived very limited benefit, she was transferred to a guidance group and the boy was placed in an activity therapy group.

The group leader, who was a man, informed her that she could come to see him in the event of difficulties. This was a compromise with our practice, but in view of the woman's situation and her helplessness, it was considered advisable in her case. At first she took advantage of the privilege and came to the leader rather frequently, but gradually tapered off her visits until she discontinued them altogether. Mr. Bernheim would occasionally talk to the leader about some situation as the group was leaving the meeting room, but did not evince any desire for individual interviews. During these fleeting talks she would ask advice on some unimportant matter of management of her son and the household.

Mrs. Bernheim attended the group sessions regularly but for a long period participated little in the conversations. She did not initiate talk, but would on occasion confirm something out of her own experience to which another member of the group had referred. At all other times she would sit quietly listening, and when the leader would turn to her in an effort to drawn her into the conversation, she would briefly state her agreement or disagreement. In time, Mrs. Bernheim began to contribute to the discussions spontaneously and, though not very bright, emerged in the role of a stabilizing factor in the group. Her comments would be of the order such as "You know you have to give to a child in order to get something from him," or, "Children are after all human beings and have feelings like grownups." She appeared to have a high degree of (symbiotic) identification with her son as though saying, "If I feel this way then my boy probably feels the same way." She was not intellectual or analytical, nor did she make any effort to conceptualize or understand. She rather functioned on the feeling level. Because she had gained so much in terms of dealing with her son, she was closed out from the group after about twenty-five bi-weekly sessions.

Several incidents as she related them to the group, however, show how much she has gained from the discussions despite her limited capacity to verbalize and her predominant passive participation.

At one of the sessions, Mrs. Bernheim seemed annoyed that despite the fact that her son was almost nine years old at the time, he still required a light at night. She said that she would leave the central light on in the living room, which would partially illuminate his adjoining bedroom, but it did not seem to satisfy him; he wanted the light in his room turned on full. This was a bone of contention between the two which was fought out every single night and created a great deal of tension between them. She could not see what there was to be afraid of in the apartment, she said.

During the ensuing discussion, the other members of the group, some of whose children were also afraid of the dark, convinced her that children are subject to irrational fears and that it was important for parents not to create conflict around it. They must give in to the child, and try to understand why such fears existed. Mrs. Bernheim seemed aloof during the harangue by the other women, not responding or participating in any way. However, as events proved later, she carefully followed the conversations and took steps to remedy situations. Not only did she allow a light in the boy's room, but she went a step further. Despite her straitened economic circumstances, she bought an inexpensive table light, placed it near the boy's bed and told him he could turn it off and on at will. He was now the "big boss," as she put it, but she turned the light on for him as she left his room that night.

At the next session of the group two weeks later, Mrs. Bernheim was beaming with joy. Her usual seedy expression, though she was a rather attractive woman, was succeeded by unaccustomed animation. The members of the group noticed the change and asked her what had happened. Mrs. Bernheim described the developments in great detail, embellishing them as she went along, but ended by saying, "You know what happened? After three nights with his new light, when I said 'good night' to him and turned on the bedside light, he suddenly said: 'Mummy, you can turn the light off. I don't need it any more.' It's wonderful!" she exclaimed. "Now we don't have to fight every night!" A check two years later revealed that the boy had not reverted to his demand for a light in the room. Apparently his behavior had not been motivated by real fear but rather represented a simple device of attracting the mother's attention and winning out against her.

¯This was only a first step in resolving conflict about going to bed, however. In the past she would urge him to retire at a certain time which he invariably resisted. This was another bone of contention between them. Following discussions at the group, she left this matter completely in the boy's hands and he would sometimes stay up a half hour beyond his bed time. She reported that she did not demur, for frequently when tired he would retire as early as 7:30 and 8:00 o'clock. The boy would say to his mother: "I'm tired today. I had a full day. I think I'll go to bed." Contrary to her former practice, she did not question him as to what had made him tired or what he had done that day. She merely accepted his statement. She did not even ask him if he did not feel well, which she used to do in the past. The latter especially is a considerable achievement for Mrs. Bernheim in view of her attachment to and keen concern about her son.

On another occasion during the group's conversation, Mrs. Bernheim reported that one week end her boy was unmanageable. He "almost tore the house apart" by his violent acting out. He was disobedient, angry, and inaccessible to her efforts to control him. Although the mother had limited him to some extent, she did not punish him for it, as she put it, "I learned here that there is always a reason why anybody behaves that way." Finally, her son revealed voluntarily that he had sustained a disappointment on the preceding Friday. In addition, Mrs. Bernheim said, the weather was inclement and the boy could not go outside and "work off his disappointment." It so happened that her sister and the latter's two children had come to visit and, shocked by her nephew's irracibility and violence, said in his hearing that if he were her son, she would "beat the hell out of him." Mrs. Bernheim calmly responded that she did not mind since she knew that the boy had a reason for being upset.

He soon stopped his annoyance, went over to his mother and

LEARNING TO BE PARENTS

asked her if he could have some money to buy a goldfish. She said she realized he was testing her as he did with the light in his room. She said that it was perfectly all right, went to her purse, and gave him fifty cents. She was almost amused by the surprised look on his face, as though he were saying: "You mean after all I did you are still going to give me money to buy fish?" She repeated the fact that she understood why he was upset and didn't see why just because he was upset she should deny him. For the remainder of that week end, and the rest of the week, he was "as good as gold."

One of her son's difficulties had been his rather extreme jealousy of her and his need to monopolize her. He would not allow her to talk to children or adults and when she did converse with someone on the street, he would tug at her skirts to pull her away, or would become so annoying that she would have to terminate the conversation. Because of her changed general attitude, her son's possessiveness had diminished to a degree, but she still felt that his needs in this regard persisted and that she would have to be careful where sharing her attentions was concerned. Because of the understanding she acquired in the group, her increased sensitivity to the child, and her rather constant refrain she often repeated: "If you give the child, he will give back to you," she had established harmony with and control over him. Her respect for her son's individuality is well illustrated by the following incident she related to the group:

Her sister was going away for a week end and asked Mrs. Bernheim to take care of her five-year-old daughter. In the past, Mrs. Bernheim said, she would have automatically said "yes," not taking into account how her son would feel about it or how he would react, though she knew full well that the week end would have been unpleasant for everyone. She now told her sister that she would first talk it over with the boy. If he felt that he would like to have his cousin she would take the little girl, but if he were negative about it she would have to refuse. Daniel "surprisingly enough" said that it was all right, he would like to have his little cousin around. "Somebody like a little sister in the family," he said. They had a very pleasant week end. The boy took care of his little cousin, played with her and was "very considerate" of her.

It should be noted that in individual treatment she was found to be dependent and submissive and retained her strong hold on her son and dominated him. She was described as being incapable of "fundamental changes in her personality, unable to reveal her inner feelings. She dealt only with everyday matters and was generally resistive." The group, in which she gained status on her own, where she could identify with other women and accept suggestions from them, helped her acquire techniques of dealing with her son. She was able to achieve this because her deeper problems remained untouched and she did not have to defend herself against the therapist through a façade of helplessness and dependence. The resulting relaxed state rendered her capable of assimilating and utilizing attitudes promulgated in the group discussions and by the leader.

We cannot claim full satisfaction with the developments in this family. The mother did require deep psychotherapy or, preferably, psychoanalysis, but her financial situation, her needs and especially her "character resistance" made her a poor prospect for individual psychotherapy. Though she developed a strong transference on her male therapist, it was entirely of a dependent, infantile nature. One can expect some regression here after guidance is terminated, but Mrs. Bernheim will not return to the level of her former conduct. She will retain some of her intellectual, and possibly also emotional growth. As a precaution the boy was continued in activity group therapy and was in addition assigned to individual psychotherapy to work through some of his neurotic elements and to reduce symbiotic dependence on his mother.

Mrs. Arthur was a co-member of Mrs. Bernheim's, whose son, about ten years old, had been in treatment in an activity therapy group. One of his difficulties was enuresis that persisted from infancy. Of special concern to her was the rather intense conflict about the boy's resistance to attending a parochial school after regular school hours which meant a great deal to her and her husband. During the course of treatment it was found that the boy was epileptic, a fact that was not known when plans for both the boy and his mother had been made. Parents of children with such specific pathology are excluded from both types of groups, activity groups for children and the guidance groups under discussion (see p. 258).

For a time Mrs. Arthur was seen by a psychiatric caseworker on an individual basis, but gained little from that experience. She was a simple, rather dull woman with limited intelligence who sought help with everyday, practical matters. The therapist found it impossible to get her into an exploration of feelings or attitudes. The caseworker, therefore, decided that a guidance group for the mother would help the boy more than would individual treatment. She was accordingly assigned to such a group. She was described as a heavy-set, slow-moving woman with a "great deal of warmth, a rather soft-spoken, motherly person, protective of her children and her husband." The latter seemed infantile and dependent on his wife. As an elevator operator he was a poor provider and Mrs. Arthur at one time took in foster children to enhance the family budget. Another motive, she claimed, was to help her son "grow up," apparently referring to the example the foster children would set for her own boy.

In the group Mrs. Arthur was rather communicative bringing in situations for discussion and consulting the group on questions of management of her home and children. She was particularly pre-occupied with problems of adolescence as they related to her girl of fourteen and the boy. She wanted to know what attitudes one must have toward children of that age, how one could reassure them, and matters of a similar nature. She frequently brought up the importance of neighbors' opinions of one and the conduct of one's home. Wasn't it one's own business as to how one managed one's home? And shouldn't others, instead of criticizing, adjust to your home? By these and similar topics relating directly to everyday situations and events she stimulated the other women in the group to explore their attitudes and acts. She was a useful instigator.[1]

One of the topics Mrs. Arthur frequently discussed in the early sessions was her boy's enuresis. There were a number of women in the group whose sons were also enuretic. At first Mrs. Arthur conveyed utter disgust and great annoyance, but in time and as a result

[1] Slavson, S. R.: *Introduction to Group Therapy*. New York: International Universities Press, 1954, p. 119.

of numerous discussions of the subject by the other women, Mrs. Arthur became unmistakenly more understanding and more tolerant. She not only accepted the symptom as something that the child could not control, but she even reassured him. She was able to report at later sessions a significant diminution in her boy's enuresis. However, the real bone of contention was the boy's attendance in the religious school. She complained that she had a lot of trouble with him on that score. The boy would create a fuss, yell, scream, throw temper tantrums, called her vile names and insisted that he was miserable in that setting and refused to go.

When she brought this matter up at a group session, the other women wondered why it was important for the boy to get a religious education. Doesn't a child have enough burdens as it is when he has regular school where he has to submit to rules and regulations, homework to do, the demands that a family always makes on a child? Why then create such tension and unhappiness by adding more burdens?[2] At the time of this discussion the boy was ten and one half years old and they agreed unanimously that if the boy did not want the parochial education, he should be left along. The boy did not have to have a full-fledged religious preparation to be confirmed, they said. There are ways of meeting the requirements without a thoroughgoing mastery of all the learnings to which boys are subjected. Mrs. Arthur held out in her position and could not be swayed.

Finally, one of the mother's asked Mrs. Arthur a striking question that changed the course of events in this impasse. "Why does your son's going to religious school mean so much to you? What makes you feel so strongly about it?"

Mrs. Arthur now revealed something about her background that never came out in individual treatment. She came from a very orthodox home, she said. Her father was fanatically orthodox. She must, therefore, "out of respect" for him see to it that the boy receive a religious training. At the same time she recalled that because of the suffering her parents' rigidity caused her and her siblings, she had "sworn" that when she grew up she would never

---

[2] It is interesting to note that the very mothers who advanced these arguments themselves pressed their children for accomplishment only a short time before.

impose upon her children as did her parents. The other mothers picked this up and pointed out to her that she was doing exactly what she promised herself she would not do, and only because of her *fear* of her father. They did not believe that she had to be so concerned about how her father felt. True, it was a problem, but her first concern was to be happy with her child and with her family, and only secondarily should she consider her parents. "Once you handle this situation with your son," one mother said, "then you split the problem in two and it makes it that much easier with your father." It was left at that.

At the following session, Mrs. Arthur came in beaming, absolutely pleased with herself. She was "bursting to tell about the whole thing," she said. Listening to the discussion of the previous session, she said, seemed to give her strength to talk this matter over with her husband and they came to a decision.[3] Her husband was able to formulate his feelings in the matter which were that he actually never wanted the child to be forced to go to school and that if he did not want to go "it wasn't so terrible; he didn't have to go." Right then and there they "discussed the whole situation with their son and told him that since school was so upsetting to him, if he did not want to go at this time, it was all right for him to drop it." But, if at some time in the future he changed his mind, he could tell them in advance, if not they would find some other acceptable way of going through with his confirmation.

One of the women asked Mrs. Arthur: "What about your father?" Mrs. Arthur replied that the discussion at the group had not only given her the courage to handle the situation with her boy, but that she now felt she could find a way to handle her father. Actually she does not care any more.

In describing this development the group leader was concerned with the fact that Mrs. Arthur was allowed to discuss her father and her attitude toward him, which is against our practice in these groups. In the case of Mrs. Arthur her resistance to accepting her

[3] In many instances consulting with a mate is a new and unique experience. One mother in another group expressed it thus: "Before I came to this group I used to think that I was to give orders and everyone had to obey me. I learned here that you can talk things over with them [the children]. You know, I even talk over things with my husband now and everybody is happier." (See Chapter VI.)

fellow members' opinions that emanated from her fear of being disapproved of by her father was overcome when she was helped by them to recognize the real reason for her inflexibility. Once she recognized it and received support from them, she was able to overcome her fears in relation to her father. The approval of the group at this point outweighed the approval of her father. The difference between the expert and the neophyte is the knowledge when to break a rule.

Mrs. Wince, a member of another group, was an attractive woman, somewhat anxious and guilty over her failure as a mother and as a person, had feelings of inadequacy and inferiority. She was confused as to her role as a mother. As a result, she dealt with her boy, twelve years of age, inconsistently: overindulged him at times, nagged him at others, and punitive on occasion. Her husband, too, felt inadequate, rarely talked, was restless, and unhappy in his work. Mrs. Wince had two miscarriages following the birth of her son. This had the effect of further increasing her feelings of inadequacy as a woman. She had also taken over a good deal of the pressure that her husband had applied to their son for high academic achievement so that he would become a "scholar and make something of himself." The boy, perpetually pushed toward intellectual pursuits and high scholarship, resisted and did as little work as possible and was "getting away with as much as he could." One of the boy's difficulties, as could be expected, was bed wetting, and Mrs. Wince often spoke about it in the group, claiming that she "tried everything." She punished her boy, beat him, deprived him of things, and scolded him and "what not." When Mrs. Wince first spoke of beating her son for his bed wetting, the reaction of one of the mothers present was described by the leader in the following words:

> You could literally see her hair stand on end. She, too, had a son who is a bed wetter and she turned on Mrs. Wince in anger, saying: "You mean you punish him for something like this?" At once she brought herself under control, apologized to the group, saying that she did not mean it the way it sounded, but she was just a little surprised because "a child cannot stop bed wetting by being punished or rewarded, or things like that. The problem was deeper than that. Parents

must recognize that the child hates it and is much more ashamed than are the parents. Punishment to stop the bed wetting would be of no use"

A general discussion followed as to the best way to approach the matter, and all felt that a bed wetter needed a lot of "warmth and understanding." He had to know that he was accepted whether he wet or not. Parents must convey their confidence that eventually the child will stop. Some suggested that parents had to "open up" and recognize with the child that he was as ashamed and upset by this as they were and to reassure him that it was nothing for him to be too disturbed about; and that it would pass. Making a fuss about it only made things worse, they thought.

Mrs. Wince once reported that the first sign of abatement of the enuresis on the part of her son was when he was ill in bed with a cold for a period of three or four days. The others asked her to describe the situation. She said she was very much concerned about him, attended him, and gave him all the things he wanted: books, magazines, and toys to play with. The other woman said that perhaps in some way these things were related to his needs; he wanted to be comforted and understood. Perhaps he did not get such attention under ordinary circumstances.

Some time later Mrs. Wince reported the enuresis now appeared periodically instead of occurring nightly, as was the case in the past. She seemed pleased by the break in the pattern and began to feel optimistic about the future. She frequently reported that when the boy was upset and the bed wetting recurred, she would comfort him. She would sit down and talk with him about it. If, for example, he had a series of dry nights, then wet his bed and felt disturbed by it, she would say: "Maybe something was bothering you. Tell me about it." The boy would then discuss situations at school with her and other matters, as well as the fact that his father was pushing him so much about school work.

Because Mrs. Wince felt so inadequate and a failure as a person and a mother, the fact that other women in the group freely admitted that their children were bed wetters, too, had a particularly salutary effect on her. Mrs. Wince's reaction to this was: "It is so wonderful to be in a group where you know that your problems are not so very much different from everybody else's." This universalization was what she needed. It was the leader's opinion that Mrs. Wince felt much more supported by the group, as a group, than from individual fellow members. At first she repeatedly accused herself of being a bad mother as though she wanted the others to agree with her and punish her, "bang her on the head" as the leader put it. But the women were not critical and the leader would occasionally and gently remind her that in this group the discussions were not aimed to show how bad mothers were, but rather how to handle things in the home. These continued reassurances helped her.

The pattern of inviting discussion with her son and help him discharge his feelings which she acquired in the group was entirely new in her life. As she was supported by the group, she passed on the support to her son. The increased tolerance and optimism was reflected in another major, and one might say, critical incident that occurred in the Wince family. The boy was once invited to a mixed party of boys and girls and came home with lipstick on his face and collar, which he proudly displayed. The parents, on the other hand, were nonplussed. The father especially became upset by the fact that the boy might become "sex crazy," neglect his studies, start "going out with girls," and look for a job as a mechanic instead of becoming a professional. "He will never amount to anything," he wailed. Mr. Wince felt that he "had to step in and break it up." The boy could no longer go to parties; no kissing games for him. He must study instead.

Despite the fact that her husband was so upset, Mrs. Wince refrained from making a final decision and checked her husband's urge to punish the boy "right then." She prevailed upon him not to do anything until she discussed it "with my group." She would do nothing until she "knew what the other women thought," and could think "this thing out more clearly."

When she presented the situation to the group, some of the women said that they too had children who went to parties and always assumed that they were adequately chaperoned. Kissing games which "had a long history from all the way back," they said, were natural for a child to want to indulge in. Because a child goes to a party and has fun and plays kissing games does not mean that he would necessarily take his mind off his studies. On the contrary, they felt that if the child had a certain amount of relaxation, a certain amount of pleasure week ends, his difficulties with studying might not be as great. Having enjoyed himself, he would be enabled to look forward to the week ends and he would do his studying much better.

Mrs. Wince took the matter up with her husband in the light of her new understanding, and insisted that there be nothing said or done in the matter and the boy be permitted to go to parties in the future.

Mrs. Wince used to be concerned about her boy's health and made a great deal of fuss about his clothing. She insisted that he wear a warm jacket when going down to the street, that he put on an additional muffler, a second sweater, and so on. The boy would constantly fight her off on this score. Even when he submitted to her insistence, he would only take off all the additional clothing when he reached the street. She was at her wits' end how to handle this "problem."

Mrs. Brown, an intellectual woman, insisted that it was best to let a child make his own decisions and give him the freedom of choice, for he would eventually strike the right choice, most suitable for him. She had applied it to her daughter, following discussions in the group around clothing. Her daughter had made some mistakes, picked out some awful-looking and unsuitable things, but nothing tragic happened. The girl did not catch cold as the mother thought she would, and no one made fun of her. Eventually the girl came around and asked the mother's advice what she should wear. The girl would never have asked the mother's opinion before, nor would she have accepted it if offered. Mrs. Brown felt that if Mrs. Wince were to give her son the freedom of choice, leaving it up to him, he would come upstairs on his own to change his jacket if he felt cold. Mrs. Wince was very skeptical. She did not think that this would work because her son was "so stubborn about such things." He always resisted her, but she would give it "a try."

At a later session Mrs. Wince exclaimed: "You know, it worked!" "What worked?" the others asked. "The business about clothes," was Mrs. Wince's reply. One day her son wanted to put on a light jacket though it was chilly outside. "I felt it was kind of cold outside and I was about to say to him, 'John, you better put on a heavier jacket,' but I stopped. I thought of what you said here and said to him instead: 'Alright, if you want to wear a light jacket, go ahead. But if you should decide that it is too cold downstairs, you can come up and change it, will you?' He said 'No,' went downstairs but came back in about fifteen minutes, saying: 'It is cold, Mom. I am going to change my jacket' and he put on a heavier one."

The perspicacity of a simple people with little education is strikingly exemplified by the following development in one of our fathers' guidance groups. It also illustrates how parents, with no special training or reading background. are able to perceive and conceptualize rather subtle meanings ιn children's reactions if they have an opportunity to interact with one another and stimulate each others' thinking. The central person in the episode to be narrated is Mr. Robbins, a dignified-looking, greying man, the only man in the group with a college education, the schooling of the others being high school or less. Mr. Robbins was a social worker in a government relief agency, while his fellow members were workers, small business-men and a salesman. Mr. Robbins' wife had been a school teacher. They had an only son, six years of age.

At the third session of a newly organized group, Mr. Robbins began the discussion by questioning what could it be that would make his child suddenly not want to go to school and asked how such a situation could be handled. He punished and even beat the child to no avail. Mr. Gilmore, who speaks in a direct, almost challenging tone of voice, said that if a child refused to go to school, a child usually gave the excuse of being sick. In such case he would handle it by telling the child that if he was sick, they would have to call the doctor and that the doctor would probably have to give him "a shot with a needle." He found that this usually had an effect on children since they did not like having injections. Mr. Frum remarked that he had experienced the same difficulty with his son Fred in the past and that his son would frequently complain of stomach-aches before he went to school. Mr. Frum said that while he and his wife tried to reassure their son about the stomach-aches, they also insisted that he go to school and it was not too difficult for them to get Fred to do so. He wondered, however, if it was a good idea to threaten a child with a doctor to make him go to school, particularly if he was fearful of doctors.

The leader asked if it might not be a good idea to get the exact situation from Mr. Robbins, the particular instance he was citing with the child since a solution arrived at in one instance may not be applicable in another. This would help the group arrive at the best solution as it related to Mr. Robbins' child. Mr. Robbins said he thought that was a good idea since it would "pinpoint the problem rather than talking about it abstractly." He went on to say that his son had been out of school for a number of weeks, first with chickenpox and later with the flu. He wondered if the long absence from school made his son feel as if he were starting all over again and made him fearful of not being able to catch up with the work the other children had been doing during his absence. Mr. Frum asked what excuses the boy gave for not wanting to go to school. Mr. Robbins replied that his son had expressed fear of being made to *participate in excessive physical activity* by the teacher which might again make him sick. He went on to say that while he and his wife had given their son a note for the teacher to limit his activity, along with the note Mr. Robbins threatened the boy with punishment if he did not go to school that morning. He volunteered that this was probably "not the best idea" but that he really had no way of knowing how else to handle the situation or what to do with his son.

The leader asked Mr. Robbins whether some unusual circumstances had occurred in the family during his son's illness. Mr. Robbins replied that as a matter of fact a great deal had happened. His father-in-law, who lived with them, had died during that time. His own mother had died the preceding week, and that he had had to go to another state to attend his mother's funeral.

Mr. Gilmore then asked Mr. Robbins if Mr. Robbins' son knew of these deaths. The latter replied that his son did know, but had not spoken much about them. The boy knew that his grandfather had been very sick since the latter had taken ill at home. Some time prior to his death the grandfather was removed to a hospital. He returned home for a brief period until shortly before he died when he was again taken to a hospital. Mr. Robbins said that they tried to spare his son when his grandfather was taken out on a stretcher and placed in an ambulance both times by taking the boy to a neighbor's apartment. The child had not been told the last time that his grandfather had been removed from the house; when he returned from the neighbor he found grandfather gone and wondered what had happened to him and later why he had not come back. In addition the mother had been taken ill with the flu during that time with many visits from and to the doctor.

Mr. Frum asked Mr. Robbins if going to school had ever been a problem for his son before. Mr. Robbins replied that it had not except when he first started kindergarten. For only a week Mrs. Robbins had to spend some time outside the classroom where his son could come out every so often and see her. Following this he had accepted school easily until recently. Mr. Gilmore, a factory worker with less than a grammar school education, remarked that perhaps the deaths in the family were in some way disturbing to the child; since the boy had been sick himself and had witnessed so much sickness in the family and the results of the sickness, perhaps he was afraid that he, too, would die.

The leader asked Mr. Gilmore if he felt that the fear of dying was related to his fear of going to school and how he saw the two being connected. Mr. Gilmore said that he could not make the connection. The other men, too, could not relate the two reactions. The leader recounted the sequence of incidents as Mr. Robbins related them: the grandfather became ill, left the house twice and did not return, then the grandmother became ill and died and the father suddenly disappeared (when he went to his mother's funeral), at the present time the mother was ill and still in bed. Mr. Robbins thought for a while and finally commented that perhaps his son was afraid to go to school out of the fear that while he was away someone else in the family might disappear and not come back, and that if he were home all the time he could make sure that they would not leave him.

The leader asked the other members of the group how this struck them. Mr. Gilmore ridiculed the idea referring to the time the boy refused to go to school when he entered kindergarten. He wondered that even if this explanation were correct how it would help get the child to go to school this week and the next.

At this point Mr. Krutch and Mr. Snow entered the room—late

because of a misunderstanding as to the location of the meeting room.
As Mr. Krutch and Mr. Snow seated themselves, Mr. Robbins commented on Mr. Gilmore's remarks that he guessed the impression his
child now had of people disappearing and his fear of death would
not be eradicated for some time, but that if he and his wife could
handle the situation in such a way as to help their son overcome this
fear, it might slowly disappear in time. He then went on to say that
if what they had discussed as the basis for not wanting to go to
school was true, he did not feel he could explain this to his son as
such, but that some other method would have to be used to convey
the same idea to him.

Mr. Gilmore remarked that perhaps the solution was for Mr.
Robbins to permit his son to stay home for a while if that was what
he wanted, to reassure him that nothing was going to happen. Mr.
Robbins wondered about the advisability of this, remarking that
perhaps the permission for him to stay home might set a pattern for
the boy so that he would not want ever to return to school.

The leader then asked Mr. Robbins what suggestions he had in
this matter. The latter said that he supposed he could tell his son
that he was going to bring him some present at the end of each day
so that he could be more certain of the fact that his father would
be returning. He said he could also tell the child in advance whenever he had to be home late so that he would not be unduly anxious.

The leader asked if the others had any further suggestions in this
area. Mr. Gilmore asked how we could be sure though that it was
the death and illnesses in the family that was causing the difficulty.
He himself had no further ideas on the matter, but that if a father
had to be aware of the meaning of all his children's behavior, the
father would sure have to be "on the ball all the time." Mr. Robbins
replied to this that parents generally did have to be on the ball if
they were going to understand what was going on with their children.
While he had been aware of the fears of death in children, it was the
first time in discussing it here tonight that he had associated it with
his son's reaction to school and thought it quite plausible.

Mr. Robbins was a rather opinionated, somewhat haughty man,
aware of his intellectuality and superiority to his group mates. He

had a tendency of making discussions involved and abstruse, quizzing the leader and the others present, and of being intellectually aggressive and condescending. As the sessions continued, he succeeded in making himself disliked, and a little feared, by the other members because of his rather caustic tongue and biting remarks. Mr. Robbins was well informed on many subjects including child psychology, psychoanalysis, and education. Despite this equipment he resorted to punishment that included beating his six-year-old child without making an effort first to understand the cause for the child's reactions. This is the habitual response of parents to any annoyance from children which is culturally tolerated and even encouraged (see Chapter I).

An examination of the above discussion reveals not only the attitudes of the participants, but also their character organization and ego functioning. One suggests threat, deceit and indirection, another punishment, still another a more empathetic and understanding approach. If properly guided, this diversity of reactions and formulations can create the dynamic interaction of minds which inevitably results in clarification. In this the leader has an important part. Note that in the hour or more of discussion, he proffered only two remarks and one question, but they were all well placed and set the direction and focus of the conversation. Each of these were so phrased that the burden of clarification was shifted to the members rather than to himself. Even when Mr. Robbins makes the obviously unsuitable suggestion that he would apprise his son of his coming home each day, the leader does not express disagreement, but rather turns to the members of the group for their opinion. He, thus, lays the foundation for the primary group code.

When the leader asks Mr. Robbins to relate the child's behavior to events in the family he is performing a basic function in parent re-education. He demonstrates that parents, in fact all people, need to understand before they react to the behavior of others, and gives them essential training in this process. This function of the leader can be designated as *evocative*. When this is repeated by the leader time and again during the discussions, the parents in child-centered guidance groups themselves eventually fall into this pattern. In another statement he points out to the group that generalizations are not always effective in child rearing: one must understand the individual child and his condition, a principle to which Mr. Robbins readily accedes. Here the leader helps these fathers to particularize rather than generalize, that is, he tells them in effect that one must understand *his* child and not only children generally, and each situation rather than blanket principles. One wishes, however, that he had not used the term "problem" but "situation" instead (see p. 45, footnote).

The fact that a man with little education and no psychological knowledge of any kind could relate the fear of death to the child's refusal to go to school, as Mr. Gilmore did, is quite remarkable. Obviously, he had sustained a change of empathy during the discussion for it was he who at first suggested threatening the child with a doctor and sticking a needle into him. However, to bring it home, the leader had to *recapitulate* the circumstances so that Mr. Robbins could grasp the significance of the succession of events leading to his child's reluctance to go to school. Having grasped this relation, Mr. Gilmore's punitive attitude at once disappears and he seeks meliorative steps.

However, two points have been overlooked in this discussion which should have been clarified by the leader. One is that the child's fear of going to school was not due to the father's leaving the house mornings, but rather to the mother's illness. He was afraid that she, too, would disappear (die), as his grandfather did during his absence. The fact that a doctor was on the scene, as was also the case with the grandfather, only served to emphasize the similarity of the two situations in the child's mind and to reinforce his *anticipatory fear* of results. Mr. Robbins, though helped to understand the situation better, was misled to believe that his absence was a threat to the child. Actually it was the child's absence from the scene when he was taken to neighbors during which people (grandfather, father) disappeared (died) that caused his anxiety. He, therefore, solved his difficulty by not absenting himself from the home, by not going to school.

Another point, a more serious one, is to have permitted Mr. Robbins to take away the impression that he could not explain to his son the meaning of the latter's behavior. This precisely is what the father should have done, and the procedure of doing it had to be outlined in great detail by the leader. In such instances even the actual wording has to be rehearsed with a parent so that he would not convey a wrong or undesirable impression. The father in this case should have explained to the child that he did not want to go to school because he thought that the same thing would happen to his mother that had happened to his grandfather, but young people like mother and father seldom die. Only old people like grandfather die. He therefore need have no fear on that score. Mother's illness was only a cold, like he himself had had a number of times. She would get better as he did. Then Mr. Robbins should have been instructed that in view of the child's age, if he insisted on staying home, he should be allowed to do so, without any question until the mother was completely well.

Parents infect their children with their fear of and discomfort about death as they do in relation to animals, darkness, thunderclap, lightning and similar phenomena. If parents take an objective and detached view of death, children will not develop fear of it. It may be interesting to relate in this connection significant episodes dealing with the attitude toward illness and death on the part of parents. These episodes also indicate that special situations, which for a variety of reasons cannot be dealt with in a group, require individual consultations. However, these should be kept to a minimum.

Little Jane, an only child, of about two years of age, whose parents were both members of the child-centered guidance group (described in Chapter I), was carefully and properly prepared for the arrival of another child. Because of a defect in placental development, the baby died at the hospital after three days. The obstetrician insisted that the mother return home at once to finish her period of recuperation because he felt that she would become disturbed by the other mothers whose babies had survived. He felt that the atmosphere in the maternity hospital would cause her distress.

Jane's father, who was a member of the group, called me on the phone asking advice as to how to break the news to the little girl. They decided to tell her that the baby was left in the hospital and would arrive later, having in mind another child which the parents planned to have as soon as possible. They were also going to bring

Jane a "big doll instead of the baby." I asked the father to come to see me before any move was made.

The plan I suggested to him, and which was scrupulously followed, was that the mother should be removed from the hospital and stay at the home of a sister whom she liked. She should not return home until she had completely recovered her physical health so that she could take up the care of her daughter where she left off. There must not be any invalidism of the mother as far as the girl was concerned, for it would mean rejection and denial of love to the child and possibly give rise to fantasies of the mother dying as well. A toy should be brought the child, but not a doll, when the mother returned. The little girl would have to be told directly, but calmly and objectively, that the baby had died. If the girl inquired what that meant she was to be told that "died" meant that he could not move like flies or bugs, or perhaps a dead dog the child may have seen on the street. It should be related to something that the child had experienced. She could also be told that there would be another brother or sister in the future.

I assured the father that the child would not understand half of what the mother would tell her in the sense that adults conceived understanding, but would get the general "drift," as it were, not so much from what was said, but from the attitude of factuality and calm with which it was said. As a further precaution I suggested that the mother move about the neighborhood without Jane for several days after she had returned, so that she could make known the fact of the infant's death to her neighbors and friends without Jane having to listen to the repetition of the tale, and especially to the reactions of these friends and neighbors. The parents reported at one of the sessions of our group that the plan worked out well in every respect, that Jane's reaction was almost one of seeming indifference, though interest, and that what might have been a serious trauma to the child was averted.

Another member of the same group sought individual advice in the matter of her only little girl of three, a rather bright and precocious child, whose grandmother suffered a heart attack while visiting the family and had to remain with them, since removing her was inadvisable. The parents were concerned about the fact that because of the small apartment, the child had witnessed the illness and the suffering and had been exposed to the doctor's visits and the resulting tensions. They accordingly planned to have the mother and child leave home and live with a relative. I advised against it, explaining to the parents that protecting a child against stress beyond a certain point could be more injurious than exposing him to it. A child of three, especially a bright and otherwise healthy youngster, as this one was, must have experience with illness. Children can see people being sick and becoming well. This adds to their security if they themselves fall ill. Again, as in the preceding instance, I explained that anxiety and fear over illness was induced by adults in the child's environment, especially the parents, and if they were calm and optimistic, the child would not be disturbed. It is necessary that the child understands, in his own limited way, what is going on around him. There must be no mystery around the tense situation. The little girl, therefore, must be told in language that she could comprehend what was wrong with her grandmother, holding out the well-founded promise that she would be well again soon. I rehearsed the actual words with the mother preparatory for this conversation. The child remained at home and in two weeks the grandmother recovered sufficiently to go home. The parents felt that it was a salutary experience for their girl.

The above two instances and the situation with Mr. Robbins bring home the fact that leaders of Child-Centered Guidance Groups should be trained psychotherapists, and mature persons whose own varied experiences have made them sufficiently resourceful so as to be able to help parents in a *practical way* with the innumerable and puzzling situations that constantly arise in everyday life with children. Another reason for requiring training and experience in psychotherapy is that the leader must be able to recognize when the group members are bordering on anxiety-provoking areas and productions and have the skill to *deflect* them from entering upon those areas. This frequently requires greater skill than in psychotherapy where free flow of verbal catharsis is permitted and encouraged.

As parents become more enlightened and more secure, they are able to take a stand with their children and become firm when the occasion arises and when it is justified. Only a few examples of this are cited below.

Mrs. Broom said that the parents' being strong and firm and knowing their place in the home was important to children. She never realized that until very recently. She now felt that she's getting to be a "stronger mother" and is having less difficulty. She described a scene that had occurred the other day. Henry came for lunch and decided not to return to school for the afternoon because the teacher had been angry with him about something. She did not become angry but merely suggested that it would be better if he returned and if necessary fight it out with the teacher and not let out his feelings through not attending school. He refused to go, however, and wanted to turn on the television set, which she prohibited. He then wanted to go out and play outdoors. She "put her foot down on this too" and told him he could not have fun while staying out of school. The boy yelled, screamed and insisted on going into the television room, but she shut the door and said she would not let him "play truant." Henry stayed in the house and at three o'clock went outdoors as he could at that time if he had gone to school.

This incident taught her that she could "really be firm on important issues" and get her son to respond, she said. She knows now what it means to be firm and for once did not mind his yelling and screaming. What is even more important is that the teacher reported that Henry was very good this year, he was well liked, there was no problem with him. In answer to the leader's question, Mrs. Broom said that she felt it was important for Henry to feel that he could not play "hooky" because he became angry with the teacher. She did not slap him as she would have done before. She was well controlled "and that's what did it," she said triumphantly. She was able to figure out how to deal with him without hurting him and that really helped him. Since that incident Henry had not stayed away from school. "Maybe he'll learn how to work out his difficulties now without running away from them the way he had been doing right along," she said.

Mrs. Broom then gave another example of determination on her part. The family was going to a birthday party of a young cousin and Henry did not want to join them. He said that he would not have any fun. In the past she would have lost her temper and argued with him; instead she suggested that if he wished, he could stay with a relative in the neighborhood and the family would go without him because they had promised and wanted to go. When the family was about ready to leave, Henry changed his mind. She accepted this without fuss. In fact when he got to the party he was happy because he had lots of fun; there were other children his age. On their way home, Mrs. Broom asked him why he did not want to go in the first place. Henry told her "something that he never would have admitted at other times," namely, that he was shy and when he did not have boys his own age to play with he felt out of place. She was surprised to learn that he was really afraid of and uncomfortable with new children. He always gave the appearance of being "so brave and courageous. You just never know," she remarked, "you really have to ask children to understand them sometimes."

Mrs. Stein said she was beginning to see that she did expect too much from Peter. Sometimes she "forgets his age" and gets angry at him as if he were much older. She should know better, she said. He cries and screams that she should let him alone, that he does not care about having friends. She had had a pretty good week after she became aware of it and "assigned" herself to act differently with Peter. She used to nag him mornings about getting up when she waked him and demand that "he do just the right thing at the right time" so that he would get off to school on time. At the suggestion of the group, she told him one morning that she was simply going to help him get dressed and ready, but not do his jobs. He looked amazed at first as though he did not believe it, but when she actually went to the kitchen to do her work, Peter "went ahead and did what he needed to and since then there has been no trouble." Mrs. Stein said she was very much surprised; maybe what she had to learn was to change her own routines and then Peter would change accordingly.

Mrs. Wolman's son occasionally asked her to move out of the neighborhood so that the boys would not pick on him. Maybe in a different neighborhood everything would be different, including the teacher and the boys.

Mrs. Gold said that her boy used to say the same thing, but now she felt that she helped him through her changed attitude and he no longer complained about these matters. He used to think that everyone picked on him the way, he said, she used to pick on him. Now that she stopped, he no longer complained about the boys. She described how she learned to be "more firm and more adult" with her children. She described how simple it was to get Jimmy into treatment once she understood what was behind his resistance. She wanted him to go, but she did nothing about it and instead waited for him to make up his mind. What was really necessary was firmness and conviction about what she decided to do. She told him that he had to go and when the time came she just took him, though he was at first somewhat rebellious. In the past she would have argued and argued and argued with him; she would have reasoned and probably to no avail. This time she simply said: "This is our bus, let's go," and he went. Since then he has been keeping his treatment appointments regularly.

Often one obtains results in a surprisingly brief time and with parents that at first glance appear to be hopeless. The case of Mr. Mathias illustrates this point. Larry Mathias, aged ten years, had difficulties in school where he acted out strong animosity toward teachers; he was inattentive, avoided doing school assignments, and failed in his subjects. In addition, Larry was socially maladjusted, had a poor relationship with his mother and was described as negative, complaining and resentful toward her. Larry had been unwanted and his mother had planned to abort him which was prevented by her husband. As a reaction to her strong hatred for Larry, Mrs. Mathias severely infantilized and overprotected him. A brother, ten years older than Larry, had been treated at the same child guidance clinic some years before.

Mr. Mathias was one of seven children in a family constantly threatened by extreme poverty. He went to work at a very early age and therefore had little schooling. Larry's mother had had a severely deprived childhood. Her mother died when Mrs. Mathias was seven years old. She described her husband as a withdrawn, taciturn man who seldom spoke to the children and who had no social contacts or interests beyond his job. He left the responsibility for the children entirely to her. In an initial interview, he was found to be an intellectually and emotionally limited person who minimized Larry's difficulties and had no desire to become involved in any way with his son's treatment.

Larry was placed in an activity therapy group and the mother, after briefly attending a child-centered guidance group, was seen intermittently by a caseworker on a supportive basis. After Larry had attended a group for a year, the father was seen again in an attempt to explore more fully his role in the family situation. Mr. Mathias was evasive and resistive. He recalled that he had been at the clinic once before and questioned why he had to come again. He seemed unwilling to recognize any difficulties in Larry and denied that his older son had ever been in treatment. However, he accepted the suggestion that he attend a fathers' discussion group which he could drop if he did not find it helpful. The group had been meeting for some time.

At the first session that Mr. Mathias attended, another member described an incident in which his son had called him a "bastard." In the ensuing discussion, stimulated by the leader, it became clear that the boy actually had not known the meaning of the word. Despite this, Mr. Mathias said the boy should be severely punished "because it's still a bad word." He also seemed incredulous upon learning that other members of the group gave weekly money allowances to their children and permitted them to spend them as the children saw fit. He emphatically registered opposition to this, exclaiming: "No, no. That's not the way. A boy has to learn the value of money!" He added that his son was too young for an allowance anyway.

At the second session two weeks later, Mr. Mathias indicated that he was particularly impressed with a group discussion of school difficulties which had been understood as sometimes resulting from a child's resentment arising from unsatisfactory familial relations. He stated thoughtfully: "I never thought of it that way." Later in the session, he proudly reported that as a result of the previous meeting's discussion, he had instituted a weekly allowance for Larry.

At his fourth session, Mr. Mathias related that he had initiated a conversation with Larry around the boy's anxiety connected with his going to a new school. With deep satisfaction Mr. Mathias said that Larry felt much less fearful after their talk.

In an interview held with the mother after the father's first four guidance sessions, she reported considerable change in his attitude toward Larry. She reported that Mr. Mathias had taken a much more active role with Larry, expressing interest in his school work and social activities and arranging to take him to basketball games. Whereas he had always slept late on Sundays, he had recently gotten up quite early to go on a bike ride with his son. In addition, he had begun to protect Larry from the mother's tantrums and name-calling whenever she would lose patience with the boy. He had explicitly told the mother that she was "ruining" Larry's treatment by her behavior.

The emerging awareness of another father's role, who had been as resistive as Mr. Mathias, is clearly shown in the following abstract from the group leader's record of an individual interview which had been requested by this group member in a telephone call:

Mr. Rosen began by stating that he had "a few problems" which he wanted to discuss with the leader but felt he had to tell him something before. In a serious and extremely thoughtful manner (which was in marked contrast to the defensiveness and resistiveness displayed by him in previous *individual* interviews with another therapist), he described that he felt some very important changes had occurred in him in the last few months. He had begun to realize that he was responsible for quite a few of the difficulties his family had been experiencing. He guessed that in the past he had been unable to admit to himself that perhaps he may have been at fault or the cause of some of the difficulties presented by his children, and also for some of his marital problems.

He said that the preceding summer his wife, for the first time since their marriage, had gone on a vacation. When he visited her, he was astonished by the difference in her manner and personality.

She was relaxed and calm which contrasted sharply with the anxiety and tenseness she displayed at home. He suddenly became aware that he must in some way be responsible for his wife's feelings throughout the year. It also occurred to him that in the past he had always gone on vacations by himself and that she had never taken any summer holidays. Recognizing some of these facts had been very helpful, he said, and that it had enabled his wife to talk freely to him about "some of the things that had been bothering her and which she kept bottled up in her for so long."

Mr. Rosen then referred specifically to his son Robert, stating that "the father's group has opened my eyes to the fact that I and Robert have been in the habit of putting on a clowning show at mealtimes for the other members of the family." He indicated that as a result of the group discussions, this has now stopped, stating specifically that he himself had stopped playing the clown at the table as he used to do. He stated that although Robert at times continued to act up, he now completely ignored this, so that the boy's clowning had no effect whatsoever, and the family meals which used to be extremely tense affairs for years have now become almost pleasant. Mr. Rosen noted that Celia[4] seemed very impressed with this change and told the father that she "was proud" of the way he acted.

Mr. Rosen then brought up several specific problems he wanted to discuss with the leader. He indicated that Robert had a severe case of acne and the father had been thinking of suggesting to the boy that he go to a skin specialist, but that he had some question in mind as to how the boy would take it. Would he be upset emotionally? At the same time, he had been thinking of spending a Sunday with the boy shooting, since Robert expressed great interest in his rifle and the father had decided to take him out to the country for some target practice. He also wondered if this might not be a good time to broach the idea of sex education. This was discussed with Mr. Rosen.

Mr. Rosen also expressed concern about Robert's wanting to kiss him excessively and indicated that he was handling this "in a proper manner," i.e., discouraging it without being blatantly rejecting. He

---

[4] A daughter who was older than Robert, and a borderline schizophrenic in treatment with another therapist at the clinic.

referred to Robert's need for having continued attention from the father, describing that the other day he had spent an hour listening to Robert play his drums, and then a half hour listening to him rehearse his lessons, but when later the father wanted to discuss something privately with Celia, Robert kept interrupting. He further expressed concern, which he had registered also in the past, that Celia seemed too dependent on the clinic, specifically her therapist, and was using it as a "crutch." The other day after her mid-term exams, Celia expressed a recurrent anxiety that none of her friends liked her and she had tried several times to call her therapist. Mr. Rosen had been somewhat upset by this. He thought this was "overdependence." The leader used the simile of the crutches when a person had a broken leg; it was absolutely necessary to use crutches for a while, so that later the crutches could be thrown away and the person could walk freely without them. He assured Mr. Rosen that when the right time came, Celia would be quite happy "to throw the crutches away," and that the clinic would be happy about it too. Mr. Rosen conveyed his understanding and acceptance of this idea.

Some of Mr. Rosen's production in this interview seemed to have the aspects of a confessional, and the leader planfully did not go along with it. Thus, when he stated that he felt that in the last four months the group had helped him to achieve this understanding, the leader replied that he was not sure of this; it was quite possible that Mr. Rosen would have achieved this understanding by himself. He seemed extremely pleased with this, first indicating that it was possible, but then reiterated that he felt that certainly his contact with the clinic had quickened the achievement of his understanding. At the close of the interview, Mr. Rosen stated that he guessed some people "went through their whole lives blind," and expressed satisfaction that he "could now see the important things." He shook the leader's hand warmly as he left.

At one point the leader had asked Mr. Rosen why he could not have brought these questions up in the group. Mr. Rosen replied that he wanted to discuss with the leader his "feelings about seeing things in their true light for the first time alone." He felt that this was somehow "too personal to be shared with the others."

Mrs. Suskin[5] said she found out that in an emergency she could "take hold." She no longer minded her "schedule being upset." Because it was his turn, she let Saul have his Boy Scout troop meet at her home even though her younger son was ill. Saul is now getting along well with the scouts and they had a good holiday week end. Saul is going fishing with her husband, "with no fuss on either side." Her only complaint against Saul is that he talks in such a loud, demanding voice and teases her now and then. She used to get upset when her husband teased her, but he stopped it.

Mrs. Kohn suggested that she pretend she did not hear the boy when he talked in a loud voice and tease him back so that he would know how it felt. Mrs. Suskin laughed and said that would give him a good reason to be even more provoking; besides, he would see through the trick. She has to set a good example and give him no reason for being provocative, not get down to his level. She used to do that. She then explained that when he had the scouts at the house, Saul told the boys they would have to be quiet because his brother was ill and sleeping. Mrs. Kohn said this was "just an act." He was probably hoping the boys would wake his brother up because he was resentful that the mother was so protective of the younger child. Mrs. Suskin said she really did not feel he was jealous but rather concerned. Saul felt much better this week when the younger boy was again able to go to school. She stoutly maintained it was not a trick and Mrs. Kohn agreed that perhaps she had found the right answers. "How did you get to understand your child so well?" she asked. Mrs. Suskin said she learned through her discussions in the other (guidance) group that when she became irritable, everything went badly. Now that she acts more "grown up" there is less tension in the house.

It may be pertinent to note that Mrs. Kohn had been in individual treatment for a year with no results before placement in the analytic therapy group.

Mrs. Wolman said she did not like her husband to be too mean to his own relatives either. Something interesting had happened on

5 Not to be confused with Mrs. Salkin; Mrs. Suskin proved to be a disturbed woman and was transferred to individual treatment for a year and later to an analytic therapy group. This abstract is taken from the latter group's record.

Mother's Day. All that Sunday she had been wondering if he would be angry if she went to see her mother, and at 8:30 in the evening she finally announced that she was going and he "did not raise any fuss." He seemed glad that she was so definite. Saturday she planned to see her husband's mother, and having made a date with his aunt, she informed him that his mother would be there too. He seems to want her to make her own decisions. Though he balks a little, he goes along. Her boy volunteered to baby sit with his younger brother and agreed not to stay up later than 10:00 P.M. At 1:00 A.M. the younger boy called on the telephone and informed her that the TV was still on. She expected her husband, who was also a member of a guidance group, would be angry, but instead on the following day, Sunday, he questioned the boy quietly. The boy said he left the TV on because he had a "funny feeling" about being alone in the house, but he did go to bed at 10 o'clock as he promised. Whereupon Mr. Wolman, very sympathetically and quietly, suggested that his son could talk with him privately if he could not admit to Mrs. Wolman that he was afraid of something.

Her husband told the boy that he understood because he, too, had been afraid when he was a child. The boy admitted that he thought of robbers coming into the house and Mr. Wolman explained to him that he had lived in the same apartment since he was fourteen years old and there never had been any robberies. The boy then said he was afraid of kidnappers and the father told him that kidnappers came only to very wealthy families. Thereupon the boy decided there was really nothing to be afraid of. Mrs. Wolman then suggested that the next time he turn off the TV but that he could leave the radio on low if he felt the house was "too quiet for him."

All the others in the group were impressed by Mrs. Wolman's sympathetic response to her son and she said that she herself was very pleased that her husband could be so "understanding and have such patience with the child." Until recently he acted as if the boy was no concern of his. Lately he told her not to assign the boy as "a baby sitter," even if she had to leave for a half hour until the boy was ready to do so without being afraid. Now the boy says he is ready and asks to be paid for it. Mr. Wolman objects to paying him for doing a service for his parents or his brother, she said. Members of families should not ask for payment for this kind of exchange of service and Mr. Wolman tries to make it up to the boy in some other way, which seems to be acceptable to him.

It is evident from these abstracts that the parents' behavior toward their children now stems from deliberative, controlled and understanding reactions and reflections instead of impulsivity and irrational emotionalism of the past. This is the focal aim of Child-Centered Group Guidance of Parents which we have been able to achieve, namely, in Freud's words, "Where id was, there shall ego be." In subsequent chapters this fact is further confirmed.

V

Toward Understanding Children

In the last chapter were quoted a number of isolated episodes that illustrated how members of a child-centered parents' guidance group help one another to deal with specific situations. These learnings, however, gradually and imperceptibly are incorporated into new and improved attitudes not only toward children's behavior, but also toward the child *as a person* and toward life generally. To illustrate these developments we are reproducing in this chapter comparatively detailed protocol records of two sessions, the twentieth and twenty-sixth; but before we do so the reader will find brief outlines of the backgrounds of the six women who were present at these discussions, two women being absent. Numbers in parentheses after the names will help the reader follow the sequence of the proceedings as they relate to each of the participants.

Mrs. Ash (1), forty-three years old, was described as a "nervous" woman, perfectionistic in regard to Alfred, intellectual, articulate, with a good knowledge of child care and aware that she was unable to apply what she had learned because of involvements in her home situation. She understood that her inconsistency had played a role in her son's poor development. At first she had been overindulgent and overprotective, but when her second son was born three years later, she became strict and punitive with Alfred, feeling that this would be the proper way to help him "mature." Her confusion as to what a good parent is appeared only in relation to Alfred. She seemed to be more adequate with her two younger boys. She blamed her husband for the difficulty. Though friendly, she was lacking in warmth, did not enjoy household activities and care of children, feeling that they were a burden to her. In general, the impression was that she was forced into the role of mother and wife and that her interests lay outside the home. Her nonacceptance of Alfred was evident from the time he was conceived.

Mrs. Ash came from Europe with her mother and sister when she was eight years old. She is the second eldest child and did not know her father until she had met him in the United States. Her mother is aggressive and talkative; her father a quiet type. She had a high school education, went to business before marriage as a secretary and liked it very much. Her marriage was kept a secret because she would have lost her job as a married woman and also because her parents were against the match. Her father had always been distant with the children. Mrs. Ash's family have not accepted her husband, who was considered by them beneath them, in addition to the fact that his economic status did not live up to their expectations. She is close to and dependent on her family and conflicted in her loyalties to them as against her husband.

Mrs. Ash dominated her husband and directed him in the relations to his children and his role in the family. She encouraged him to participate in activities outside the home, having adopted her family's attitude toward him and regarded him as an inferior person. However, she appreciates his efforts and attempts to maintain the family comfortably.

Mr. Ash also attended a fathers' group on an exploratory basis. He was found to be very tense and was difficult for the group. He was, therefore, transferred after one session to individual therapy from which he withdrew. It was felt that he was overwhelmed by his homoerotic impulses and by his maternal rather than paternal role in the family, particularly in relation to Alfred, and that he therefore could not subject himself to treatment. He was a compulsive talker. The diagnosis established was psychoneurosis, obsessional, compulsive type with very strong dependency trends. He is in perpetual fear that his wife will leave him if he is not adequate. In general, his relationship to his wife is one of insecurity and lack of acceptance. He is extremely dependent on a sister with whom he is in a business partnership. Mrs. Ash was openly critical of her husband in regard to his weakness, his indulgence and so forth. There are also open quarrels regarding the relationships and status of their respective families.

Mr. and Mrs. Ash were constantly arguing about what was the right thing to do for their children, the father preferring to be in the home and taking on the maternal role. Both parents were either punitive or rewarding in relation to Alfred. For instance, both were interested in raising Alfred's achievement in school; both tutored him every evening after the younger children had gone to bed, and on week ends; both parents seemed to be more accepting of the two younger children. Mrs. Ash was especially pleased with the "friendliness" of the younger boys. However, father and mother were as involved in their own activities as they were with those of Alfred.

Alfred was ten years old when he was referred for treatment. He was "extremely quiet," unable to defend himself against his peers and against his younger brother. He cried easily, lied, and was difficult at school. Alfred was considered uncommunicative, inarticulate, and guarded against self-revelation. A diagnosis of character disorder with a passive, feminine personality was established. Alfred was treated in activity group therapy exclusively.

Mrs. Ash had the uncomfortable feeling that Alfred might turn out to be like her own father—withdrawn, quiet, ineffectual. Her disappointment with him became more marked at the birth of the younger boy who appeared to her to be more outgoing and "manly," the kind of boy she had wanted. Alfred had had a severe asthmatic condition when he was two but it gradually disappeared by the time he was five. Although she had talked of being overindulgent with him, it is to be questioned what that meant in view of the fact that she is not a warm, demonstrative person and had really rejected this child from the time he was born. His asthmatic condition may very well suggest the rejection that he felt. Further unconscious rejection of him is revealed by her perfectionistic demands on him which are in contrast to the complete acceptance of whatever the two younger children did. To her, then, Alfred represents her weak father and her weak husband. Until she came into the group, she had constantly compared him unfavorably to his brothers and in this way set up his brothers against him.

Mrs. Friedman (2), a woman of forty, kept herself well groomed and attractively dressed. She was intelligent, ambitious for her children to attain high scholastic standards. A rather tense, rigid person, she was inclined to be overprotective and dominating of both her children and her husband. She made attempts to enlist various community resources to learn how to understand her son better. She maintained an attitude of inadequacy and self-blame, with accompanying hostility and guilt. Mrs. Friedman had a pleasant personality, was soft-spoken and inclined to depend on authority for guidance. She was friendly and sociable.

She was born in Europe where she suffered extreme physical and economic deprivation in early childhood, the youngest of five children with two older sisters and brothers. When her father migrated to America with one older brother and one older sister, Mrs. Friedman remained behind with the rest of the family. She had a difficult time adjusting to her father when she arrived in the United States at the age of eight, but gradually developed a warm relation with him. Her parents were extremely religious and her mother was eager to raise her grandchildren in an orthodox fashion. Mrs. Friedman was close to her family. Two of her siblings lived in the same apartment house.

Mr. Friedman was a cab driver, friendly, easy-going and good-natured. He was the oldest of three with a younger brother and sister. He, too, suffered early economic deprivation, having had to assume financial responsibility at seven years of age, when he worked as delivery boy. He was eager to provide for his son what he himself had missed as a child and has gone along with his wife in overprotecting the boy against all hardships and difficulties. He was not able to set limits for Morris and in general has sought a sibling-like relationship with him. Occasionally, he would beat the boy up because of his inability to cope with him. Mr. Friedman has been in a guidance group, as was his wife.

Morris was referred to the child guidance clinic at the age of nine for nocturnal enuresis persisting since birth, temper tantrums, poor relationship with his mother and some stealing from her. He had friends but did not get along with them too well, was a restless sleeper, had some fear of the dark and was a nail biter. He has been treated in activity group therapy where he had gained ego strength and had become better adjusted socially, but we believed that his basic sexual difficulties as well as some other internalized neurotic problems needed to be worked out in individual treatment.

Morris was not welcomed by either parent because of their financial difficulties at the time of his birth. The mother had not wanted her second child, a girl, either, because of the burden this child would be to her, but as soon as she was born accepted her. The girl's development progressed much more normally than her older brother's, who was exceedingly rivalrous with her. He always insisted on receiving as many presents as were given her. Whenever the father brought his daughter a present, Morris insisted that he receive either money equal to the cost of the presents, or presents of the exact same value. Although Morris could at times be friendly with his sister, he would more often destroy or hide her toys and play with them himself for long periods, thus depriving her of her fun.

Mrs. Friedman had always found fault with Morris except for the fact that he was sociable with friends of his age and with adults. Unconsciously she feared that he might be like her husband's brother who had lived on the margin of the law. This could partly explain her overprotectiveness and the fact that she had little confidence in his ability to do things on his own. Before he came for treatment, she bathed him and minimized the importance of privacy for a boy of his age. She had been frequently punitive, especially when she felt defeated by her son, particularly around his bed wetting.

Mrs. James (3), forty-five years old, was a tall, heavy-set woman of average intelligence, aggressive and dominating in relation to her peers, on the one hand, and submissive and conforming to people in authority, such as teachers and the leader in the guidance group, on the other. She was unable to recognize her part in her difficulties, particularly with her son, using projection as her main defense. She had a strong need to be in the right and to be accepted. Her rigidity and inflexibility were marked in her contact with the clinic, but more recently she had shown some degree of amenability. Essentially, she was a phallic woman, whose satisfaction as a mother had been gratified only in the development of her first son. She had three sons, one twenty-two years old, another nineteen, and Stanley who was ten years of age.

Mrs. James was born in the United States and graduated from public school. Her father, who died when she was thirty-two years old, was described by her as "a good-natured man in every way." She currently contributed to her mother's maintenance, whom she described as a "quiet kind." Mrs. James had two younger sisters, one two years her junior and the other eight, the latter unmarried and living with her mother.

Little was known about Mr. James other than the fact that he was manager of a small business. He was used by his wife as the punitive agent in her disciplining of Stanley. From him we knew that he played checkers with his father who never lost to his son. The impression one got from his wife is that he was a hard-working person and liked a quiet home. Mrs. James dominated and directed him and he was submissive to her. She described what appeared to be a warm relationship between her and her husband and that they were affectionate with each other even in the presence of their children.

According to Mrs. James her family was a close-knit group. They frequently gave parties. Particular stress was laid on the older son who was married and who, with his wife, visited the family once a week. This boy had been most gratifying to Mrs. James in that he had been a good student, outgoing socially, and had done well according to her standards. The middle boy was withdrawn and she found it difficult to understand what caused the difference in the development of the two boys. He could not make friends with girls and did not have too many boy friends either. He was friendly only when someone else took the initiative. The two older boys had been chummy until the older, in his adolescence, had become interested in the girl who later became his wife. Since then, according to Mrs. James, the middle boy has been like a "lost sheep." His interest in Stanley becomes activated only when the latter initiates it and then he becomes annoyed with him. Because Stanley wet his bed, the two older brothers did not want him in their room. This is the reason she gave for keeping Stanley in the parents' bedroom against everyone's better judgment. It is not known whether Stanley's siblings did not accept him because of their mother's attitude or not.

Stanley was referred to the clinic by the school at the age of ten because of poor work, unsatisfactory conduct, viciousness with children, infantile behavior and mother's complaint that he was a chronic bed wetter and unable to establish close relationships. His I.Q. was 83, according to school reports. He was considered a dull child, reacting to neglect and rejection on the part of a dominating mother with high achievement standards and a punitive father. There was some internalization as indicated by fears. Treatment goals for this boy had to be limited because of his low mentality, and he was treated both individually and in activity group therapy.

Stanley was unplanned and unwanted. Although this was true for the other children as well, there was specially intense rejection of him because he was not a girl. The mother had chosen a girl's name in advance and, after he was born, used it for him for a long time. She tried in other ways to prevent his acting like a boy. His bed wetting has been a source of great concern to her and she consulted various doctors and clinics, used punitive methods, embarrassment before people, whippings by her and her husband, but to no avail. Another disappointment was the boy's poor school work of which Mrs. James was greatly ashamed. She cooperated with teachers and school principals in pressing him to achieve beyond his ability, but made little or no attempt to understand him or his limitations. The indication of extreme rejection of the boy was evidenced when the family had a wedding party for the oldest son and he was kept out of the family photos that were taken on that occasion. Mrs. James talked readily about the "burden" Stanley had been to her at a time when she had reached an age where she could expect to be free and no longer have to care for a child, especially one like Stanley. Further evidence, which was later revealed in the group, pointed to the fact that she was inordinately seductive toward him and sexually involved with him to such an extent that she once confessed of having "the same feelings" when Stanley kissed her as when her husband did (see p. 217).

Mrs. Kling (4) was a woman in the early fifties, heavy but well-groomed, presenting a good and neat appearance. She spoke with a marked European accent, but was articulate and expressed her thoughts adequately. She was inclined to be domineering and controlling, but kindly and friendly. She exerted herself to gain approval, had strong drives for a higher education and achievement for her children. She contacted school authorities, was active in parent-teacher groups and interested in children, generally. Her attitude toward her three boys as well as her husband was one of overprotection. She made "sacrifices" for the boys and said she enjoyed being a mother. She was a woman who once she felt accepted became amenable and cooperative and made a real effort to understand how she could do better with her children. She appeared to have a strong ego and had guided the family through many difficulties.

Mrs. Kling was the youngest of five children. She came to the United States alone at the age of sixteen to join an older sister already established here. Her family suffered extreme deprivation in Europe after World War I where there was widespread hunger. A brother and two sisters who remained in Europe have not been heard from. There is the possibility that they died under the Nazi regime. Her father was described as warm and intelligent. She explained that she was conflicted about coming to America alone, fearing the separation from her parents on the one hand, and very eager to be free on the other. Mrs. Kling had a difficult struggle in the new country and had attended evening school while working during the day. She had been rather aggressive and unafraid of new situations when young.

Mrs. Kling described her husband as a hard worker and a good parent who was always bringing things for the children and the home. He was a laborer and had made a fair living for the family. On the other hand, he needed much attention from his wife. She said he was like a little boy and she did things for him that a mother usually does for a child. She did not begrudge him this, however, because he had had a very deprived childhood, she said. He left his family at an early age to get away from "miserable conditions." His mother never cooked, nor did she attend the children properly. The implication was that his mother was a psychologically ill person. Occasionally Mrs. Kling would say that her husband was too old to have patience with a young child, or that he was not a "father type," because he showed little interest in the children. He merely wanted to relax and take it easy. He left the rearing of the children to her, but was at the same time critical of her. Mrs. Kling was very eager for her husband to join a guidance group "for the sake of the children more than for him." The siblings in this family seemed well adjusted to each other; there was a close tie between Jacob and his younger brother.

All three children were unplanned. Mrs. Kling attempted to abort the first son, but did nothing about the pregnancies following that.

Mrs. Kling was overly attentive to the children's body functions, their interests, and their schoolwork. In the intake interview she talked of her marked interest in the anal functions of her children, such as asking the children not to flush the toilet so that she could examine their stools. Good manners, proper behavior and conformity were very important to her, which she constantly "preached" to her children. On the other hand, she permitted a great deal of aggression and resentment directed toward herself, but could not "talk the children into behaving themselves better." She was less disturbed about what went on in the home than the children's behavior outside.

Jacob was eleven years old when he was referred through an educational clinic. His difficulties at the time consisted of generalized fearfulness, reading inability and withdrawal from children. He had been a very sickly child with frequent gastrointestinal symptoms such as cramps and vomiting which occurred when some upsetting situations in school arose. His I.Q. was 93 and he had been in special classes until the time when psychotherapy was initiated. He was compared unfavorably by his parents with the older and younger brothers both of whom were more alert in all areas and had always been physically sturdier.

In addition to being an overprotective mother to all her three children, Mrs. Kling was especially concerned with respect to Jacob because at the age of four weeks he had a convulsive episode. He had been an ailing child, running high fever and complaining of stomach upsets until about the age of eight years when he had an appendectomy. She had considered him the weakest of her three children, had followed his school adjustment more closely and had worked with teachers in an attempt to cushion the pressures on him. She was concerned with the fact that Jacob would never become a self-sustaining person able to deal with his life adequately.

Jacob was treated in group therapy. He had made considerable gains in the group in that he was able to express some aggression and seemed less threatened by the activities of the other boys. However, he had indicated a fear of losing control of himself in this permissive atmosphere and, together with his mother's overprotectiveness and identification with him in this respect, he withdrew from the group. He reacted in a similar way to summer camp. He was accordingly assigned to individual treatment at the clinic.

Mrs. Salkin (5), the mother of two boys, Harris, ten years old, and a younger boy of five, was in her late thirties, born in the United States. She was a woman of more than average intelligence, was anxious, particularly in relation to her husband and Harris, had continually sought help in understanding their difficulties and trying to work them out. She took her responsibilities as mother and wife very seriously and far more maturely than did her husband. She tended to keep her anger under cover but seemed to be aware of it and adjusted in a socially acceptable way. She had a pleasing personality and was well liked. There was a tendency to be dependent; she sought to improve her knowledge of handling herself in relation to her home.

Mrs. Salkin's parents were divorced after a life marked by continual friction and quarrels. There was a time when she had allied herself with her father and was able to "wind him around her finger." He became blind when she and her brother were young. Her mother was a strong person, the father a disturbed and weak one. Her brother had a mental breakdown during the war and was receiving psychiatric treatment. Nothing more was known about her life with her family other than that she married young "to have a strong man to depend on."

Mrs. Salkin described her first two years of marriage as fairly happy; difficulties appeared only at the birth of Harris to which Mr. Salkin reacted in an extremely infantile manner and with jealousy at her handling the child. He spent much time on his hobby of model electric trains which angered Mrs. Salkin. Mr. Salkin continued to display his resentment of Harris. The mother had at first tried to appease her husband and hide her hostility, but in recent years had become able to react to it more directly. There had been occasional discussions about separation, usually initiated by Mrs. Salkin on the basis that her husband was too inadequate as a parent, and her need to continue to be the mainstay in the family. In addition to being infantile Mr. Salkin had violent temper outbursts particularly in relation to Harris. He himself came from a disturbed background in which he had a very tense and hostile relationship with his own father who was very punitive. Mr. Salkin preferred the younger son who was "more conforming and easier to get along with." However, he was not too close with the latter either, was perfectionistic, and found it difficult to accept anything that Harris did without criticism. There were some traces of paranoid thinking. He was distant from his wife and children through his excessive preoccupation and absorption with his hobby.

The two boys were in constant rivalry with each other, Harris being very cruel to his younger brother. The impression one gathered was that this was a pretty tense household, with mother constantly on the watch to keep the peace. It is to be noted that Mr. Salkin joined the fathers' guidance group and continued to attend. Mrs. Salkin was aware of the causes of Harris' difficulties with his brother, taking most of the blame on herself since she did not sincerely accept him which she showed more clearly at the birth of the "more attractive second child."

Harris, above average intellectually, was not working up to capacity in school. There was marked aggressive behavior toward his mother, openly expressed death wishes against her and marked aggressiveness toward his younger brother and constant fights with his father which were usually provoked by the latter. He was restless, was a severe thumb sucker, did not get along with children by provoking them into fights, had anxiety around injury and death. He had 40 per cent hearing. According to the hospital, there was a possibility of a mild "organic deficit" due to an intrauterine condition of the mother during pregnancy. He had individual therapy for four months, then exploratory group therapy, but his destructiveness made it necessary to discharge him from the group. Individual therapy was re-initiated.

Mrs. Salkin brought Harris to the child guidance clinic on the recommendation of a local hospital. She was afraid that he tended to be delinquent and tried to understand what motivated his difficult behavior. It is to be noted that Mr. Salkin opposed payment for the boy's treatment and Mrs. Salkin paid a small fee out of her household allowance.[1]

We are omitting the case history of Mrs. Cross (6), another member of this group of mothers, because it appears in a more expanded form in the next chapter. All that the reader needs to know at this point is that her son Sol was a persistent bed wetter and that she disliked him to such a degree as to express it in the following terms: "My stomach turns each time I see him." The father was extremely punitive, consistently administering severe beatings to Sol.

We have then a group of parents—mothers and fathers—who have all come from economically poor families, who have had difficulties as children themselves through family tensions, material, emotional and educational deprivations, and who as a result of these deficiencies in their lives were unprepared or inadequately prepared to undertake parental functions. Their own affect needs and frustrations caused them to make demands which could not be met by children. The parents expected from their offspring a level of maturity and achievement, especially scholastic success, of which they themselves were incapable. Their lack of clarity and their ambivalence are clearly seen in the inappropriateness and their overconcern and overprotection as compared to the demands described. Nearly all of them sought self-fulfillment through their children, thus depriving them of the individuality and autonomy which are the right of every human being. To achieve these ends, these parents,

[1] For additional information on this family see Chapter VI.

in their own immaturity, employed direct repressive and punitive methods which not only antagonized the children, but made them even less capable to grow and to achieve that which would otherwise have been possible. The personalities of most of the children were deviant to greater or lesser extent and all of them had behavior disorders which were both means of retaliation as well as getting attention (love) from their parents.

The children's responses, and in some instances also their personalities, further activated and intensified the parents' resentment and demands with the resulting "vicious circle" being set in motion. Children and parents were in opposition to each other, struggling to attain opposing aims—one forcing the child into their own mold, the other seeking to retain his autonomy. Instead of mutually cooperative effort, with all that it involves in a family circle, the children and adults were at loggerheads—some overtly, others covertly. Both the adults and the children were urged on by their infantile, narcissistic feelings of omnipotence and personalistic drives. There was little mature objectivity and realistic appreciation as to what was involved in growth and personality evolvement, nor was there much understanding of what children needed to attain the very aims the parents had for them. There was direct imposition of demands buttressed by scoldings, punishment, threat and humiliation, on the one hand, and overprotection and infantilization on the other.

The evil of the situation lies in the fact that the parents' values and attitudes accord with those prevailing in their culture. In their own childhood they had been treated as they now treated their children which is, unfortunately, tacitly and overtly approved by their society. The vicious circle engendered by this value system must be broken, which can be done by demonstrating methods of dealing with family situations other than they had learned and employed. Out of this, a new value system can arise. It is necessary to re-emphasize the point that these objectives cannot be achieved when there exist in the personality of the parent psychoneurotic or characterological states that block this reorientation. We shall see that a few of the mothers of this group fell into that category and had to be removed.

What follows are reproductions of the discussions at two sessions twelve weeks apart. The group met on alternate weeks for twelve months with a four-months interval between sessions (which was unnecessarily long), thus a period of sixteen months has elapsed between their first and last sessions. The group leader was a woman.

Session 20

Mrs. Kling (4) phoned in the morning to say that her husband was ill with the flu. She had just had the doctor and was unable to leave her husband alone. She hoped the leader would not think she was not interested in attending, although she had been absent several times in the last few months. She has had her apartment painted, and had many things to do which interfered with coming to the meetings. However, if the group and the leader did not mind, she would like to come next time and then continue regularly. She giggled a bit and said perhaps she could be replaced by someone else. She was assured of the leader's interest in having her continue and told that the group would want her back, but the decision was for her to make. Mrs. Kling said she liked the agency for that very reason: she was allowed to make decisions for herself. Mr. R— (the boy's group therapist) also helped her son decide for himself rather than tell him what to do. She said she did not interfere with that. She did not even know what they, Mr. R—and her son, worked out together. It was all right with her. She then asked that the leader leave word with the business office and she would come in to make her payment as soon as she could. She had expected to make this payment today.

Mrs. Friedman (2) phoned before the meeting to say that her little girl was ill with the grippe and she had no one to leave with her. She asked if the leader would send her the "minutes of the meeting." She missed the meetings very much when she could not attend. She had missed only one other before. The leader said she would probably catch up next time.

As the session opened, Mrs. Cross (6) started by saying she would like some help with her problem, around Sol's new interest in a pet chameleon. When Mrs. James (3) wondered about it, Mrs. Cross described it as a lizard-like animal the size of a mouse. She simply cannot bear the sight of it. It is long, green, and ugly. She cannot tolerate turtles and would more readily take a parakeet; but not this. Her face showed revulsion. Sol has already built a cage for it and has told his mother he would have it covered up and that he would look after it. She would not have to touch it or look at it. She is nonetheless miserable when she thinks of it being in the house. Sol told her about a friend whose mother felt the same way, but gradually learned to like it and take care of it. It was his plan to get it on his way back from the skating party he was going to attend with his club (therapy group) that day. She really would like the group's help in making a decision. She has been thinking of it for at least ten days since Sol had brought up the question.

Mrs. Salkin (5) tried to talk Mrs. Cross (6) into accepting this the way Sol did. She referred to how she was repulsed when her children wanted to bring in tadpoles and that when she finally accepted their need to have pets, she became interested and even read up on their growth process, etc. Her problem had been in doing so much work for these pets in addition to everything else in the house; her children too had promised they would take care of them but never did. There were times when she was tempted to teach them a lesson by throwing these things out, but then she decided it was childlike. They were enjoying the animals. It was fun and she was learning something about them. It really did not hurt her too much to take care of them a little each day.

Mrs. James (3) said it reminded her of the husband who wanted his limburger cheese. She hated the smell of it. How to give him what he wants and still have pleasant odors is a problem. Mrs. Salkin (5) said she dealt with that problem when her husband brought home limburger cheese and had a good deal left over by wrapping it well in tinfoil and put it out on the fire escape rather than in the refrigerator. She did not show any anger. He had a right to what he wanted.

Mrs. James (3) said she would suggest that Sol bring in this little pet and if he should tire of it soon, mother should not take any responsibility as Mrs. Salkin (5) did, and it would just have to die. He would throw it out and then it would be out of his system.

Mrs. Salkin (5) said she could appreciate how Mrs. Cross (6) felt because she herself had the same "repulsive feeling" against a hamster which is a mouse-like animal. Mrs. Salkin (5) had told Harris how repulsed she was by it and since he did not seem too firm about it, he accepted mother's request not to have it in the house just to please her. She had already pointed out to him that she was compromising on other matters and asked if he would compromise with her on this matter, and he did. She thought that maybe it would be good for Mrs. Cross (6) to speak to Sol that way too, since she too has made so many compromises for him. Mrs. Cross (6) giggled and said she had talked Sol out of the hamster, but she could not talk him out of this. He already has the cage. Mrs. James (3) said it sounded like a contest of wills and she wondered who was going to compromise first.

Mrs. Salkin (5) gave another example of how she was able to help her boy accept certain limitations when she compromised. Harris was very much enamored of a set of toy trains that a friend of his had gotten for his birthday and Harris thought he would like to have them too. He referred to the fact that his father got him only little trains, that he was big enough now to have the larger trains. She pointed out that this was a very expensive set. It really took a lot of money out of their budget and perhaps if they could all save maybe by next year he could have it for his next birthday. The boy and she are saving together and even the little brother said he would like to contribute because he would be able to play with the trains. This had become a family project.

Mrs. Salkin continued that she thought her boy had learned a real lesson: he understood now that parents sometimes denied something because of the reality of limited funds and not because they did not like their children. She gave a very vivid description of how she said to Harris: "Do you think we don't love you and that's the reason we don't give you these toys?" Harris cried a bit and said he did not know why he did not get the trains, and it was then that Mrs. Salkin told him that she would cooperate with him in saving along with him. She almost tearfully said she could understand his frustration. First she let him explode and cry and that was good and then when he "spent himself," she talked with him. She said that she knew how he felt because she had also been frustrated when she was young in so many ways and yet only as an adult did she begin to understand that her family had not done things just to be hard on her, but rather because they did not have funds. She did not understand it then.

Mrs. Cross (6) said this was a very important time in her own development. In the last few months she had been saying to herself: "Don't say 'no' so fast." She first listened and tried to understand what the children wanted. It is not too difficult to help children accept the fact that you actually cannot give them what they want. She gave examples of how she and the children now can face limitations because her denials are not based on just being contrary as she used to be. When she does not have a ready answer or does not want to say "No," because her boy at that point is not ready to accept it, she does not stir up more bad feelings than already exist. Sometimes she simply says, "I'll think about it." This short delay, she said, helps a lot.

There was a brief pause.

Mrs. Salkin (5) said she would like to talk a little more about Harris and the situation she had brought up two sessions back. For the last two weeks Harris has again been forlorn in relation to friends. That very same boy who had kept friends from him has again done it. She looked at Mrs. Cross (6) who said she had not yet worked out her own problem (which she had just raised) and wondered if the group could talk about it just a little longer before Mrs. Salkin's question was discussed. Mrs. Salkin (5) agreed that there was time to bring her "problem" in later.

Mrs. Cross (6) wondered whether her boy was being persistent about this little chameleon to get even with her for her demand on him to attend parochial school afternoons. There had been some difficulty around this. He has decided to go back to school until he is confirmed, and now comes this request for something he knows mother does not like. Maybe it is like what Mrs. James (3) said, it is a matter of wills and he feels sure that he will win, as already indicated by the cage he brought in. Mrs. James (3) said she could not see the connection between the mother's demand that he attend school and his punishing her with the pet she did not like.

Mrs. Cross (6) explained that she thought he was just showing her his strength, being like the mother, and making his own demands. He did compromise and does attend parochial school and now wants his mother to compromise for him. Mrs. James (3) nodded to indicate that she now understood it. At this point the leader said perhaps Sol just wanted a pet and did not have anything special in mind.

Mrs. James (3) said that the mother's preference here should be considered. If she felt so badly about having that pet around, then the child should be told in no uncertain terms that he could not have it. Did the mother not sometimes have a right to this kind of attitude? Mrs. Salkin (5) again told how she had handled the matter of a parakeet which was a problem since it ducked all over the house. Her boys decided they would not have it when she pointed out to them how much work it would entail. She also referred to her past compromises. They accepted this.

Mrs. Ash (1) who came in at this time was briefed by Mrs. Cross (6), who was encouraged by Mrs. Salkin (5) to tell what happened, so that Mrs. Ash (1) would be in a position to give her a "fresh opinion."

Mrs. Ash (1) thought that the child should have his pet. It is as harmless as a turtle, she said. The boy will wear himself out after a while and then they could get rid of it. She thought it would be better for the mother to make the compromise. She described some of the turtles that her children had had for a while. What a nuisance they were! How irritated she was with them! Then, after a couple of days, they either died or got lost and the "kids were no longer interested." She was angry at herself for having made such a fuss about them.

Mrs. James (3) said it did not pay to argue. You either have to accept what the children want, or just put your foot down, "but arguments are bad." The leader asked why arguments were bad and Mrs. James (3) said, "Well, they just go on and on, and you never get things settled." Mrs. Ash (1) said sometimes you had to tell a child it would please you to have him do something for you.

She described how that very same day her boy put a scarf on just to please her. She was glad he was well protected against the rough wind. Mrs. James (3) said she liked that kind of an attitude on the part of a child, namely, doing something nice for mother; just to please her. It did not hurt the child and it was good for the mother. This, she thought, was the way a child developed responsibility for others. (She probably meant "sensitivity" but the leader did not pick this up. Apparently Mrs. James is becoming sensitized to her child's needs.)

Mrs. Cross (6) said she had some ideas. She thought she would make some decision before she went home, since Sol definitely said he would bring that "little thing" back from his skating party. Two of the women here said that they hoped she would tell them about what she had decided to do at the next session.

There was a pause; then Mrs. Salkin (5) asked whether she could now talk about Harris and whether everyone was ready for her discussion. All agreed. She once more referred to her son's being so unhappy about not playing with children that he again began to suck his thumb. "Isn't there something a mother should do?" she asked with emphasis and turned to the leader. The leader said: "Maybe there is something a mother should do, let's see."

Mrs. Salkin (5) said it had become so bad that he was moody again and did not feel like going to school. She told him that she thought he ought to fight his own battles, and that she had been wrong to intercede for him in the past. He has some little girls with whom he always played in the house. It is all right with her, but she did not think it was good for his development.

There was a bit of a pause during which the leader asked how Harris had developed socially, in terms of peers.

Mrs. Salkin (5) readily brought the group up to date, starting with the time he was "sort of forced," she said, to be on his own when his brother was born when he was four and one-half years old. Actually he never had played well with children, even until then, always taking their things, being very aggressive. He became worse when his brother was born. She always was able to understand his aggressiveness as directed at his brother. She had often told him he was simply jealous of his brother and that if he played well with children, he would have friends. She now thought that maybe she was "too intellectual" with him, blaming him for not having friends, always being angry and pushing him. He was always aggressive. At home, as well, he was dominating in that he always wanted anything he laid his eyes on and she usually gave it to him for otherwise he would go into a temper tantrum. They had financial and other difficulties and she could not bear his crying. Giving in was an easy way for her. She now knows it was wrong. When he started school things had worked out better and he began making friends. She recalled how he sometimes bribed them with toys, which he would later take away. Then they would not talk to him and he would come home crying asking them to forgive him, but they would not.

Mrs. Ash (1) and Mrs. James (3) said they had the same situation with their boys. It would be very helpful then to concentrate on Harris. Mrs. Ash said her boy had always been a very meek, mild, little boy. Now he is asserting himself but he is having trouble from time to time because boys "cannot take what he hands out." It is too rough at times.

Mrs. James (3) said her boy had not reached that point yet. He was not even ready to go out. Mrs. Cross (6) said she did not have any such difficulty. Her children always played well with each other and with their friends. Mrs. Ash (1) said that her boy thought that he was not good enough to play. He sometimes complains that he is not strong enough and feels miserable that the boys do not want him in their games. They say he has to practice first by himself and there is no one to practice with him. He wants to be athletic. Maybe that is something he really needs—practice, "but on the other hand, why don't they give him a chance?" What can she say to him?

Mrs. James (3) said her boy always wanted to be the leader. He does not even want to play. He would like to be the umpire, the captain. The boys do not want him for anything, and so he stays away altogether. "When will he ever learn to socialize?" she asked.

Mrs. Salkin (5) said her Harris was athletic. He is a fighter, can defend himself; he can even provoke, but evidently there must be something in him that causes the whole group to turn against him, even when only one boy is angry at Harris. She has been thinking that maybe he is just too rough but does not know how to take their roughness in turn. She described how roughly he played with his father, but then maybe it was the father's fault. He likes to "sort of roughen them up—to toughen them up." She thinks her husband has given Harris a feeling that he is not strong or capable. Her husband's hobby is electric trains and he does not like either of the boys to come near him when he is working on them. She referred to him as being "perfectionistic." However, he has been able to help Harris to get a set of airplane parts for himself, but Harris prefers to be near his father and his work.

Mrs. Salkin continued that she knew that Harris must have suffered when his brother was born, because the latter was preferred by everyone. He was a bigger baby, more fun to hold and play with than Harris had ever been. This too must be affecting Harris, she said. She recalled that when the baby took the bottle, Harris wanted it, too, and although he had long ago stopped taking the bottle, for fully a whole month, he wanted a bottle every day, like the baby. She permitted this in order that he might work out the jealousy that he had had but it did not seem to help him grow into a stronger boy in relation to his age group. He never really played with friends, was always either fighting them or running away from them. At home, he had temper tantrums which she thought was wrong. She just expected too much from him and so he just never learned to play.

The leader said that since Harris was now attending a club (therapy group), he probably would learn how to work his way into a better relationship with children his age. She indicated that children go through different phases where they are sort of feeling their strengths and weaknesses. Sometimes it is better when a mother does nothing but accept the fact that the child is going through a trying period.

Mrs. Salkin (5) looked relieved and said, "You mean that is all I sometimes have to do? I don't have to talk to him and sympathize with him?" Mrs. James (3) said: "What can you do to sympathize? You can tell him you are sorry he has no friends, but on the other hand, you are not really sorry, because he doesn't know how to play with them." Mrs. Salkin (5) replied: "Well, I could sympathize with the fact that he feels unhappy." At this point, since it was the end of the session, the leader said that confidence should always be conveyed to a child. This helps him to continue to work out his difficulties, secure in the knowledge that his mother at least has confidence in him.

As the women were leaving the room, Mrs. Cross (6) said she had decided on the matter of her boy's pet. She would ask him to hold off his decision for another time. It did not have to be today. She did not know why she had not thought of it before, except that she felt that his demand for it had to be met today.

Mrs. James (3) giggled and said, "Why didn't we think of something so smart? Whenever you are in doubt, postpone your decision." She looked directly at the leader as she said this.

This session is characterized by a concerted effort on the part of the mothers to *understand* the behavior of their children and by a considerable degree of empathy with them, in addition to the usual procedure of helping one another to unravel their confusions and guiding each other toward appropriate action. We are impressed with Sol's (6) mature approach to his mother when he assures her she would become accustomed to the chameleon as his friend's mother did. All the mothers recognized the importance of tolerance, suasion and compromise which are now displacing their previous authoritarianism, domination and inflexible measures of dealing with their children. They spend a great deal of time exploring more satisfactory ways of dealing with situation at hand than by mere arbitrariness. Mrs. Cross (6) exemplifies this to a high degree when she controls her negativism, delays saying "no" and avoids it, if at all possible.

All the mothers present function less on an impulse (id) basis and exercise more of their control (ego). This change is one of the major values of these groups, namely, emotional re-education so that the source of the parents' ways of dealing with their children that formerly stemmed from their impulses (id) is now replaced by appropriate ego functioning. This has a maturing effect on their personalities and one wonders, therefore, whether Child-Centered Group Guidance is not a form of limited (ego) psychotherapy. Because there is a change in the available quantum of ego strength and an altered relation betwen the id and the ego, one is justified in speculating that there may be some therapeutic effect here of a more or less permanent nature. We shall have the opportunity later to suggest further evidence of this possibility (see Chapter XI). However, it is of utmost importance that this relation remain in a latent state and not be acted upon by the leader. Group psychotherapy and group guidance *as techniques* must be kept strictly apart.

The degree of identification and universalization, which prevent guilt, is personified here by Mrs. Salkin's (5) situation with Harris. All have a similar problem, and therefore decide to "concentrate" on him. In the course of the discussion, Mrs. Salkin (5) discovers why her son has difficulties. As she and the others speak about the same problem, it becomes *clear* to her that it lay in her manner of dealing with him when her younger son was born.

This discussion reveals the mothers in a state of considerably increased objectivity as they relate disturbing incidents without emotion. Vastly greater ego strength is apparent as they face their own part in the genesis of their children's difficulties. There is also increased self-control in dealing with their impulses and with their children, greater strength and a more hopeful outlook upon life to which their improved self-confidence (self-image) contributes. All these spell maturity, a maturity evidenced by a greater tolerance of each other, as demonstrated by Mrs. Salkin's (5) delaying the presentation of her "problem" until Mrs. Cross (6) is finished, and by their more tolerant acceptance of their husbands as demonstrated by Mrs. James' (3) incident with the limburger cheese and Mrs. Salkin (5) in relation to her husband's model train hobby.

Session 26

Mrs. Cross (6) said, "What with the nice spring weather, it is time to think of summer vacations." Sol liked camp very much but this year he said he would like to be with the family and has been urging the parents to rent a cottage in New Hampshire. They had visited a relative during Easter week who rents a cottage and her children seemed to enjoy very much the freedom of being at the lake and hiking. She could not figure out why Sol encouraged her to do this except that she thought maybe he felt sorry for her the preceding summer. She had written to him and had told him how hot it was in the city but that it was a vacation for her anyway to have the children at camp. It would be good for Sol to be with a group again, but she was not "pressuring him." She was thinking about it, she told him. Another reason why he does not want to go back to camp is that a friend of his is to be confirmed in July and he wants to attend the party, and he would not want to go to camp in August "because the materials are all used up by that time," he said.

Mrs. Friedman (2) said that her boy did not want to go anywhere. He only wanted to work. Mrs. Salkin (5), on the other hand, reported that she was really happy her boy liked camp and wanted to return. He is already registered, but she would not press him if he did not want to go. Mrs. Friedman (2) was not sorry that her son refused to go again because last year after his return from camp he began wetting his bed even more than before. It was awful that morning. He wet worse than ever. Following camp, he had also developed a tic of the shoulder that lasted a few weeks. It was not a good experience for him and she thought it was wrong to have encouraged him to go.

Mrs. Cross (6) said that she was no longer concerned about the matter of wetting. She hardly thinks of it. It happens maybe once a week or even less and is just so casual no one pays attention to it. Mrs. Friedman (2) said that somehow Morris had his mind made up about wetting. For instance, when he goes to bed, he tells her not to bother changing his linen because it is going to be wet in the morning anyway. It is a sort of defeatist attitude that he has. That is his way about many things, come to think of it. He is always certain of failure when there is a test in school or when he is playing ball in a tournament, etc.

Mrs. Salkin (5) said: "That's it; the boy probably has an inferiority complex like my boy still does occasionally." She knows that when he feels certain of himself, he wants to outdo himself and be the best. That is her trouble. As soon as he develops strength and understanding and a good feeling about himself, he stops at nothing. However, when he is feeling low, he does not want to do anything. The two extremes are bad and she is working on that.

Mrs. Cross (6) said that she had a ray of hope about Sol really getting to be a completely independent boy, but "maybe that is expecting too much." She described the incident during Easter week when Sol had been invited by a relative to stay overnight. He had never been away from home because he feared his bed wetting would interfere with his having a good time. He went with his "little package of pajamas, etc.," but at 10:30 he complained of a headache and came home. She accepted it and told him it was too bad, but maybe it was best to come home if he had a headache. She had an idea that he had developed the headache because he was afraid to sleep away from home. He just was not ready, yet it was good that he even accepted the offer and made the gesture. She felt pleased with herself that she did not discuss it with him and call him down as she might have done in the past.

The leader turned to Mrs. Friedman (2) and asked her to tell a little more about what had been happening with Morris that his bed wetting and his restlessness became worse. Mrs. Friedman said she recognized that he was "nervous" at camp, but became more intensively so on his return, "a sort of jumpiness." Sometimes she thinks that he bears his parents some resentment for sending him to camp when he really was not quite ready; they were not sure he was not ready. On the other hand, she thinks some of his restlessness is due to his age, as some of the mothers previously mentioned. She knew by this that it was sexual restlessness and that it was good for him to be active, but not the way he was. He overdoes it; wears himself out.

Mrs. Salkin (5) said she wondered whether at his age, thirteen, he was also worried about his bed wetting. He has not gotten better. He probably is wondering if he is going to be a real he-man, doesn't know how to stop the wetting. Maybe his nervousness and restlessness are also due to worry. Mrs. Cross (6) said that's true, how could he feel like being a man, that he is growing up to be one, if he still wets his bed.

Mrs. Friedman (2) stated that the matter of sex is something that she is sure he is bothered about. For instance, the other day he told her to be sure to put pants on the baby, that he was annoyed with her bare legs. He did not like to see them. He did not like to look at legs on the TV either. He often studies girls' forms on the screen and in the newspapers and he revolts against what he calls "disgusting legs." Mrs. Salkin (5) laughed and said he really wanted to see those legs, only they stimulated him sexually so he wanted to cover them up, and his business activity of selling soda pop and making money was a very good cover-up. Athletics, she said, would also be very good and maybe even better. Here she talked knowingly, as did some of the other women, how athletics reduced inner tensions.

Mrs. Kling (4) explained how it helped her when she was anxious about something. "It does not have to be sex," she added smiling, but when she got a little nervous, washing the floor or dishes helped her a lot. She felt better after that.

Mrs. Ash (1) asked whether the boy was conscious of having those sex urges.

The leader *diverted* the sex discussion to Morris's defeatist attitude toward himself which his mother had pointed out before. She wondered why Morris had this attitude and whether Mrs. Friedman knew how it had gotten started. Mrs. Friedman (2) smiled and said she was a defeatist; "my boy is like I am." She recalled how everything he did, if it was not perfect, she would be annoyed with him because that was the way she was with herself. She was a very perfectionistic person but was now "working" on herself to relax and be less demanding of herself and of others. It's hard; she does not like her way, and yet it is not easy to change. She recalled her attitude toward Morris's bed wetting before she came to the group. She would say to him: "You'll never change. I guess I'll just have to put up with you forever."

Mrs. Salkin (5) remarked that if Mrs. Friedman changed her attitude about bed wetting, maybe she would help Morris toward a new attitude toward himself, too. She pointed out that if he was so strongly affected by his mother, he could probably be affected in a positive way as well as in a negative, and suggested that Mrs. Friedman "talk to the boy, tell him that it is a problem." Maybe she could then help him with this and other problems.

Mrs. Kling (4) suggested: "Don't talk sex to your boy, nor should your husband. Let the doctor do it." Mrs. Friedman (2) responded by saying that the doctor did talk to the boy when he recently had a physical examination for camp, and that she had asked the doctor to do so. All that happened was that the boy told the doctor that he got an erection and the doctor said: "Don't worry about it." She does not think that this is "sex talk" or of any help to a child.

Mrs. James (3) changed the subject by saying that she has been worried about her boy's school since she no longer put pressure on him but was keeping her fingers crossed. Mrs. Cross (6) gave illustrations of how the relationships in her family have been so much better since she relaxed her pressure on her children. "In fact, it's good, it's almost perfect. I am so happy," she added. Mrs. Friedman (2) wished that she could say that too. She knows that if she had confidence in herself, her boy would have it too. She then described how sensitive he was to her feelings even when she said nothing. For instance, when she and her husband are talking, he would come over and say: "Are you talking about me?" He is always sure that he is the cause of their difficulty because that's the way it used to be; they always argued about him. He sometimes says he feels as if he were a burden on them; that he was miserable about it and did not want to make them so unhappy.

Mrs. James' (3) son, Stanley, came to the door. He had an appointment with his caseworker and they had arranged that he would meet her in the office. She called him in and introduced him to everyone. When he left, the women turned to her and said: "How could you speak so harshly about such a nice-looking boy?" Mrs. James blushed, but seemed pleased and said: "That's the way he is to everyone—nice, but not to me. I only know how he acts toward me."

Mrs. Friedman (2) said she would like to return to the matter of sex. She wondered if masturbation would stop bed wetting. The doctor had mentioned that to her, but how can you ask a child to masturbate so he would stop wetting? Wouldn't it be worse? Mrs. Kling (4) said with firmness; "You ask Morris why he thinks he wets. Tell him if he makes up his mind not to, maybe he won't."

Mrs. Friedman (2) responded that she was not going to follow the doctor's advice concerning masturbation of course, but she would have to decide on something more definite about his not wetting and might take Mrs. Kling's suggestion. She has often suggested to him that he would not wet his bed, but maybe her heart was not in it; maybe it is not now either, but she will have to work up a positive spirit about it. She must admit she is a defeatist about this whole matter.

Mrs. James (3) was puzzled. There are times when her Stanley wets his bed when he has had a glass of milk at bedtime and at other times goes dry after drinking a quart of milk. It does not seem to have anything to do with what he has had before bedtime, but she knows that if he says, "I'll wet," he will and that is because he is angry at her. Mrs. Kling (4) said: "That's just it. Children like to hurt their mothers and this is one way they can do it, even if it hurts them too. Therefore, if you tell a child it won't hurt me if you wet, but it might be better if you didn't because you'd feel better about it yourself, it will give him a feeling it has nothing to do with his mother."

Mrs. James (3) turned to Mrs. Kling (4) and said that it was a good idea to make the boy feel that it had nothing to do with her and not to argue.

Mrs. Ash (1) averred that it might be better to talk to Morris about wanting to help him. "Maybe he could give you suggestions." She found that she has been successful of late in getting Alfred to tell her what he thought would help her; and he is usually "darn right." It took her a long time to believe that it was possible for a child to understand but she followed Mrs. Cross's suggestion despite her own doubts, and it worked.

The leader asked Mrs. Ash why it worked. Mrs. Ash (1) responded: "I developed confidence in myself and made up my mind that it was going to work. When I didn't have a feeling that it would, the children got that feeling, too. It's funny, those feelings you don't put into words but they are there" (meaning the children know they are there).

The leader then asked Mrs. Friedman (2) to give an illustration of what happened on Sunday. (It was a little difficult to pin Mrs.

Friedman down until now as to what was really happening. There was only a general picture of her feelings of failure which the boy too developed about himself.) Mrs. Friedman (2) readily responded: "He was out all day; just selling his sodas and there was no talk. He didn't have any friends; he didn't want to go with the family to visit relatives. When we came home at night and he finally returned in the rain, I urged him to bathe and have some supper. He didn't want to do either. My husband was a little disappointed that Morris didn't want to join us at the little party that the family had; but what he was angriest about was that when we came home, Morris was still out selling sodas and my husband felt very badly about it. Morris came back when we had been home for some time."

Mrs. Ash (1) said maybe Morris felt he was not wanted anywhere. Mrs. Friedman (2) responded by saying she could not understand this because they have always assured him of their interest in him. Mrs. Ash (1) said maybe that was not enough. Maybe he felt that the parents did not think well of him and so he did not want to be with them. Mrs. Friedman (2) confessed she never thought of that but she did know that he had never really been close to his parents. He has never talked with them in an intimate way about things that bothered him. Mrs. Ash (1) said she found in her experience something else that might be helpful to Mrs. Friedman. She found that she had really never gotten a feeling of Alfred being close the way Mrs. Friedman described Morris. She used to wait for Alfred to come and make conversation with her, but now she does the opposite. She starts the conversations. Usually the talk is around something he is doing. She shows interest and encourages him to tell her about it. That has worked wonders and he is such a happy child now. She just cannot understand how she could have been so blind to such a simple little thing.

Mrs. Friedman (2) thought about it, too, but she felt a little embarrassed when all this time she has been silent waiting for him to take the initiative. It is a little hard for her to do it also because he might think that she is just trying a trick on him; trying to win him over in nice ways and maybe then pressure him.

Mrs. Ash (1) assured her that this was not so at all. It is only Mrs. Friedman's feeling. She used to feel that way too. She used to feel that if a child did not come to her there was nothing to do. She would just have to wait for him; but that is not so. The child waits for the mother, because, as in her case, she has not really been fair to him. She has always made him submissive. Now it is her turn to get him to talk up and show him that she is interested. She now listens to him; not only to him, but to the younger children, as well. She must admit that her housework is now secondary but is glad because now her relation with her children is so much better and she is having so much more fun. "It's patience and perseverence that is so necessary," she added. She then turned to the leader and said that the leader had once said: "What else can parents offer children if not food, shelter and patience?" Well, she, Mrs. Ash, did not know at that time what the leader meant by "patience," but now she does. It is good to have it. Children know and thrive on it. The other day Alfred received 100 in spelling and 80 in arithmetic. She never would have believed it! And he did it all on his own, no pressure from her.

Mrs. Cross (6) testified to "wonderful" report cards, too, because there was no longer any pressure. She continued: "We never gave the children any satisfaction that they can do well on their own. Now we appreciate them, have confidence and so they are doing their best." The other day Sol came home and asked her what mark in arithmetic would satisfy her. She said: "Well, you had 65 and that was good because you passed and you had not been doing even that well last year. Maybe you got 70 now; and he hugged me, saying I was absolutely right, that was exactly what he got. This without any effort on anyone's part but his own."

Mrs. Salkin (5) said her boy, too, had improved tremendously and the teacher had noticed it too. She knows why, and maybe the teacher does, but she is not going to tell the teacher and the teacher did not ask her. Her son is now the class monitor. He is so pleased with the teacher's personal interest that he is willing to do anything. It only means to Mrs. Salkin that he still needs "that individual touch." She'll give it to him and let the teacher do so, too, until he has had enough.

Mrs. Kling (4) reported that was true with her Jacob too. He is still improving because the teacher in school is showing such an interest and no one at home is pressuring him either. Mrs. Ash (1) stated, "Now I know what we mean about treating ourselves as parents. We then get the proper reaction from the children. If we correct ourselves, we correct what's wrong. This was an eye opener. I should have come here years ago. In fact, all parents should come here before their children are born."

Mrs. Cross (6) replied to this by saying: "Children often test out their parents and in my case it's frequently around schoolwork because I still have a need for my children to do well in school. Not as much as before, but still they know that I would like them to do well." She said to them once when signing their report cards that she loved them even if they should fail. She then talked about how she really meant it. "It doesn't matter, an error here or there or a low mark here or there does not destroy the whole thing. All I would tell a child now if he fails is that I would help him out and I really mean it. That's what counts. Children want to know if your feelings are real."

Mrs. James (3) said she was still pessimistic, she still had to get the kind of progress that Mrs. Ash has been talking about. She is still pessimistic like Mrs. Friedman about bed wetting and also about school. The work would not be so bad if her boy's behavior were better. The other day he was demoted and does not want to do anything about it. He fights bigger boys in the street. Recently he did not want to go with his parents to visit the family and when they came home, they found he had been beaten up by an older boy. They were not away very long either. Stanley was very unhappy and accused his parents of not being interested in him. Yet the week before he came with them to visit another relative, though he complained bitterly; when he got there, he fixed the radio and enjoyed himself. Mrs. Salkin (5) added: "This matter of social-izing is a problem, yet it could be worked out and that's what Mrs. James's Stanley needs—a working out so that he can learn to play with children." She then talked of how she used to side with her parents when there was a complaint about her Harris. Now she tells them to let the children alone and fight it out.

The leader turned to Mrs. James (3) and asked her about Stanley's earlier social development. Mrs. James said that Stanley had never been really interested in children; but maybe it was her fault. He was a cute little boy. She was usually very busy with the house and wanted him near her. This is in contrast to the way she handled the older one whom she trusted to play alone. The reason for it, she thought, was that the older was so resourceful, capable and well able to handle himself and his brother that she could trust him. Stanley was born so much later in her life and she was so much more concerned about him that she kept him close to her.

Mrs. Friedman (2) asked if Stanley liked sports. Mrs. James (3) said he did not. She wished he could develop such a liking but now she could see that maybe she did not let him do so.

Mrs. Kling (4) said that her oldest boy didn't have friends either. Once when one of the boys picked a fight with him and he fought back, as a result he became interested in boys' activities, especially since he won out. The leader stated that usually children become interested in playing with other children around the age of four or five when they could play away from the mothers a little. Mrs. James (3) responded by saying that this hit her very hard. She knew that Stanley did not want to go to kindergarten and found it hard to separate from her. Mrs. Ash (1) advised Mrs. James that it would be better to let Stanley fight it out with whomever he is fighting and to encourage him to bring friends to the house. Mrs. James asked: "How could I possibly have those fights in the house?" To which Mrs. Ash responded: "You will see. They will become friends because you have invited them into the house. They won't fight."

Mrs. Salkin (5) then reported that since she had talked with the group about her Harris's difficulty with friends, things have cleared up, only because the mother of one of the boys accepted him into her home and did not think Harris was such a bad child after all. Now Harris has this friend and together they can face the other boys on the block who used to be Harris's enemies. She believes that as a result Harris will make friends also with the others. She has since talked to the boy's mother who told her that Harris was really looking for companions and that she could help him by be-friending him. This helped.

Mrs. Ash (1) said: "You have to sacrifice time, your housework and many things, if you want to correct the things that have gone wrong. Give your child a little time." She then proceeded to tell Mrs. James (3) to stop what she was doing in the evenings and play a game with Stanley or ask him to tell her what is on TV, "so that he would get a feeling that you're interested in what is going on and his activities are of interest to you. I did it with Alfred and I know what I am talking about. I never believed that a little interest like that on my part would change the relationship; but it did!"

Mrs. James (3) reflectively averred that from now on she would do what Mrs. Ash suggested. Everyone has improved except she, and turning to Mrs. Friedman (2), she said: "You did, too, for a while, but now it's bad again, but maybe it will get better."

Mrs. Ash (1) repeated that a mother's interest in a child helped him feel that he was worthwhile. He can then go out and play with friends. That is her understanding of what she has gotten from what the leader had said some time ago about a child feeling that he is okay if mother gives him such a feeling. He is then able to face his friends.

Mrs. James (3) said she wished she had patience, but like Mrs. Ash (1) did, she would have to find the time. She is going to make a job of this. It is true, she used to show Stanley she was annoyed with him, that he was like a fifth wheel, that she was more interested in her older boys. Now she has to show that she is interested also in Stanley. She'll try. Mrs. Ash (1) advised: "Don't try a whole evening; just a few minutes' worth; ask him just once what's going on TV and he'll be delighted, especially if you ask him at the right time when he can tell you what is going on. You make him feel important. That's so necessary."

The session ended on this note. As the group was leaving, Mrs. James (3) passed around a picture of her grandson, a month old. The leader said: "Well, it is going to be pretty difficult for Stanley now to compete with his nephew as well as with his brothers." Mrs. James said that she was aware of it. She thinks that Stanley probably will feel people are more interested in the baby than in him, and it will be true and right. However, she knows she is going to have to work on this and she will. "If Mrs. Ash can do it, I can too," she said with determination.

In Session 26, we find all the women bending their efforts with seriousness and persistency *to help* Mrs. Friedman (2) eliminate her son's enuresis. Their identification with her and their genuine desire to be of help are as striking as is their feeling of oneness. This deliberation took up most of the ninety minutes. It is evident that Mrs. Friedman's (2) discouragement and feeling of failure, after a period of improvement, stem from her own and that of her husband's inner problems. In fact, she recognizes this when she reiterates the idea that her son's failure reflects her attitude. While in the past she was incensed by her son's irresponsibility and carefree approach toward money, she is now annoyed by the fact that he gives his attention, at thirteen years of age, to making and saving his money. Although Morris had a period of respite from the pressures in the home so that he had become a more mature and more independent youngster, her neurotic difficulties that were held in abeyance through the ego support from the group now reasserted themselves. Obviously she cannot be expected to retain the operational improvement she gained from the group which she was able to utilize for a period. She requires a more fundamental change in her psychic organization which now interferes with her functioning. Accordingly, individual or group psychotherapy rather than guidance were recommended for her.

In contrast to Mrs. Friedman (2), we see Mrs. Cross (6) who despite her earlier discouragement and intense rejection of Sol now feels satisfied with her son's progress and is optimistic even about his weakness which he revealed in the matter of sleeping in a friend's house. Mrs. Salkin (5) has a high degree of intuition and intellectual penetration and even Mrs. Kling (4), a very simple and uneducated woman, understands and is able to accept the fact that children "like to hurt their mothers." That a simple, European-bred, unschooled, elderly woman can accept this spells considerable intellectual unfoldment and emotional flexibility.

Mrs. James (3) too has not made as much progress as the others. Like Mrs. Friedman (2), her personality blockings interfere with the improvement of her son, but not to the same degree as in the latter. For Mrs. Ash (1) to consider talking to a child as an equal, as she suggests, represents great strides. She recognizes that as she develops confidence in herself, it is reflected in her children. Both Mrs. Ash (1) and Mrs. Friedman (2) were constricted in their relations with their children, but this was not a part of Mrs. Ash's neurosis, she was able to overcome it in relation to her son through the guidance group, while Mrs. Friedman (2) could not achieve it.

The fact that these women with their educational, religious and cultural backgrounds are able to tie up some of their children's reactions with sex and discuss it in an impersonal and unembarrassed way is quite remarkable. Note that the leader diverts too personal and too involved examination of this subject that may create tensions and anxiety in the women (see Chapter VIII).

The general improvement in the children's social behavior stems in no small part from the parents' attitudes toward them.

One doubts that Mrs. James (3) will be able to carry out her emphatic resolve at the end of the session without individual help. However, she has made a step in that direction for we read in the minutes of the next session, two weeks later, the following:

"Mrs. James (3) wondered if there would still be a little time to bring in her 'assignment.' She has been trying to get closer to Stanley and doesn't think she has succeeded yet. After our session last time, she told Stanley at an appropriate moment that she was interested in the stamp collection he was working on; she had an hour and would he like to show her a little bit and maybe she could work with him on it. He was delighted and for a whole hour they sat together and he explained what he was doing and what he hoped to do. Since then, she has made other suggestions in a rather formal way. For instance, she would say to him: 'In an hour, I'll have a little time and I'd love to talk with you.' He would say he was busy, he wanted to ride the bicycle or that there was something on TV he would like to see.

"Mrs. Salkin (5) asked: 'Why should he spend a whole hour with you? It's too much for any boy his age to want to be with his mother so long. You've got to be casual.' Mrs. Ash (1) said: 'Sure, the child doesn't even know when you want to be with him.

You watch for what he says and you find that he will give you the high sign [signal] to be with him.' She agreed with Mrs. Salkin that an hour was too much. Mrs. James (3) said she must admit that her boy probably was afraid that if she sat down with him it would be to talk about school or to criticize him, as she used to in the past. He still says: 'What do you want to talk to me about, school?' She says: 'No, you know I'm not going to,' but evidently he does not believe her.

"Mrs. Friedman (2) said she used to have to face the same situation with Morris. He is afraid to sit down and talk with her. He is always on the run, fearing that she will talk about school. However, like Mrs. Ash (1), she has found that when he shows an interest in talking to her, she lays aside everything, and stops to talk with him. Things had been better in the last few weeks. She thanked the group for helping her out last time. He is just as hyperactive around his sodas, but she is not bothering about it too much; at least he now comes home to eat his meals on time and he want to talk with her, which is even more important."

CHAPTER

VI

Ameliorating Family Tensions

Mrs. Cross applied to the Child Guidance Clinic for help with Sol, age eleven years, because of persistent nocturnal and intermittent diurnal enuresis at school. Mild encopresis on the average of once a week was also reported. Mrs. Cross could not recall whether he had ever been dry. She thought there might have been a brief period of it before, but definitely not since he began attending school. A thorough physical examination at a hospital ruled out organic causes. Mrs. Cross said that the boy was ashamed when his blankets and sheets were hung to dry, which was almost continuous.

Sol bit his nails. He did not accept any responsibility in the home and resisted every request from the mother. The mother described severe tension between herself and Sol. When the mother was home with the boy and asked him to do something, he would always resist and become resentful, as though, as the mother characterized it, "the world owed him a living." However, when the mother was away from home and left Sol a note asking him to do something, it was always done. In the long run, the boy always did what the mother requested from him, but "there always had to be a fight first." If he did not get his way, he would go into a tantrum, use abusive language against her, run screaming into the bathroom and slam the door behind him.

Sol was a good-looking, sturdy and neatly dressed boy, with a degree of bravado and feigned nonchalance. When asked about school, he said that school was "no good; the kids were all right, but it was the teachers." The arithmetic teacher was giving too much homework; the English teacher was a bore. "All she does is talk," he said. The music teacher was criticized because only she sang and never gave any of the pupils a chance. His one good class was gym. He complained that he hardly had any spare time because he attended parochial school every day and did his homework. Concerning his relationship with his brother, Sol categorically replied, "No good." He was not interested in clubs. When the case-worker who first interviewed him mentioned casually that the clinic had clubs for boys where they meet and made whatever they wished, Sol remained silent but reflective.

Social adjustment appeared to be quite adequate in that the boy had friends, was liked and accepted for both his personality and athletic abilities. At this interview, and contrary to what was learned later, Mrs. Cross claimed that there had never been any school problem; in fact, the boy was liked by the teachers and was considered responsible and dependable. He fought with his siblings, but she did not consider it to be inordinate.

Sol was a planned child, born two years after marriage. The mother described a good pregnancy in which she worked until her sixth month. Delivery was somewhat difficult and she recalled that "the ten hours seemed endless."[1] The child was bottle-fed and described as a happy infant who ate well. Toilet training began at six months, and immediately led to tension. The child would not co-operate, would sit on the toilet without doing anything but later would soil his diapers. Sol shared the parental bedroom until the age of two years when he was moved to his own room. He was later joined by his siblings in the room. Currently, Sol and his brother, two years younger, and a sister, five years younger, shared the room. The mother bathed the three children together for a time. At first the boys questioned her as to why the girl did not have a penis, but later appeared to accept this. Sol had no fears. He was always able to sleep without a light in his room.

Mrs. Cross said with some embarrassment that she did not recall too clearly details of Sol's early development since she was very busy with the second child at whose birth Sol was a little over two years old. She considered him an adorable baby. Very deliberately,

1 See p. 40.

when the sibling was born, both parents "made a fuss" over Sol to prevent jealousy. When he was two years old and his mother was nearly ready to be delivered of the second child, she stayed overnight with him in the hospital for his tonsillectomy. When he started school and the two younger children were still very small, she left them in someone else's care, so that she could stay with him for the first week to help him with his adjustment, since he refused to remain there without her. In the intake interview Mrs. Cross understressed her concern about his enuresis. She said she used to get very angry and scold him for it, but when she found that it was of no avail, she decided to ignore it despite her annoyance. She said that somehow she could never get Sol to respond to her the way the younger children did. Sol was even more distant with his father. Mrs. Cross attributed this to the fact that the father worked nights in a post office and was therefore seldom home. Later, however, in the group interviews, she revealed herself as being inordinately hostile toward and rejecting of her older son. Besides, Mr. Cross made no effort to relate himself to the boy even when he was home.

Mrs. Cross was a tallish, slender woman, thirty-six years old, seemingly pleasant and intelligent, neatly and conservatively dressed, alert and friendly in a quiet way. She gave the impression of being calm. She talked easily and articulately and seemed to choose her words carefully, but lacked spontaneity. Her voice was gruff, somewhat raspy and had a masculine timbre.

Mrs. Cross was the youngest of four children. Two of her siblings were brothers. Her sister was the eldest child. She recalled many fights with her next older brother, especially during his adolescence when he did not want her "tagging along after him." She was now closer with him than with her other brother. She said she had little in common with her sister before they were both married. The father was described as a stern disciplinarian of whom the children were frightened. Mrs. Cross's mother was not very demonstrative, but more easy-going than her father. While the children's physical necessities were met, there was a lack of warmth and love in the family. Mrs. Cross's mother died a year before. Her father now lived in her neighborhood and came for his evening meals to her. He was inclined to be domineering and critical of her and her husband.

Mr. and Mrs. Cross met while they were both holding civil service jobs. She spoke of herself as only slightly more social than her husband, but not "too aggressive." She added that a "group of strangers can just floor me." She appeared to be the dominant and guiding personality in her home and in relation to her children, as well as toward her husband.

Mrs. Cross said little about her husband beyond the fact that he was impatient with Sol and that he had very little to do with the boy. She also indicated that there was intense conflict between the two of them and that not infrequently the father beat Sol.

We have here a boy whose symptoms may or may not indicate a serious personality disturbance. This is a child who has reached the age of eleven with continued enuresis and who is also given to occasional encopresis. The possible seriousness of this was recognized by the intake worker when he stated in his report among other things that "these symptoms may be indicative of serious pathology and of an extremely infantile personality." However, after reviewing the material we recognized that the mother did not present serious neurotic symptoms, nor could we trace strong castration drives on her part. Rather, she was a person who found herself in a position that necessitated her dominating the family, partly due to the fact that her husband's job allowed minimal participation in the family, and partly because of her rivalry with a male sibling as well as a result of the specific culture from which she came. The relation toward her brother stamped her personality with masculine strivings which did not seem to us intense or overwhelming. These strivings were revealed, in addition to her role in the family, by the masculine timbre of her voice.

The fact that the parents were sufficiently sensitive of the boy's feelings to make a "fuss" over him when a new sibling was born, that the mother stayed overnight at the hospital when he had his tonsillectomy, and that she was willing to stay at the school the first week of her son's attendance, indicate basic warmth, but she was evidently not able to accept her son's growing autonomy and self-determination as he grew older. She protected him only when he was a baby or in difficulty and distress, but under ordinary conditions acted out her rivalry with her brother upon her son.

Sol did not appear to have been exposed to intensive pathogenic experiences. His difficulty was one of reactive behavior to both a demanding, somewhat masculine mother and a strict, neglectful and rejecting father. We can therefore consider his enuresis, encopresis, and temper tantrums as retaliation against the parents, and possibly more so against the father. As a result of both the early toilet training and his need to act out against his parents, he retained many infantile character traits and habits. Nevertheless, the impression one gets from the first interview was that the boy's basic ego development—as revealed by his general demeanor as well as his ability to talk with freedom even in the first interview concerning his siblings, school and teachers—was wholesome. The fact that he did not attempt to deny or rationalize his failures indicated basic ego strength. We also considered important that while he was disobedient and challenging to the mother in her presence, he had always accomplished what was expected of him in her absence. This seemed to us to be the key to Sol's life pattern, namely, that he had the ego strength to mobilize his forces to deal with reality on his own level, but refrained from doing so because of counterhostility toward his parents. Our diagnosis at the time was primary behavior disorder, preoedipal type.

Activity group therapy presents the child with a new type of personal relations; it has a maturing effect because of the corrective interaction among the members of the group; it places responsibility upon each for his own conduct which necessarily results in improved ego and superego functioning. When there are no internalized severe neurotic conflicts, these corrective adaptations are effective in producing a more socialized and more integrative character. We therefore decided that activity group therapy was indicated for Sol, provided we could ameliorate the pressures on him from his parents, particularly the father. What was necessary here was to help the boy to mature by accepting his own aggressions and find a new way of interpersonal adaptations as well as to alter the climate of the family.

Mrs. Cross was placed in a newly formed guidance group which met on alternate weeks for ninety minute sessions. There were five other women in the group, all of whose boys were being treated at the clinic either individually or in groups. The age of three of their boys was nine to ten years and three others were between ten and eleven. Mrs. Cross attended all of the sixteen fortnightly sessions held before the summer recess with no absences.

During the first session Mrs. Cross was more guarded than any of the other women. Though quiet and friendly, she waited for the others to take the initiative. Only when asked a specific question by the leader or by one of the other members of the group did Mrs. Cross respond with a nod of the head. When one of the group members presented her difficulties with a son who was a bed wetter, Mrs. Cross stated that she, too, had a similar difficulty. After inquiring whether this boy had had a physical examination and hearing that the findings had been negative, Mrs. Cross said she wondered whether the bed wetting was due to jealousy among the children in the family.

Her younger boy was born two years after Sol, "and maybe the baby in him still persists." Sol still talks about the fact that she favored the younger brother. He makes no attempt to get up during the night even when he is wet. He merely rolls himself over to the dry side of the bed. She thinks that he is "just lazy." She has talked with him, cajoled him and shamed him, but with no results. In the same session, Mrs. Cross responded to another member of the group who presented her "problem" of feeding, namely, her child did not want to eat what was given him. Mrs. Cross said it was like bed wetting; maybe the child also wanted to hurt his mother. Maybe that was what Sol was doing to her; just getting even with her for having had a younger child. Mrs. Cross identified with the other woman who felt that her child's feeding problem developed when a sibling was born. Both women then said that maybe they wanted their first children to grow up too fast so that they could devote themselves to the younger children's needs without taking into consideration that their first ones were not yet old enough and capable enough to look after themselves. Mrs. Cross said she understood all of this and had tried "to reason with Sol," telling him she knew why he was wetting, but why couldn't he stop it? It doesn't do him any good; it only makes it more difficult for her to like him. Here she shuddered with the "smell of urine in my nose continually." She just can't respond to him when she thinks of the "stink" she has to put up with every day. "If Sol ever wants to win my love, why can't he do what will get the necessary results?" she asked with heat.

In the second session, Mrs. Cross was again quiet for the first half of the session. When one of the mothers complained that her boy did not defend himself at school against teachers and children, Mrs. Cross stated that Sol did not want to go to school, nor did he want to do his homework. He just about passes and she knows from the school that he has a good brain and could do better. Sometimes Mrs. Cross leaves him alone in the hope that "his own inner drives will come through and give him the necessary incentive," but at other times, especially near midterm and at the end of the school year, she must admit that she pressures him quite hard. When another mother reported that her child fought with children, Mrs. Cross expressed surprise and asked whether he did not like to play with them. She thought that all children liked to play with others. Mrs. Cross was very thoughtful when the other mother explained that her boy fought with children because he fought with his brother, too. Maybe the children represent his brothers.

Mrs. Cross, smiling and more relaxed than was usual for her, said that all the mothers present seemed to have problems though they manifest themselves in different ways. She then asked: "What can we do now to correct the errors we made that caused these problems?" She did not regret having a second child so near in age to Sol, but how could she make it clear to him, as all the mothers needed to do to their children, that this was not done with a view of rejecting him or preferring another or a better child. In response to a fellow member, Mrs. Cross agreed that it was strange that "although we don't have problems with the younger children and know better how to handle them, this has not carried over to our handling of the first. Something keeps you back, I don't know what it is. There must be some reason as to why the first continues to be difficult."

The other mother, Mrs. Solon, talked about restoring the love relationship with her boy, rather than expecting him to do it. It was she who owed something to the child and now she was trying to figure out how to do this. Mrs. Cross agreed that it was the parents' duty to make peace with their children. She then suggested that she would discuss her boy fully in the next session. Hers would probably take a longer time, she said, because her boy was the quiet type who kept everything to himself. (It so happened that at this session the women discussed boys with symptoms of overt behavior.) As Mrs. Cross left at the end of the session she talked with Mrs. Solon so that others could hear her. One of the things she said was: "How can you 'about face' and not lose your status with the child?" She laughed as she said this.

In the third session, Mrs. Cross initiated the discussion about her boy. She said she had always tried to explain to Sol that she did not willfully neglect him when she was busy with the younger children. In response to Mrs. Solon she agreed that it wasn't easy, for each child wanted his mother for himself as long as possible. Her boy seems to wait for her to take the first steps toward a better relation. It is very difficult for her. She waits for the children to come to her first. They know she will respond. But Sol does not come to her. She is beginning to suspect there may be something about her that prevents him from doing it.

The preceding week all three children had been sick. This was a good time for her to do what she had been attempting to; namely, to get close to Sol. She figured out a way of giving each of them in their respective beds a little of her time, "just for fun." They chose the time and Sol showed more affection and more friendliness toward her than ever before. She was very pleased. One of the other members commended her for this and asked whether she enjoyed it as much as did Sol. With tears in her eyes Mrs. Cross said she certainly did and added, "children are children no matter what the age."

In response to one of the mothers who was defensive toward her children, Mrs. Cross said, "You must tell children the truth and it would be very helpful to tell them the purpose for your coming to the group." She then described how because of a discussion with the leader of the present group over the telephone she was able to tell Sol that she joined the group to get help in getting along with children. This, she said, was very good. Besides, she added, she was that kind of a person; she did not like to tell lies because children learn to do so from their parents. When one of the members of the group said that her boy paid the treatment fee to the case-worker each time he visited her, Mrs. Cross said this should be the responsibility of the mother. Although the child should know that there is a fee being paid, because that means that the mother is considering it important, the bill should be paid by the mother and not by the child.

In the fourth session the women were talking about the improvement in their relationships with their children and the children's improved behavior. One of them said that she thought she had reduced her pressures on the boy. Mrs. Cross said that maybe she, too, has pressed her children too much. She must admit that she had been pressuring, especially in the matter of homework and getting to school on time. She had the feeling that unless she was behind Sol he would not do anything that happened to be displeasing to him, such as school. Mrs. Solon asked at this point: "Why should a child have less confidence in himself than the mother has in him?" Mrs. Cross said she used to think that if a child knew of his mother's concern about him, he would dwell on it himself. On the other hand, it also meant to the child that she did not trust him. She added: "Maybe Mrs. Cohen was right about the fact that pressure means being babied. That's what Sol tells me." Maybe she thought of it only from her point of view and never his. (This was the first recognition on the part of the women that a child too has a point of view and that parents seldom allow them to express it.)

In the seventh session, Mrs. Cross reported that she had had a very successful experience (which seemed to show what the group discussions have meant to her). She described how she worked out the problem of waking Sol in the morning. This and getting Sol ready for school were always very trying periods. She told him the night before that she would no longer call him, but set the alarm clock in his room. The rest was up to him. Sol accepted this new arrangement "and it worked!" Once when he did not respond he was late for school, but she said nothing.

Sol came back that afternoon to report that he had been late. She was not angry with him; in fact she was pleased that he could talk to her about it, for in the past he always covered such things up. She pointed out to him that maybe he needed a little more time in the morning. He has not been late since. Mrs. Cross said "it is strange."

Now she realizes that she acts better with the children and has no anxiety about their getting to school on time and doing their work well. Responding to what another member said, Mrs. Cross stated she was not really a rigid parent except where such pressures like school called for it.

She described how enjoyable the Easter vacation had been. In the past, she anticipated every school vacation with anxiety as to how things would work out. This time she decided to take the children into her confidence and plan with them an enjoyable vacation for all. The children, particularly Sol, were excited and made good suggestions which she accepted. Later in the session when punishment was discussed, Mrs. Cross said that hitting a child only "pushes him away from you." Sometimes she is tempted to use force but she has to "discipline" herself. She used to lose her temper much more quickly than she does since she attended the group.

At another session Mrs. Cross described how Sol came home one day for lunch and asked his mother what she thought had happened when he left home a little later than usual, and she said "When you make up your mind to be on time, I guess you were on time." He answered smiling: "You are right, I was not late. You are very different from the way you used to be. You always thought I was late and you always thought the worst of me."

In response to Mrs. Friedman's complaint that her boy refused to have lunch at school, Mrs. Cross said that he probably felt that Mrs. Friedman preferred her daughter when she suggested that he have lunch at school instead of coming home. Mrs. Cross added that maybe he wanted to come home and see what mother and sister were doing together; maybe he's missing out on something.

She figured this out for herself in her own family. She interpreted this as jealousy of each other: maybe their brothers and sisters were getting something that they were not. The other members of the group agreed with her and concurred with her suggestion that Mrs. Friedman should have her boy come home for lunch. She should even take the time to eat with him and find another time for the younger child when he leaves.

In the eighth session Mrs. Cross advised Mrs. Kling not to insist that her son go to summer camp because "maybe the child has a good reason for not going." She should ask him. "We should do with camp what we do with other things," she added. Maybe Mrs. Kling's boy is afraid to leave home and is not yet strong enough to be on his own.

Reacting to another member of the group who was discussing with the leader how to help her bed-wetting son in the matter of camp, Mrs. Cross spontaneously broke in and said that she had "an idea." She would tell Sol that he was missing fun by not going to camp and would question him as to why something like bed wetting should cause him to miss what he was entitled to. In a sort of challenging way, she suggested to the other mother that she do the same and see how it would work, since both of their boys were bed wetters and had never been to camp before because of it.

In the ninth session, Mrs. Cross joyfully reported her success in getting Sol to go to camp. She told him exactly what she had told the group the previous session. She found an opportune time when she was alone to talk with him. She also said that perhaps she could help him overcome this difficulty. She proceeded to show him how to make his own bed and how to change the linen if he had to do it. Sol was very enthusiastic. She then helped him to see that if he could feel comfortable about the bed wetting, he could now make his application for camp. He had asked her to make the telephone call, but she told him that she thought it would be better if he did it himself. This he did. Mrs. Cross said that in the past she would have made the call and filled out the application for him. She seemed very happy because it was "a step in the right direction." It gave Sol a feeling of responsibility. She now knows better how to help children assume responsibility.

At the same session Mrs. Cross reported her difficulty around handling a situation when a child breaks or destroys something. Sol had broken his glasses while playing and she told him he would have to pay for repairing them from his allowance. He ought to know that he should leave his glasses home when he goes out to play. Others in the group discussed this situation in terms of what an allowance means to children and how to deal with restrictions on allowances. When asked by the leader about Sol's feelings about wearing glasses, Mrs. Cross smiled and said that she had been thinking about it, too. She knew when she took him to the eye doctor that he was not going to wear the glasses because he said he would not. She imagined that he would find ways for not wearing them. She then recalled how she would occasionally find the glasses on the floor and other unsafe places. Apparently he just wanted to break them, she said emphatically, and maybe paying for them was not going to help at all. Sol is probably rebelling against her pressure to wear them, but she better clear this up with him. It was not her idea; it was the doctor's, but unwittingly she was helping the doctor against Sol. She ended by saying that she thought she could work it out with Sol.

At the eleventh session, Mrs. Cross talked of how she found it interesting to observe the children's play and general behavior and figure out what they meant; also she did not mind what was going on. Her husband, too, is now interested. He is no longer puzzled or annoyed. In response to Mrs. Salkin's difficulty as to how to plan Sunday activities with her boy, Mrs. Cross said that she and her husband seemed to have found a way to work it out with their family. She would like to describe what has happened. They, too, used to make the children go along wherever *they* went. The Crosses now start the day by asking the three children what they would like to do. Children and parents make suggestions. If there is agreement, then there is no problem; but if there is any disagreement, each child can have his plan carried out on different Sundays. Thus, each in turn gives up his preference for the others. Mrs. Cross said that this worked because the children recognized that "daddy and mother would like very much to have a day with all their children." So far many Sundays have turned out to be very nice and pleasant. After describing a pleasant day in Coney Island, Mrs. Cross said: "It's wonderful to be on your toes. Why not, when you get such results?" All laughed good-naturedly and agreed.

At the thirteenth session, Mrs. Cross related how she came to recognize that being alone with his mother even for short periods meant a great deal to Sol. He considered it a sign of personal interest in him, and therefore, love. This is reflected even in his attendance at the club (therapy group). She talked again of how she had always looked for opportunities to be alone with Sol, not just to reprimand him or criticize him, as in the past, but to have fun with him a little bit. He now wets maybe once in two weeks, sometimes for a few days at a time and then he stops. She does nothing about it. She thinks now that it will take care of itself when "other things have been taken care of."

At the fourteenth session, Mrs. Cross reported that Sol's wetting had increased again, but she did nothing about it because she thought maybe there was something bothering him and he let it out in wetting. Some children turn to thumb sucking and he turns to bed wetting, she said. She thinks it may be due to the anxiety around his new school; he is in junior high school now, where the work is more difficult. She has been pressuring him again about his homework, particularly in math, because the teacher tells her that he will have to keep him back if Sol does not pass. When criticized for this by another member of the group, Mrs. Cross turned to the leader asking her what else she could do to help the boy pass his subjects. The leader again helped Mrs. Cross by a series of questions to clarify for her the fact that Sol had been using his school studies again as a means of annoying and defeating her. Mrs. Cross then came to the conclusion that it might be better if she left the whole thing alone so that he could work it out for himself.

At the fifteenth session, Mrs. Salkin talked about the miserable day she had had when she spent a Sunday alone with Harris. Her husband and younger child had gone off to visit someone and she had the day which she thought would be welcomed by Harris, as in the past, but instead he was very critical of her. Mrs. Cross said that she thought Mrs. Salkin had too long a day with her boy. Young boys do not like to spend too much time with their families, particularly alone with their mothers. Mrs. Cross suggested that Mrs. Salkin should have asked Harris what he wanted to do instead of assuming that he wanted to spend the whole day with her. Mrs. Cross talked with much confidence and understanding about how children grow up and separate from their parents. "And you have to let them," she said emphatically. Her boy now prepares his own bath, whereas just a few months ago nothing she could do or say would make him do it. She had to make all the preparations. "Maybe he's dressing up for girls," she said with a smile and blushed. She responded to Mrs. Friedman's description of how her boy was amazed and annoyed when she walked into his room while he was dressing. Mrs. Friedman did not think anything of it. She is the mother, why should he feel so embarrassed? Here Mrs. Cross talked of how boys were maturing sexually and should have their privacy.

At the sixteenth session, Mrs. Friedman discussed her difficulty with her little three-year-old girl who refused to eat. She had never had this problem with her older boy. Mrs. Cross said the trouble was that mothers felt as though children were not grateful enough for all the trouble they took in preparing food and therefore got annoyed. She figured this out about herself and remembers how she would get angry. Yet she knows that children should not eat just because they have to be grateful. "Aren't we big people in the same position at times?" she asked. Her problem with Sol was not around food, but around toilet. Evidently wetting for him is still part of the toilet training which was strict, and he is still rebelling. The leader asked Mrs. Cross how she felt now about her son's bed wetting. She said she no longer thought of it with "disgust," nor did she react to it with "revulsion" as she used to. She can now walk into the boy's room, even when he had wet the bed and not be angry at him. She described how in the past the feeling of anger toward the boy for wetting always made her very tense and she always looked for the worst in him when he came home for lunch. His wetting is not regular and she knows from the way he is relaxed about everything, about his newly acquired friends and his improved relation with his siblings, that he is on his way toward complete improvement.

The only problem she has now is how to help him with "that

arithmetic." With the help of the leader, Mrs. Cross worked out a plan. She would face him with the fact that he had a problem, and tell him that she would like to help him with it but would not press him beyond that, come what may.

The group delayed in starting after the summer recess and there was an interval of about four months before it met again. Mrs. Cross seemed to have retained the progress she had made. She has become aware of the change within herself as well as in Sol. She spoke a number of times at the sessions about the absence of tensions and conflicts. She stated that she now understood the significance of her son's behavior and this understanding made it possible for her to accept it and not to flare up. In fact the change in her attitude, she said, was once verbalized by Sol when he said: "Mommie, you don't blow up any more like you used to." She could now see why Sol reacted to her "pouncing on him" the way she used to do and the way she would ignore his and her other children's desires. She stated that she now liked to ask the children for their opinions on matters that concerned them and the family and frequently she even asked them to explain why they did a specific thing. She does not do it critically, but that it was a genuine attempt to understand the child and get his point of view.

It also came out during these group talks that not only had Mrs. Cross's approach to the children changed but also her husband has been drawn into the pattern. Now that the home is much quieter and Sol does not present so many difficulties the father enjoyed the children, and the two of them frequently talk things over between themselves and find it extremely enlightening as well as interesting. She then exclaimed: "This group taught me that you can talk things over even with your husband!"

During one of the sessions she made the point that, "You have to have more than patience. You have to have faith in children. Words alone do not convey this faith, but somehow children do understand if you really have it."

Instead of telling Sol not to be anxious and disturbed she is now careful not to create situations that would cause him disturbance, for, she added: "A child is sensitive and anxious even as much as adults and should be handled carefully. It pays off. A parent should give a child the proper incentive and not exert pressure. We should train the child to work things out for himself." She herself is working on this especially in the school area. She must admit that she is concerned about Sol's poor arithmetic work and she still is at a loss how to reduce her anxiety and keep the good relationship between her and Sol intact.

During one of these discussions she said something that seemed significant. "If a parent exhibits anxiety the child will defeat the parent. He will defeat the parent when she is most anxious in order to get even for all the wrongs the child *thinks* the parent had committed against him." Parents must be constantly on the alert, she continued. She has developed a great deal of confidence in herself not only in relation to Sol but in relation to her other children. She now understands what a struggle Sol had had around his bed wetting and therefore she no longer is angry. Now that she does not feel so angry with him she does not seem to mind the odor as much.

Sol has practically stopped bed wetting. Sometimes three weeks will go by with the bed remaining dry. Occasionally an "accident" occurs, but she is no longer exasperated by it. Sol now willingly takes baths. She does not even have to remind him about it and he is generally cleaner about his person. He gets along much better with his brother and does not seem to go around "with a chip on his shoulder" as he did in the past.

Mrs. Cross's progress as a parent and the rather rare understanding the group had awakened in her continued. It was therefore decided that at the termination of the group season, her membership in the group also be terminated. She attended all of the twenty-nine sessions of the group.

The first interview with Mr. Cross took place two months after Sol's entry into the activity therapy group for the purpose of exploring Mr. Cross's role in Sol's difficulties and in determining the need for treatment for the father.

Mr. Cross is of average height, heavily built but not stout. Although his features conveyed an impression of intellectuality and mildness, this was quickly dispelled by his sharp and rather sar-

castic manner of speech. He began the interview by asking the
worker questions before the worker could question him. He observed
that Sol had been bringing home arts and crafts materials from his
club and wondered whether this was allowed: he was ready to assume
that the child had acted wrongly. In acknowledging that Sol liked
the group, Mr. Cross commented with heavy sarcasm that the reason
for this was that it enabled the boy to miss parochial school. He then
went on to express more openly a coldly negative attitude toward
Sol, characterizing him as "arrogant, self-centered and selfish" and
hoping that one day Sol would have "a rude awakening."

Mr. Cross verbalized his open preference for Sol's younger
brother, a more passive and conforming child. In his own words,
"I wouldn't trade Jack for seven Sol's." A general lack of understanding of children's feelings and motivations was reflected in
Mr. Cross's criticisms of Sol's activities and interests. Thus he expressed dissatisfaction with Sol's playing with cap pistols and his
interest in Western movies on television. The father was especially
critical of Sol's use of his allowance and gave the following illustration.

Recently when the parents felt that Sol needed a hat, the boy
insisted that the only kind of hat he would accept would be the
Confederate Army style cap which was apparently in style at the
time. When the parents refused to buy this type of hat for him,
Sol used his allowance to buy one for himself. Caustically, Mr.
Cross remarked that Sol has worn the hat only a few times. He was
extremely dissatisfied with the child for having bought the hat
for himself. He cited several instances of Sol's disobedience, such
as his refusal to wear a hat when going out into the rain. After a
scene, the boy agreed to take the hat but upon his return, it was
apparent that he had stuck the hat into his pocket instead of wearing it. With a somewhat baffled gesture, Mr. Cross indicated that
he did not know how to handle these situations with Sol. He felt
that Sol got along better with the mother although he was often
negative toward her as well, but in general the boy seemed to accept
orders and reprimands more easily from her than from him.

When the worker directed the discussion toward Mr. Cross's own
background, he related a lonely and unhappy childhood in which

his father was always too busy to have any time for the children. For the first seven years of his life, the family lived in a neighborhood where there was rarely anyone with whom he could play. He guessed that he had never been a boy himself and he thought that this might have something to do with his inability to get along with Sol. In discussing his job in the civil service where he was in a supervisory position, Mr. Cross gave evidence that he had difficulty in dealing with the staff and complained somewhat bitterly about their insubordination, and also of the fact that his superiors would not always back him up when he had reported infractions of rules.

Membership in a guidance group for fathers was broached to Mr. Cross as a channel toward bettering parent-child relations. Mr. Cross accepted this idea and showed interest in attending the next session. At the close of the interview, Mr. Cross expressed appreciation for having been able to talk to the worker and then added, "Perhaps I now won't have the itch to strangle Sol so often."

Mr. Cross joined the fathers' guidance group consisting of seven members that met alternate weeks for ninety minute periods. He attended seven of the eight remaining sessions before the summer recess. Upon arriving at his first session and seeing the other men seated around the table, Mr. Cross commented: "I see now that other people have troubles, too." At this first session he seemed initially intent upon almost defiantly publicizing his poor relationship with Sol. Thus, he described with bravado how Sol had approached the mother for sex information, confiding to her that he had not asked the father because, as the child said, "he would knock my block off." Questioned by the other group members as to whether he had ever threatened the boy, Mr. Cross casually replied that he had and that he had also hit him, adding that when Sol answered the mother back, Mr. Cross got "an awful itch to wallop him." When another group member, Mr. Salkin, who had been in the group for some time, gently chided Mr. Cross with the statement that walloping was not necessary, Mr. Cross, a little defensively, replied, "Well, if he's trying to get under my skin, he certainly is succeeding." Here the leader asked the group why a boy should want to get under his father's skin. Mr. James then addressed

Mr. Cross, saying, "Maybe he wants your attention." At this, Mr. Cross grew thoughtfully silent.

When problems connected with school and homework were raised, Mr. Cross ruefully recalled that once after helping Sol with his homework, the boy returned from school with a failing mark and had told the father, "See how lousy you are!" He then added in a somewhat sarcastic vein that Sol was like "Sam Levenson's child" in that he did his homework with one eye on the book and the other on television.

Another member described an extremely frustrating situation that arose each morning with his son when the boy's mother left for work quite early and it fell to him to get the boy off to school. The child just dawdled and the father kept telling him to hurry up. The boy is unable to find his books and then blames the father; screaming and conflict between them becomes quite intense. Here the leader pointed out that the boy seemed to be making the father react to his pattern each morning by this "button pushing," and that the boy was getting the father to act on his own level. Mr. Cross expressed interest in this, saying that the leader's remark about pressing buttons reminded him that Sol would do the same thing with his mother and she would get panicky. However, after a while (as a result of group discussions) the mother began to ignore situations and this worked out.

Later when another member of the group said that his son received both a religious education and piano lessons in addition to regular public school, Mr. Cross asked if this wasn't too heavy a schedule for a young child. The other replied that his son attended parochial school only three times a week. Mr. Cross commented that the boy was lucky; Sol had to attend school six times a week and only got out of going one day by going to his club (group therapy).

Another father described how difficult it was to get his son off to school in the morning but that there was no problem at all at lunchtime when two boys called for him. The leader commented on this as illustrative of the importance of peers to children at this age, that at times friends may seem to be much more important to a child than his family. This compliance to the desires of friends is based on the fact that the child is sure of his parents but is not nearly as sure of the acceptance by his friends.

One of the men, Mr. Salkin, stated that perhaps children displayed all these difficulties because of some weakness they have inherited from parents. Another laughed and said that everything is traced back to parents, but that it was much easier to change a child than it was to change two parents. Here, speaking quite seriously for the first time, Mr. Cross said that the changing of all three was a very difficult task indeed, and added that his son got away with much more than he, himself, ever did as a child.

At his second session, Mr. Cross's participation in the early stages of the meeting was marked by his empathic espousal of a *laissez faire* attitude toward children which, however, was expressed with a negative, rejecting intent rather than in terms of respect for the child's autonomy. Thus, when Mr. Salkin said that his son left his pajamas and socks around in the morning, Mr. Cross remarked in a resentful tone: "Why don't you let it irritate the boy instead of you? Just leave them there until he gets sick and tired of it."

Mr. Cross then brought up the subject of homework, recalling that he and his wife used to nag Sol about this but now (again, as a result of her membership in the group) they decided that this was up to Sol and the school. He then indicated that he actually did not care whether Sol did his homework or not. He followed this with a critical comment that Sol could not be bothered with his arithmetic problems and that the boy was too lazy to change feet into inches. At the same time he noted that Sol recently worked hard on a science report. Here the leader noted that Mr. Cross had described Sol as lazy in one subject and yet diligent in another. Mr. Cross acknowledged that Sol was interested in science and that his attitude toward math was probably one of not being interested enough rather than of laziness. He continued by critically describing Sol's slipshod handwriting.

After an interval, Mr. Cross presented several situations apparently designed to demonstrate that his younger son was much more ambitious, sociable and generally more intelligent than Sol. As he continued to stress the differences between the two boys in a fashion that was quite uncomplimentary to Sol, the leader finally asked him why there should be such a difference between two children in the same family. Mr. Cross appeared thoughtful, did not respond immediately, and then stated in a serious manner that he really did not know.

Mr. Daws then reported to the group that he had noticed his adolescent daughter's sensitivity about wearing her glasses and indicated that he could understand this in a young girl of her age. Mr. Cross responded by describing that Sol had had a habit of telling his parents that he had not worn his glasses in school as he was supposed to do. However, inquiry revealed that Sol did wear his glasses there. Mr. Cross concluded: "I guess he's trying to irritate us in some way." At this point, Mr. Friedman addressed Mr. Cross: "The problem is that you irritate your boy and he is getting back at you." In a simple, humble manner Mr. Cross remarked, "I know I have irritated him." (This was the first time Mr. Cross admitted to his part in the strained relation between him and his son.)

When the subject of enuresis was raised for discussion by several group members, the leader responded to the group's interest by listing in layman's terms some of the various underlying reasons for this symptom and what it may represent to the child. From the half dozen or so possibilities listed, Mr. Cross singled out the one which suggested that enuresis could constitute a resentful reaction against repressive parents. As if thinking aloud, he said slowly: "In my case, Sol's wetting could be a way of getting back at my wife and me because of our strong reaction to him when he first began to wet."

In the third session, Mr. Cross was attentively silent as another father described a situation where his son refused to do an errand for his parents. After a group discussion, the leader pointed out that an act of disobedience was not an isolated incident between parents and children, but rather part and parcel, an expression of, the whole relationship between them. One of the men said that he now understood his son's pattern. He seems to irritate him in various ways. At this point, Mr. Cross said sarcastically: "My guy is going in for experiments. He tries to see how mad he can get us." Sol tested the mother by telling her that he had overspent his allowance but later revealed that he actually had not. Now that he and his wife are aware of his intent, they ignore it. He explained that he now realized that this testing had been going on for a long time but only in the last few weeks had he and his wife become aware of it. When asked by one of the men how he came to this understanding, Mr. Cross said the idea came from his wife's "discussion group."

Mr. Albert, a new member, presented his family situation describing that of his three sons, the eldest was the difficult one. Mr. Cross commented that it always seemed to be the first who was "a problem." Mr. Albert guessed that the first child was the "experimental one." Mr. Cross added that because one did not have enough time to give to the second and third children less fuss was made over them, and "somehow this is better for them." When a discussion of physical punishment of children came up, Mr. Cross made a telling contribution as he recalled that once after hitting Sol, in order to press a point home, he had asked the boy sharply: "Do you know why I hit you?" To this Sol retorted bitterly: "Sure, because you're bigger."

Mr. Cross was absent from the next session. At the following one, his fourth, he again reverted to presenting Sol in emphatically critical tones, describing him as "self-centered, arrogant and uncooperative." However, a new trend was observed in that Mr. Cross began to participate freely in the mutual helpfulness within the group, expressing interest in the communications of other members. To one father whose son was distrustful, Mr. Cross suggested taking the boy to a baseball game; he mentioned specifically that the Yankees were playing a double header the forthcoming week end. In another situation where a father could not get his son to accompany him in visiting relatives, Mr. Cross offered the following: "Why don't you ask your boy what he wants to do and then go ahead and do it!"

Later in the session, another member made the observation that children were at times amenable to and quite friendly with almost complete strangers and this frequently contrasted to their resentful behavior toward their own parents. The leader made the point that children were not born friends of their parents but had to be made friends of; where this effort was not made, parents and children did not get along. A somewhat shocked silence ensued broken after a while by Mr. Cross, saying very thoughtfully: "The best I can say for Sol and myself is that an armed truce now exists."

His next comment was a complaint against Sol's uncooperativeness, specifically the boy's refusal to help with the shopping for the family. The leader asked if there ever was a time when Sol had enjoyed helping the father in repairing things around the house. Mr. Cross replied that he could not remember the last time this had occurred, and added that he no longer asked the boy to do anything. He recalled that several months before when he was painting a wall in the house, Sol was watching with interest and Mr. Cross guessed that on this occasion Sol would have liked to help, but that he probably had not asked since he assumed his father would refuse. (This awareness was significant for Mr. Cross.)

At the close of this session, Mr. Cross, seemingly anxious, remained with the leader and asked about the possibility of having Sol attend a summer camp. He also asked about camp for the younger two children and then proceeded to describe the two as extremely well adjusted. To relieve Mr. Cross's tension the leader remarked supportively that two out of three was a good batting average. Mr. Cross laughed and said that he guessed that was right and then added, "But I think we can rescue the third child, too."

At the following session, Mr. Cross spoke ambivalently of Sol, first expressing sympathy with the boy's anxiety about going to camp for the first time and then describing that in the morning, after Sol had wet the bed, they needed a deodorant for the house. He stated with pleasure that in a recent quarrel between Sol and the mother, the child "really got paid for all the back numbers." He followed this with the criticism of all three of his children for demanding new toys which held their interest only briefly. This led to a discussion by the group on children's hobbies. The point was made that parents who took over the care of a child's hobby, such as fish, did not help develop a sense of responsibility in the child which the parents ought to see develop. Mr. Cross who had not participated actively in this conversation criticized Sol's activities, describing that while on an errand he had overpaid two cents on an item. Mr. Cross summarized resentfully, "I guess he thinks more of his own money than he does of his father's."

Immediately after this, Mr. Cross remarked that just the other day he had obtained Sol's help in doing something around the house by casually asking, "Do you want to give me a hand?" This was the first breach in "the cold war" between father and son.

In response to several comments about children's demands which apparently had been touched off by Mr. Cross's earlier statement on the subject, the leader asked the group whether parents ought to meet these demands for a while so that children could reciprocate later. Mr. Cross rejected this idea by quoting the case of a relative who had a bad relationship with his son despite having given his child "everything." Another member countered by relating a situation that illustrated that children needed to receive before they in turn could give. Mr. Cross responded to this with a report on how his three children chipped in for a Mother's Day present. They also decided to get a present for his "wife's anniversary." He quickly changed this to "our anniversary." He again criticized Sol for having undertaken both these financial commitments and at the same time buying gold fish, all out of his allowance. The leader remarked here that Sol was embarking upon his beginning experience in sharing and in a sense was "just going into business," and yet Mr. Cross appeared to expect him to operate like J. P. Morgan. The group laughed. Mr. Cross smiled in an accepting manner.

One of the group members described his son as unwilling to leave the house after school, despite continued urging to do so by the parents. This led to a definition of respect for children as meaning that the child be allowed to grow at his own pace and be accepted for what he is today with the knowledge that he will progress to the next stage when he is inwardly ready to do so. This father became aware that he was not showing respect to his son by constantly pestering him to go out and play on the street. Mr. Cross responded by describing that for a long while he used to badger Sol about doing his homework neatly but that after a "big fight" with the boy, a few weeks ago, he decided to leave him alone. Just this past week end Mr. Cross noticed that Sol suddenly put in about three hours on his homework voluntarily, and he did it all quite neatly.

At the last session before the summer recess, Mr. Jenner who had sensed Mr. Cross's initial resistance to the group, congratulated him for "sticking it out." Mr. Cross, pleased, said he was glad he had done so and remarked that it had "borne fruit." He described that Sol had been quite favorably impressed when the parents told him that they were also going to groups in order to find out how everyone in the family could get along better. With pride Mr. Cross added that there had not been a fight with the boy for weeks.

In the fall, Mr. Cross was seen individually by the group leader. He reported that Sol had recently been dry for two weeks, but then had begun to wet again. He thought that the regression might be due to anxiety connected with the boy's approaching confirmation. He noted Sol's eagerness to be done with parochial school and indicated that if he were in the boy's place, he would feel the same way since the teacher did little to make the work interesting. He described two incidents that are of special significance in evaluating the effect of the guidance group on him. While alone with Sol recently, the boy had commented that he liked Spanish, a new subject in school, but that he did not know certain words. The father, a college graduate, suggested in a friendly way that Sol ask him about them. The boy did so and Mr. Cross made the correct translations. Mr. Cross's comment on this was, "We ironed that out quite easily and I think Sol liked the idea." The second situation revolved around Sol's attempt to make an arts and crafts project for school. Twice, when the job was almost done after considerable effort on the boy's part, it broke. After the second failure, Sol reacted with a severe and prolonged tantrum. Not without pride, Mr. Cross described that he was able to ignore the tantrum, and Sol then went ahead to a third attempt and this time was successful in finishing the project.

When asked how he might have handled this situation a year ago, Mr. Cross grinned and replied unhesitatingly: "I'd probably have murdered the kid."

At the first session when the group reconvened in the fall, his eighth, Mr. Cross described an incident which reflected Sol's awareness of the positive change in his parents. Mr. Cross first stated that he had been somewhat dissatisfied with the way Sol spent his allowance every now and then on an expensive model airplane. Generally,

Sol goes out and buys one model at a time, but last week he went out and "blew his allowance" on two airplanes. When he came home with them, neither father nor mother said anything and after a while Sol said in amazement: "Here I went out and bought not one but two models and no one blew a gut." To this, Mr. Cross commented that he guessed that Sol is now getting the idea that his parents are "not out to pick on him all the time."

Mr. Cross later reported that Sol went without wetting his bed for several weeks at a time and that the parents permitted him to stay out for a party with his friends as late as 1:30 A.M. They felt that because the other boys were allowed to do so, they should not deprive Sol of the same privilege. Mr. Cross also said at one of the group sessions that Sol bought presents for him and his wife during Christmas week, though Mr. Cross added sarcastically: "It is lucky he got gifts that I could afford." With considerable satisfaction he addressed the leader, saying, "I think there is something which would interest you. Sol was able to save money for something he wanted very much. He could not do this in the past, since he would always spend the money as soon as it was given to him and sometimes in large amounts, too." (The boy's impulsive spending of money has been one of the points of contention between father and son. In the past Sol used spending of money as one of the means of irritating his father.)

At the eleventh session he attended, when one of the men said thoughtfully: "I sometimes wonder who needs the cure—the parents or the kids," Mr. Cross said very seriously, "After coming here for a while I am sure that if the parents were okay the children would have no problems. I sometimes think that the child grows up in spite of adults." He then proceeded to develop the idea by saying that "while people would not attempt to fix a radio because it is too complicated an instrument, they will go ahead and do all sorts of things with children who are much more complicated than radios."

At the same session Mr. Friedman said something about luck being involved in bringing up children and cited the case of a boy who although neglected by his father nevertheless grew up and became a successful lawyer. Mr. Cross said, "Maybe the boy's father had enough sense to leave him alone so that the boy made his own way in life." Mr. Cross also described Sol's better application to his homework which was both surprising and gratifying to the father. He then reported a new interest the boy had recently developed, namely, photography.

Mr. Cross reported to the group that Sol had gotten 100 in mathematics and asked the leader if he should "make a fuss" about it. The leader in turn asked Mr. Cross if he had made a fuss when the boy received poor marks. Mr. Cross smiled broadly and said he thought he got the point; if he had emphasized failure, he should also note effort and success. In this same session, he criticized Sol's carelessness about money, both when he ran errands for the parents and in the management of his allowance. Though Sol gave up bed wetting for many months, he regressed at that particular period (which Mrs. Cross discussed also at the mother's group). But instead of violently attacking the boy for it as he would have done in the past, Mr. Cross now understood that it was brought on by the parents' denying Sol a pet on which he had his heart set and expressed the optimistic belief that he would stop when he got the pet and especially when the anxiety connected with his pending confirmation had passed.

During some of the following sessions Mr. Cross has shown an interest in the literature dealing with children which was completely outside of his consideration in the past, quoting examples of good parenthood. One of these was from "The Parent's Prayer" taken from a bulletin of a child welfare agency. It consisted of a parent's prayer to God, couched in biblical language, in which he prayed that he would not lose patience with, interrupt, nag, or demand adult behavior from his children. Mr. Cross appeared sincerely touched by this and said that after reading it, he had seriously asked his children to read it and tell him what he was "guilty of." His children, he said, took this rather flippantly. Another idea that arrested Mr. Cross's interest was that a child comes into the world as a blank canvas upon which adults make their impression, some softly with loving care, some roughly, some carelessly and some impatiently. Once Mr. Cross described an incident of his son's effort at shaving with the father's razor, but instead of being annoyed, the father talked about it humorously and good-naturedly.

When another father, a newcomer, told of having decreased his son's allowance as punishment, Mr. Cross said that he had learned in the group that an allowance was one thing and punishment another and that the two should be kept separate. He then related two incidents that seemed to please him very much. One was concerned with Sol's enthusiastic response to an invitation to join a neighborhood center with his father, ending his narration with the remark, "Well, maybe Sol is growing up after all." Another occurred at the circus where the children wanted hot dogs, but Mr. Cross pointed out to them that the hot dogs were carried on plain trays, instead of heating units, and would probably be cold and tasteless. He suggested to the children that they should not buy them. Sol accepted this suggestion and Mr. Cross remarked that a year ago the boy would probably "have thrown a terrific tantrum." When Sol had recently received the new English bicycle he bought for himself, he brought it to the father at the subway station and insisted that he take a ride. Mr. Cross said he was really pleased.

Despite the definite constructive trends in Mr. Cross's attitudes and understanding of his children, his basic underlying ambivalence was still lurking. From time to time there was a resurgence of his criticism of Sol, yet this was differentiated from previous negative statements by a change in tone and manner. In the beginning these comments were marked by a cold and biting sarcasm; they now were uttered with less vehemence. He seemed consistently more tolerant, more accepting, and more casual in his criticism. Thus at one session he remarked matter-of-factly that Sol had "slipped back a little" in his behaivor. Occasionally a note of rejection of his good relationship with his son crept through, as was the case once when he said in a calm manner that he did not think that he and his son were getting along any better, but that the bed wetting had certainly improved. (This was actually not a true depiction of the situation.)

At the final session of the season, the leader suggested to the group that they evaluate their experience in the group. When one member said that it helped him to accept calmly behavior in his son which previously would have caused him to lose his temper, Mr. Cross remarked that he was "always" ready to lose his temper with Sol, but now he found that he could control it; and when several of the members complained that the leader had not given them enough specific advice, others, including Mr. Cross, disagreed on the grounds that because of individual differences in children, direct advice could not always be helpful. Substantiating this argument, Mr. Cross said he observed that the same children could even be different at different times of the day, and as far as he was personally concerned, aside from the improvement in Sol's bed wetting, he felt that there had been improvement in his relationship with the boy. When questioned by one of the members whether he "blew up" at the boy, Mr. Cross replied that in the last three months he had completely refrained from being critical in the child's presence, adding that in the past he had always worked week ends and had had little time to spend with his children. He then added somewhat sadly that it was difficult for him, because "Sol has no use for me," adding seriously, "I think the trouble is that this group did not begin to meet fifteen years ago. By now the damage was done." He reiterated his statement that parents were entrusted with the highly complex job of bringing up children without adequate preparation, knowledge, or experience.

Despite the general improvement in Mr. Cross as a parent, and the transformation of his relation with his son from open hostilities, to "an armed truce," as he characterized it, then to a marked effort to being tolerant and understanding, Mr. Cross's basic personality inadequacies stemming principally from his relation with his own father and his early deprivations, it was doubtful whether he would be able to retain improvement. The occasional resurgence of his negative feelings, ambivalence and obvious inability to accept his son because of his own affect needs would, in our opinion, require "working through" of some of his traumatic background in individual psychotherapy. Because of his own deprived childhood, Mr. Cross unconsciously re-enacted his own father's role in relation to Sol, although consciously he wished to be different. Never having received love himself, he was unable to give love to his children. Though the entire family had gained from Sol's and his parents' group experiences, and though the boy and Mrs. Cross could be closed, the father was referred for individual treatment.

Because of the demands of his job that involved evening work,

Mr. Cross was able to attend only nineteen out of the possible thirty-two sessions of the group.

In accordance with this decision Mr. Cross was seen individually by the group leader. When individual treatment was broached to him, Mr. Cross felt he had gained enough from the group to continue on his own. In explaining his position he said among other things: "About Sol, as I look around at other boys, I now see that he is pretty much like all the others and I think the main trouble is with me. Maybe because I had to obey my father immediately I expect the same thing from him." He then said that Sol had played a major part in the children having recently given him and his wife a nice gift for their anniversary. Then, as if offering the leader tangible proof of his worth as a parent and the affection and esteem in which his children held him, he showed the leader the envelope in which the children's anniversary gift had been enclosed. It was addressed, "To two wonderful people, From the three pests." Mr. Cross reiterated several times that it was Sol who had really initiated the idea of the gift and had probably contributed most of the money to buy it and had also written the card.

The changes in attitude of the parents were achieved by the child-centered group guidance technique without dealing with their personality problems. The mother in this instance was amenable to the influence of the discussions in the group and the suggestions that came from its members. After the very first session we see her attempting to "get closer" to her children "as an experiment," as she put it, and because the experiment had met with a little success as Sol responded to her overtures, she was understandably pleased with it and continued to act in accordance with her newly evolving insights of the child's needs which, "pays off," as she put it.

The father, as we became aware, had more serious personality difficulties and his early defensive hostility and sarcasm prevented him from moving as rapidly and as willingly as did the mother, but he could not remain unresponsive to the changes in Sol's personality, as well as his wife's efforts at working things out with him and making him more a part of the family group. This appealed to the natural, almost instinctive, parental cravings which, when given a favorable opportunity for finding gratification, are easily activated.

Although we are not justified in claiming that deeply-affecting intrapsychic changes occurred in either of the two parents, particularly the father, their functioning as parents and mates had improved and the relationships in the family grew more healthy and more constructive which in turn favored wholesome personality development in all the children. It is not unusual to find in such families that children, other than the one referred for treatment, also have difficulties requiring attention. It is our feeling that we have probably prevented developing behavior difficulties in the other children as well as correcting those in Sol.

Attention should also be called to the fact that comparatively little was known at the beginning about the background of the mother and father, or their personality structures, beyond what was gleaned from the intake interviews. In preparation for psychotherapy we allow ourselves to go much deeper into the exploration of the backgrounds and character of parents. In group guidance we eschew doing it because questioning and uncovering of intimate and painful facts in their lives activates the need for a psychotherapeutic resolution of these. Since the group guidance as described here is not designed to enter into these areas or offer the participants this experience, we avoid activating such memories. Another reason for this avoidance is that such exploration sets a pattern for interviews which the parents may carry over into the group talks. In other words, it determines the primary group code in advance. This is, however, not an insurmountable difficulty since a skillful guidance worker (leader) with experience in psychotherapy can change this code quickly enough. A greater hazard is the parents' coming to the group in states of disturbance and in need of having them allayed or worked through. This emotional need cannot be as easily side-stepped by even the best of therapists.

This rather lengthy report illustrates the possibility and the importance of altering attitudes in parents in certain selected cases where the parents' ways of dealing with their children are not too deeply charged with psychoneurotic content. Of great value in working with this family was the fact that the three leaders were in communication with each other on the material produced by all three members of the family and frequently exchanged impressions. The fact that the treatment and guidance was under the supervision of one person aided in the integration of their efforts. It prevented errors and facilitated the smooth dealing with this family.[2]

About three years after the closing of this family, a follow-up was held with the parents. The father was the first to be invited to come to see his former group leader but both parents arrived and came into the worker's room together. Mr. Cross explained that he had brought his wife along because she saw much more of Sol and, therefore, would be able to give a better picture of him.

The mother was the more articulate of the two during the interview. The parents reported that Sol presented no special difficulties. He got along very well in school, participated in extracurricular activities, and was one of the editors of the newspaper at his high school as well as in the neighborhood center, which he attended regularly. In addition, he was holding a part-time job. The teachers spoke very highly of him.

Encopresis stopped completely and has never reappeared. Enuresis occurs intermittently mostly following a sharp conflict between him and the mother. The parents recognized this as a retaliatory act. The mother reported that she still had to "correct him in many ways." However, as the parents talked, the mother stated quite spontaneously: "Perhaps it is us." By this she meant that it may be that the parents' personal difficulties are projected upon the boy. At another point, the father said, "Maybe we expect too much of ourselves and probably expect too much of Sol." This would seem significant in view of the fact that the father, who had trained to be a high school teacher, has been working as a post office clerk.

When the boy was seen by the caseworker, he reported substantially the same activities and adjustment as the parents had. Just as the mother complained about him, he also complained about the mother who he felt was still exerting too much pressure upon him. He got along better with his father, he said, because his father did not scream at him and did not attempt to control him. Sol still felt considerable hostility toward his younger brother.

[2] For a report on the effect of activity group therapy on Mr. and Mrs. Cross's son, see Appendix, pp. 311-328.

In appearance Sol presented a picture of a normal adolescent. He is a handsome youngster and his manner and general bearing gave the impression of an adolescent with no particular personality problems or social maladjustment. He seemed well set up, not unduly anxious and as communicative as one could expect considering his basic personality structure and the background from which he had come.

VII

Effects Upon the Family Climate

Any group of persons in a more or less intimate relation strike a state of equilibrium. This may be real equilibrium or "equilibrium under tension," which I have described in my book, *Child Psychotherapy*.[1] The matter of group or interpersonal equilibrium is particularly pertinent for families where the role of each member is sharply defined, where each occupies a particular place in the group constellation and affects it in a special way. Thus traditionally, at least, the father occupies the position of authority and functions as the disciplinarian. His contribution is, or should be, one of security and stability. The mother, on the other hand, is the nurturer and the giver of love to the children and to her husband. By the same token, sex of, and the order in which children are born affect the role and position of each in the family. These roles emerge by virtue of their antecedent presence in the family, the relationship existing between the child and his parents, by the latter's unconscious attitudes and system of values as well as their emotional state during the various stages of the child's growth.

It is understandable that, by and large, the oldest child would occupy the attention of parents and be a source of greater anxiety to them than the subsequent offspring. The attitude of siblings toward each other are determined, among other things, by the fact that the older has to give up the mother to the younger. Thus, rivalries, hostilities, aggressions, as well as positive attitudes, inevitably emerge. This network of feelings and relations is increasingly complicated by

[1] New York: Columbia University Press, 1952, pp. 68 et seq.

the advent of subsequent children, each one fitting into the gestalt or emotional complex of the family group. The situation is further diversified by the presence in the home of relatives: grandparents, aunts and uncles.

When a family carries on its daily living, meets responsibilities and functions as a unit in a more or less integrated way, the equilibria resulting therefrom are in evidence. Equilibrium in human groups is never static, for jealousies, struggles, conflicts, dissension, and hostilities constantly emerge. However, a group can remain intact for any length of time only when the disturbances are brought under control and some degree of stability is alternately re-established. As already stated, this equilibrium may be one "under tension," a dynamic which is described in detail in the book to which we have referred. Should it be impossible to re-establish equilibrium, the group becomes disrupted and a "break-up" results.

In family group tensions, as in all other constellations of forces, the resultant is one of equilibrium. When a change occurs in any one of the components, there is a corresponding rearrangement or change in the other forces in the constellation both in intensity and direction so that equilibrium is again re-established. In families, a change in personality, role, or effectiveness and power on the part of one or more persons inevitably modify the roles, power and relationships of all the others. It is for this reason that a change of any member of a family through psychotherapy—the father, mother or a child—results in a set of new forces and therefore the need for a new equilibrium. Psychotherapists and guidance counselors have found it necessary to work with members of families other than the patients or clients in order to re-establish such a workable family equilibrium. Changes in children as a result of emotional rehabilitation frequently require or affect some personality or attitudinal changes in the parents as well. One often finds that a change in the husband, for example, requires that the wife, too, make some realignment in her attitudes, behavior and functions. *Total family therapy* is therefore becoming increasingly accepted in mental hygiene practices.

This was one of the considerations in referring the child and both parents to groups, for it was found that in many instances a change in one of them would not assure a wholesome family climate without a change in the others. To produce a wholesome home atmosphere, it was necessary to eliminate the existing or potential conflicts and tensions in all the others. In a clinic referrals are not made to "guidance groups" alone. According to indications, parents, as well as children, may be offered individual treatment, group psychotherapy, or group guidance, or a combination of some of these.[2]

Much of the effect of total family treatment, as in the case of the Cross family, for example (see Chapter V), was evident in the subtle change in the *family climate* as well as in the functioning of the individuals in it. This improvement in the total climate was observed in other families as well. However, in some instances it was possible to obtain evidence of these changes, while in others, because of the restrictions of personnel and our technique, this was not possible or advisable.

Although we directed our effort toward altering the relation between the parents and children, it soon became evident that the relationships between the parents themselves had automatically undergone definite improvement as a result of one or both of them being members of our groups. For example, in one of our discussion groups, we had a father (Mr. Daws) who was brought up in a near East country and who therefore was traditionally a strict disciplinarian and a tyrant (see Chapter III). He lorded it over his family, particularly the children, with an iron hand, punishing them severely, and calling upon them to perform tasks far beyond their abilities and readiness. His wife was an American woman who had been in individual treatment because of a serious personality disturbance. It was easy to understand why the two were in frequent conflict about ways of dealing with their children and that the consequent tension between them seriously affected the latter.

Through the criticism, pressure and aid of the other members in the group, this man was forced to acknowledge that his approach was unsuitable for wholesome development of his children in our

2 Perhaps this is what is meant by the phrase "breaking the vicious circle." The reader will recall from preceding pages that in some instances one parent was treated either individually or was a member of a group while another may have been either in group guidance or in individual treatment. The child, too, may have been in individual or group treatment or in both simultaneously.

culture. He soon mended his ways. Once when in a discussion another member of the group talked about the difficulty he was having in applying his newly acquired ideas on child development because of his wife, Mr. Daws said: "Now, there are no two schools of thought in our family about how to bring up our children. My wife and I talk things over and we come to an understanding."

The reader will also recall Mrs. Cross's statement that she had felt in the past her function was to tell her children and her husband what to do and they had to obey her. She then said that she had discovered through the group that she could now talk things over with her children, adding with an expression of surprise that she now talked things over even with her husband. Before that, they had never discussed anything with each other, but as a result of their experience in their groups they began to talk things over and came to an understanding concerning all matters requiring their joint attention.

We are understandably interested in the effects of Child-Centered Group Guidance of Parents upon relationships between the adults of a family. A parent who is preoccupied primarily with his personal problems and pressures—the father with earning a living, the mother with the details and chores of housework and child rearing—frequently shares little of the several common interests, and when situations arise that affect them both they have no *modus operandi* by which they could cooperate and unify their efforts for the benefit of their family. Each is wrapped up in his own pressures and resentments against his fate and against each other. Characteristically, the parents who came to our attention had scarcely a common basis for getting together to discuss or to cooperate.

The discussions in our groups stirred the parents up so much that their thoughts and reflections flowed over into the family circle. Mothers would impart to their husbands the ideas acquired in the group that seemed meaningful and stayed with them. In nearly all instances, the fathers listened and responded, and friendly discussions between husband and wife resulted; not the resentments, hostilities and quarrels of the past, but a real exchange. This had clearly occurred in the case of the Ross family, as a result of which Mr. Ross asked to join a group or to see a caseworker so that he, too, could keep up with his wife's newly evolving ideas and development (Chapter X). A number of the mothers who had been in groups asked that their husbands as well be included in a "fathers' group" so that there would be a greater community of feeling, which in turn produced a more harmonious family atmosphere.

To illustrate this development, it may be useful to summarize briefly the effect of Child-Centered Group Guidance on two parents, each attending separate groups, and the interaction of their group experiences.

Mrs. Salkin (5) (Chapter V) who had been moody at the early sessions caused the leader some concern, because these moods may have constituted symptoms of depression. Mrs. Salkin, however, gradually overcame them and appeared more cheerful as the sessions progressed. From the very start she revealed an awareness of children's needs and a sensitivity far above that of the others in the group. She was more permissive than the others and not as impatient. At one session she related that Harris occasionally still took toys into the bathtub, but she did not mind it. To her it meant that he had skipped this type of play when he was younger. She knew he would outgrow it after he had had this type of gratification. She observed that he gradually took less time to bathe than before, which meant that he was paying more attention to bathing and less to playing with the toys.

There was talk at the same session about how some situations upset mothers while others did not. Mrs. Salkin said one of her difficulties in the past had been that Harris had not wanted to eat the food she gave him. As a result, he was "very skinny." This had hurt her because she felt it reflected on her ability to take proper care of him. Since coming to the group, she has stopped bothering him about it; she has not worried, because, in addition to what she learned in the group about managing the feeding of children, she sometimes felt that maybe age alone would correct his eating habits; as he grew, he would require more food. She felt it may have been the emotional tension she imposed on him that prevented him from eating normally. Now he talked about wanting to be big and strong and so he eats "man-sized portions." She gives them to him willingly.

She talked very articulately and clearly about helping children with what they wanted to be and do.

Mrs. Salkin had never been absent. She was invariably punctual, alert, responsive, but not always ready to initiate discussions. This may have been a reaction to her preoccupation with a difficult husband rather than a primary feature in her personality.

When Mrs. Salkin was first interviewed (see pp. 126-128), she was emphatic on the point that her husband would not respond to any effort at treatment. We, however, felt from the outset that the chief source of the difficulties in this family was the father and that we would have to direct our efforts toward him. The caseworker, who was also the leader of the fathers' group, therefore invited Mr. Salkin to come in to see him. Mr. Salkin had a very youthful appearance, boasting a small moustache, and quite evidently immature; though he was in his middle thirties, he looked like a man in his twenties. The caseworker described him as inordinately tense with a "pervasive" anxiety. The interviewer emphasized in his report Mr. Salkin's intense discomfort and tension, and described him as a person who "definitely induced a negative countertransference."

Mr. Salkin was suspicious and thought he was being cheated and taken advantage of by his customers and partner in a small business they owned. He was critical and found fault with everyone around him. His compelling interest, of which we learned from his wife, was model trains. These he kept locked in a room to which no one was admitted and where he spent nearly all of his free time.

In the interview he revealed a cold, hostile attitude toward his son and concentrated on the fact that the boy was "fresh to his mother." He evaded involving himself, claimed he was very busy and got home late evenings. When a group was suggested, he said he would like to take advantage of it, but was much too busy. He promised he would call the caseworker sometime later but failed to do so.

Mrs. Salkin had been in a mothers' guidance group for some time and had made considerable progress herself, but kept reporting that her husband was extremely punitive toward their son, beating him constantly. He grew particularly vicious when disturbed by the children at his model trains. No doubt, because of her newly acquired security in the group, once, when the father beat Harris, the mother decided to take a stand. She told him that if this kept up, she would leave him. This aroused intense anxiety in Mr. Salkin and he telephoned the leader to say that he would like to come to a group, explaining that a crisis had arisen in his family with which he needed help. The group had been meeting for some time; two of the fathers in it, Mr. Cross (6) and Mr. Friedman (2) were carried from the year before.

"His whole manner and carriage suggested that he may be more ready for a mental institution than for a guidance group," is the way the leader described Mr. Salkin's appearance. "I have never seen such a tense, frightened, anxious and hostile person in my life." Mr. Salkin sat quietly for about twenty minutes listening to the others talk, smoking one cigarette after another and moving about in his seat with extreme discomfort. Unable to keep himself under control any longer, he began to talk in a very tense, almost compulsive way. Mr. Salkin's first contribution was offered in a discussion around permissiveness when he made the statement: "If you let kids get away with too much, it's no good." He then followed this by referring to a report in the newspapers of a son killing his mother, supposedly over a few dollars which she had refused him.

He later said that his own son had almost broken up his marriage. He wanted to know what to do about it; he was at a loss. He proceeded to say that had the window been open at the time of a recent fight in his family, he would have thrown both the boy and the mother out the window, but now he "did not know what to do." The boy showed no respect whatsoever. He said with intense hostility that the child "does not listen and shows no respect." His concept of respect on the part of a child was that "a child should listen [obey], should not slander his father, should be quiet when his father is trying to sleep, should do anything he is told." Mr. Salkin, with feeling, said that children were too soft these days and proceeded to compare the present ways of growing up with his own childhood on the East Side of New York where he had had to fight all day. He said that his father used to beat him severely; yet he still loved his father. He strongly criticized Harris for telling another child about a surprise birthday party for him, as a result of which all of the children on the block ostracized Harris.

When the leader made the comment that he had described a very unhappy child, Mr. Salkin seemed astonished and then became thoughtful. He said after a moment: "I guess he *is* unhappy, although I never thought of it that way."

Later Mr. Salkin attempted to implicate his wife by describing that she had a brother who was in a mental hospital and that "she is afraid of my instilling fear in Harris because he might turn out like her brother." He strongly criticized his wife for not giving him free reign with the boy.

The other men in the group told Mr. Salkin that since they had come to the group they had been successful with their boys in different ways. They confronted him with their achievements, as it were, which only added to Mr. Salkin's feelings of failure and frustration. Almost appealingly he asked: "Isn't there any answer to all of this?" The others told him that he would have to learn to control himself and that instead of counting to ten, he would have to "count to fifty." They assured him from their own experience that he "would learn," as they did, that if he let the boy alone, things would be far better for all concerned. However, while the men boasted of their success, they were not critical of the newcomer, nor did they convey disapproval of him; there was evident underlying acceptance. They gave him the feeling that they were interested in his situation, inquired as to the duration of the conflicts and conveyed a friendly and warm feeling. Mr. Salkin left the session in a highly distraught state and did not return to the next session two weeks later.

The leader wrote him a friendly letter inviting him to the following session, adding a statement that he knew that the first session had been a difficult one for him, but he thought that Mr. Salkin did very well. When Mr. Salkin came to the session his first remark was, "I got your letter." (This was evidently a way of saying that he was helped to come back through the support and encouragement he had received from it.) Mr. Salkin presented a completely different picture. He was much calmer, more relaxed and more friendly. In fact, one of his fellow group members commented: "Boy, you're relaxed now. What happened? There seems to be improvement right away."

With a very pleased expression Mr. Salkin said that things were a lot better. He rationalized by saying that at the time of the previous session he had been having troubles in his business. His next statement was that he had been getting along wonderfully well with Harris. The boy was now seeking him out; they were playing and going places together. What was still bothering him was the boy's fighting with his younger brother. "Is that normal?" he asked. The others assured him that it was. Mr. Cross told him that (at that stage) his three children also were fighting and that they were continually making alliances of two against one. He never knew who was going "to get killed." He said all this in a humorous manner. The leader then made a comment, specifically for Mr. Salkin's benefit, universalizing the fact that brothers and sisters have been jealous of each other since the beginning of time.[3] With an expression of great relief, Mr. Salkin said, "I'm certainly glad to hear that!" and he offered cigarettes to all present.

He then commented, "They say that kids reflect what parents are. Is that true?" and repeated that being in business for himself involving long hours kept him away from his children. He implied that this was the cause for his difficulties with Harris. The others disagreed and Mr. Daws explained that a child had problems because of something he had missed in his life, something which the parents had not given him. Mr. Salkin seemed to take this statement seriously. He appeared thoughtful and then remarked, "Maybe there is something wrong. I'd like to find out." During the same session Mr. Friedman remarked to Mr. Salkin approvingly, "You're much more relaxed than you were a month ago. I think you've really made progress." Mr. Salkin appeared pleased and acknowledged that he felt more relaxed.

At the following session Mr. Salkin's first comment was to the effect that he and his boy were still getting along well together. Then, in an almost casual, tolerant way, said: "Of course, he is still murdering the younger boy, but I know that's pretty normal and usual. I can't expect a perfect child."

At a later session, with surprise in his voice he said that he had never realized that Harris was self-conscious. He had recently observed that the boy was shy about two slightly protruding teeth. He

[3] Retelling the Biblical stories of Cain and Abel and Joseph and his brothers is a very effective and convincing device here.

also raised the question of whether to stop Harris from reading in the bathroom before going to sleep at night. After some discussion of this in the group, Mr. Salkin smiled and remarked, "Come to think of it, I take a paper to the bathroom myself and that's probably where Harris gets it from."

Once when another father criticized his son for being ungrateful and throwing a tantrum because he had received confirmation presents which he did not like, Mr. Salkin commented, "In your mind he's ungrateful but maybe he's just upset about something." This was a totally different attitude Mr. Salkin now presented.

It was apparent that in addition to the guidance he had been receiving relative to his behavior with his children, the social values inherent in the group had great significance for this man. He would sit close to the table and look around attentively as the others spoke. The leader had the feeling that Mr. Salkin did not always follow the content of the talk but was rather responding emotionally to a social situation. He seemed glad to be with a group of men. He would offer cigarettes all around, soon began to offer to drive fellow members home after the sessions, and would ask the others where they had parked their cars and tell them where he had parked his.

Mr. Salkin became increasingly freer in communicating and in his relationships to the other men. He grew receptive to their suggestions and opinions, but seldom sought direct advice from them; this he did from the leader. Time and again he turned to the latter for advice and suggestions which were given him always gently and helpfully. He continued to report improvement in Harris and in his own relations with him. He was growing closer to his children, tolerant of their self-assertiveness and pleased with the fact that Harris frequently sought him out for conversation, advice and play. Mr. Salkin who had always been distant from his children and very infantile in his demands so that his wife would frequently and quite automatically refer to "my three boys"—two sons and her husband—now spent more time with them and less with his model trains.

He once invited the children to go to an amusement park where there were "all sorts of rides" and other types of diversion and excitement typical of such places, but Harris did not want to go. He said he would rather play with a friend. Mr. Salkin said that while he was "a little disappointed in one way," he knew that it was more important for the boy, who had social difficulties, to spend time with a friend than to be with him.

Mr. Salkin had, on occasion, talked about his own background. He once commented that when he was nine years old a boy had shown him how he masturbated. He said this in such a casual way that one got the impression that the experience had not affected him too deeply. He had brought out the fact that he had been very jealous of his sister and had once threatened to cut her up with scissors. She had been so frightened by this that thereafter he left her alone. He narrated how his father had beat him, thrown things at him, and placed him in a children's shelter as a young child. He described himself as "a wild boy" when he was young. He referred to the fact that at times "I blow my top at my wife," indicating that his wife "sees things differently" than he did. As the discussions progressed Mr. Salkin implied that she was more mature and certainly more patient with the children than he was and praised her for it.

No small part in the improvement of Mr. Salkin was played by his wife who was a bright and perceptive woman fully cognizant of the situation in the home and her husband's character. She recognized from the outset that while she needed to alter her treatment of her children, she could not go far without some change in her husband. She once conveyed this thought when she said laconically, "I don't know that I can go very far with my boys." Her threat to separate from him when he attacked Harris was the *critical event* in this situation; it drove him to seek out the clinic for help. He would continually quarrel with her, demanding, "Why don't you get these brats out of my way when I am working on these models?" He had his own special tool chest and though he got Harris a little tool chest too, the latter preferred to work with his father's tools. There was always bickering and commotion on that account. After Mrs. Salkin had been in the group for some months she told her husband directly and emphatically that she was not interested in raising him to be a man. She would raise her boys to be men, but not her husband. (This information was elicited during the few times she had seen the leader individually and not in the group sessions.) In a sense Mrs.

Salkin prodded her husband through this into seeking help in the clinic.

There were also indications that Mr. Salkin sought in the leader a person in authority who would help him but not *use* authority to crush him, as his father had done. He needed an authority but one that would accept him and be kind to him. The leader, unlike Mr. Salkin's father, evidently represented a positive father figure, and his wife now became the good mother figure who guided him toward a source of help and who was ready to stand by him while he was growing. Mrs. Salkin unquestionably was greatly encouraged by the fact that her husband sought out help and treated him with greater consideration and respect. We can also assume that Mr. Salkin was guilty about his rivalry with his son, as he was guilty about his rivalry with his own siblings. We can also assume considerable homoerotic trends in Mr. Salkin because of his early developmental history, but such libidinal difficulties are not touched in guidance groups. When they interfere with the group process the member is removed and referred for individual treatment.

The improvement in the family atmosphere did not leave Mrs. Salkin unaffected. As already related, she was observed to be withdrawn, quiet and pensive in the early sessions of the group and at times sad and even depressed. These states gradually disappeared and she became enlivened and participated freely in the discussions, enriching them with her rather unusual insights and understanding. Similarly Mr. Salkin was characterized by his group leader as "poised, relaxed and without a trace of his earlier discomfort and extreme disturbed state." The group has helped him assume a different role in the family than he had occupied before. Instead of being a sibling in relation to his own children and regarding his wife as a mother figure whom he expected to pamper and protect him, he was helped through identification with the others in the group to see his role in a new light. This is one of the important values of guidance groups; namely, parents motivate one another to function in a parental role instead of a sibling relation. This is made possible by the fact that all are fairly well matched: all are parents of children of the same sex and nearly the same age. By *mutual induction* they become more aware of the parental role and abandon their earlier patterns in which they re-enacted their own parents. For example, Mr. Salkin's father used to throw things at him and beat him; he did likewise. When these habit patterns and identifications are brought to awareness by the group and the leader and the light of reason and understanding is thrown on it, the "habit" is eliminated. Of course if there are present inner resistive forces preventing the emergence of this awareness and control salutary results cannot be expected.

Parents in the groups are placed in a new kind of family, with a new type of relation which, as in the case of Mr. Salkin, they have never experienced. They discover a new way of dealing with human relations which had been alien to them. The group, as a new family, serves as a model for their own families. The leader is a good parent figure, tolerant, accepting, understanding, permitting free expression and encouraging each to be himself; the fellow members are good siblings who do not beat one down—hence each strives to emulate these newly discovered and pleasure-giving relations in their own families. Mr. Salkin's extreme discomfort at the first individual interview and at the first group session and his fear to return stemmed from his fear of being beaten down and criticized, as he had been in his father's family. When this did not occur and the leader evinced his interest in Mr. Salkin through the letter, i.e., showed that he *wanted* him, a new pattern of human relations was revealed to him in the group; he felt secure and became accessible to the group influence. There was considerable improvement in the relationship between Mr. Salkin and Harris, since the former attended the fathers' guidance group. The mother was exceedingly pleased with this. For her it was as if "he had grown up overnight to be a father," as she once expressed it. In the past she had frequently talked about her husband being like a child, and "a greater problem" to her than her boys. Now the total relationship within the home has greatly improved; the atmosphere was more relaxed, she said.

Mrs. Salkin, too, seemed to have benefited greatly from her group experience. She had acquired further insights and modified her attitudes. Considering her own family background, which was very difficult, her own dependency needs appeared to be still unmet, but her ego strength had been greatly increased.

In an interview with the follow-up caseworker, Mrs. Salkin stated that Harris and his father had been getting along well. Things seemed to be going better between them and Harris had even once told her: "You know, Mother, Daddy seems to be much nicer to me these days." Mrs. Salkin then added that she, too, had observed improvement in her husband. Instead of being physically punitive with the boy, the father now used verbal means to control the child. Somewhat sadly, she said, she guessed that it would take a long time to work things out, but that she did see improvement. She related that after his first group session he had been adamant against going again. He now liked it, but spoke little about it to her.

The improvement in the relation between the husband and wife continued. The highly destructive emotional backgrounds of the two prevented their being very close to one another, but the channels of communication between them had been opened up. Mr. Salkin and his wife exchanged opinions and discussed their children which they were unable to do before. The total relation sustained considerable improvement, according to Mrs. Salkin's report in later follow-up interviews.

Another type of change in the relationship of parents is illustrated by the Wolmans. The family consisted, in addition to the parents, of three boys.

Carl was referred for treatment at age nine through the father's analyst because of "difficulty in managing him at school and at home," seemingly fighting against all rules and regulations. The school described him as "a nonconformist." In relation to the mother, he was provocative; he teased her until she lost control of herself and would yell and scream at him "almost hysterically." As a child he had sucked his thumb. Masturbation had increased during the few months prior to referral for treatment. He had been enuretic between the ages of three and a half and eight years.

Mr. Wolman did not want children. The mother planfully neglected to use contraceptives, and Carl was conceived. When the father learned of this he was "furious." There were feeding difficulties, the boy sucked his thumb and held on to his blankets. She overprotected and infantilized the child and fed him baby foods until he was well within latency.

Mrs. Wolman was the oldest of three children, having a sister four years and a brother ten years younger than herself. There was conflict and constant friction between the maternal grandparents. The maternal grandfather apparently had had an affair with another woman. When Mrs. Wolman was fifteen years old, her mother had a "nervous breakdown" which led to her attempting suicide. She was committed to a mental institution for two years.

Mr. Wolman was the dominant parent. He rejected Carl from the moment of his conception and made it obvious to the mother and to Carl that he was not interested in the boy and that the total responsibility for him would have to be borne by her. He has been openly hostile to the boy throughout and at the same time constantly criticized his wife for her emotional involvement with her son. Prior to treatment the mother attempted to deal with Carl by herself and hoped that his negative behavior would not come to the attention of the father and add further friction and tension to the marital relation. When interviewed at intake, she displayed strong feelings of inadequacy, worthlessness and a weak self-image as a person, wife and mother.

After fifteen sessions in a guidance group, Mrs. Wolman changed. She began to deal with her children in a more mature and more appropriate manner. In addition, her former submissiveness to her husband was diminishing which reflected her increased feelings of self-adequacy. She no longer passively accepted her husband's constant criticism of her handling of Carl and of her general demeanor. Instead, she faced him with the fact that he had joint responsibility in the upbringing of their son and pointed out to him that his neglect of his responsibilities toward the children was damaging to them. In a particularly violent quarrel, Mrs. Wolman told her husband that she was willing to bring up her children, but definitely refused to cater to him as though he were a baby and if he continued in his ways she would leave him. She was not going, she said, to solve Carl's problems alone. He would have to take a part. Her unaccustomed assertiveness created a panic in Mr. Wolman. But the consistency of her changed attitude and her refusal to discharge both paternal and maternal functions brought home to Mr. Wolman the inevitability of the need to alter his own role in the family group.

Despite the temporary tension between husband and wife, a new relation emerged between the two that had salutary effects upon the family atmosphere and the children in it.

At the follow-up interview with Mrs. Wolman, she recognized that one could make up for the past and that she actually was not as strong and reliable as she thought she had been even though she attempted to create that impression. She knew that her husband still put considerable responsibility on her in relation to the care and guidance of the children. However, there had been considerable improvement in his attitude toward her. He no longer stayed away from home evenings, as he had in the past, but remained in the house. The two frequently had rather pleasant conversations concerning matters outside of as well as in the home. In the past he had hardly ever talked about anything and when he had not gone out— a rare occurrence—he had remained silent and withdrawn. She recognized now that she should not prod him and demand that he act in a more outgoing manner because he may be preoccupied with "what is going on in his analysis." In the past, when he kept quiet and was withdrawn, she had considered it as anger and displeasure with her. Now she understood that he must be preoccupied with many things. The relationship between her husband and herself had been greatly improved and she felt much happier about it, she said.

At one of the group sessions Mrs. Kling elaborated on how fathers could make things difficult for their children. Her husband had been greatly deprived as a child, had had little education and had worked very hard to make a good living. He therefore could not understand why his children should not put forth some effort to earn at least their personal expenses. He told their son that he could leave school if he wished, but if he continued, he would have to earn enough at least for his clothes. Her husband said he would provide him with food and shelter, but if he really wanted an education he would have to help himself a little.

Mrs. Kling could see that her husband was partly right, but on the other hand her son had also been working very hard. In fact, he worked so hard, that he lost interest in school. But she could accept her husband's disapproval of the boy's using the money he earned not for his personal expenses but for taking girls out. She then narrated how she sat down with her son one evening when no one else was around and explained to him the reason for the father's complaints. Her boy was very unhappy, she said, and had complained to her about his father, but she told him that he should try to understand the father's position: he worked very hard and could not really afford all that the boy was demanding. Mrs. Kling felt that if she had not intervened, her boy, past sixteen years of age, might really have left home as he threatened to do as a result of the conflict with his father.

VIII

Pitfalls

To be able to keep the discussion at the group sessions within boundaries of the operational level and prevent its overflowing into the psychodynamic sphere requires skill, a high degree of alertness and the capacity to anticipate a line of inquiry that may emerge from a move on the part of the leader. A reaction or response to a remark or a question from a group member detonates a chain reaction of associative ideas, feelings, and thoughts. This may lead the conversation into useful channels, divert it from its desirable course or, even worse, may generate guilt and anxiety among the participants which would defeat the entire effort.

Another skill required is the ability to arrest or divert a trend in the interchange among the group members which, according to the leader's judgment, may take the group along unfruitful, undesirable or even destructive paths, but this he must do without seeming arbitrary or authoritarian. It has already been pointed out that the effectiveness of our technique depends almost exclusively on the primary group code, or the understanding the members have as to what their aim is and what their own role should be. Unsuitable demeanor by the leader generates misunderstanding, and errors on his part may undermine the values of the group deliberations and even threaten the group's existence. It is his behavior, role and responses that set the atmosphere for easy communication, free interaction and mutual benefit. If he assumes an authoritarian role and a didactic manner, the reaction to him, as we shall see in a further discussion of this subject, vitiates the intent of

Child-Centered Group Guidance. The results are especially poor when the members of a group become guilty and anxious.

Parents in these groups continually expose leaders to the temptation of embarking on theoretic and intellectual discussions and to explore and analyze anxiety-laden topics. This the leader must avoid. To recognize these digressions and successfully avoid pursuing them without arousing suspicion or resentment, is a skill that has to be acquired through training by someone who has had experience with this technique.

In this chapter we shall present several instances where leaders have been trapped either by the group members or by their own lack of prescience that could have had or actually had undesirable outcomes. We take the following from a guidance group of fathers:

Mr. Ginn, with a note of complaint in his voice, said that his son Sheldon had been "confirmed" this fall. Since then he had become even more independent and wanted his own way. He "listens" to (obeys) his parents even less than he used to. The leader asked Mr. Ginn what being confirmed meant to his son. Before Mr. Ginn could answer, Mr. Fine commented that it meant the boy "became a man." Mr. Ginn appeared to shake off this interpretation and said that it meant that the boy "has to respect his parents even more." Mr. Kent made the point that, on the contrary, the child should probably be more independent after his confirmation. Mr. Ginn, however, stubbornly held to his thesis that the boy should be more "obedient" to his parents and recalled that even his teacher had told Sheldon he should "listen" to his parents and have "respect" for them.

At this point, the leader asked the group what respect was and how a child learned to respect others. Mr. Ginn defined respect as "obedience," adding that a child learned respect by seeing the parents "listen to and respect one another." (Mr. Ginn's wife was a powerful, domineering woman.) Mr. Berk joined the discussion at this point, stating in a somewhat intellectual, though sincere, manner that perhaps there was another aspect to it. "What of parents showing respect for the child?" he asked. He continued by saying that at times he had been guilty of disrespect toward his son and become cross or impatient with the boy. He illustrated this by recalling that recently he had very impatiently and crossly ordered his son to shine his (the boy's) shoes, whereas it would probably have been much more respectful to the boy if he had said in a calm way that a shoe shine helped preserve the leather. Mr. Day said that as he saw it, respect was "the boy's wanting to be like and emulate his father." Mr. Jasper added that perhaps that was admiration rather than respect.

There followed several other interpretations of respect, most of which hovered in the area of obedience. The leader then remarked that he thought a little story might be helpful in defining the idea of respect and related an incident in which a child was allowed to make his own decision. The group seemed impressed by this. Mr. Bernard appeared quite thoughtful at this point and described the story as "very pertinent." Mr. Ginn nodded his head approvingly and then with some eagerness hurried to tell the worker that that was exactly what his wife (who was a member of a guidance group) had done with their boy. She told him that he could make up his own mind about the matter; and the boy did.

Mr. Kent recalled that the leader had once said that in matters where the health of the child was concerned, the parents had to make the decision and narrated that recently his son who had just had a shower wanted to go outdoors immediately thereafter. He had a cold at the time and so Mr. Kent kept him from going out and asked if that was right. The leader said yes, the father was right provided that the child was also given the right to be mad for not being able to go out. The group seemed surprised at this and a pause ensued. Mr. Bernard asked for a clarification. The leader responded with the brief comment that just as we adults had the right to have at times angry feelings, so did children, too. Generally we as adults allowed them to express only the feelings which we considered good, such as affection and kindness, and squelched the "bad" feelings in them. Mr. Bernard said he had never thought of that part of the matter.

This passage illustrates how the leader fell into the error of initiating a purely theoretic dissertation on respect, rather than encouraging Mr. Ginn to narrate specific instances of his son's "disobedience and lack of respect," which might have helped him recognize on his own the impropriety of his values and the unreality of his expectations. We have already seen in previous illustrations how clarity and change of values occur when a situation is mulled over, as it were, by a number of participants. Clarity emerges from free discussion of a *specific* topic or event common to the experience of all. Here we have instead an abstract analysis with considerable semantic confusion and differences of opinion stemming largely from varied personal backgrounds. In these groups exploration of a concept detached from an event can never be as helpful as the analysis of an actual situation.

Once the trend in this direction was started, the leader was forced by Mr. Kent to go deeper into the morrass of ideation. Here a rather difficult concept is presented to a group of uninitiated men that a parent has a right to inhibit his child but owes the latter the privilege to be angry. Understandably the fathers were stumped by this. First to recover from the shock was Mr. Bernard (a man who held a doctorate in the physical sciences). This forces the leader to go into an explanation which without doubt must have appeared to the men as esoteric or remained at least incomprehensible. The leader has allowed himself to fall into the role of teacher and borrowed a page from classroom instruction which is inappropriate in our method. This does not mean that on occasion the leader cannot clarify some misconceptions in the minds of the group members. Discussion of abstract subjects have to be resorted to very seldom, however, in order that the primary group code of investigating empirical situations in the child's life rather than theory and philosophy be firmly impressed upon the participants. Another disadvantage in failing to keep the group to this line is that the parents would escape into theory and sophistry out of their own anxiety that may arise from confronting their family problems and their own part in them.

The following is another example of inappropriate dealing with a situation because the leader permitted himself to become involved in a conversation that aroused anxiety.

Mrs. Ross questioned with some concern the right of children to make decisions on their own, and cited as proof that there were certain things she did not feel children had a right to decide for themselves. She said that there were times when children had to go to a doctor for some reason or another, and she did not feel a child could make his own decision in this. The other mothers were inclined to agree with her and remarked that there were certain things children did not like to do though they were necessary.

The leader agreed with the women and went on to say that even in such areas as taking a child to a doctor when he was opposed to it, we still had to recognize that children feared and were apprehensive about such experiences, and if we recognized this with our children, it would help in achieving what we were after.

At this point Mrs. Ross began to relate some of her son's fears and referred specifically to radio and TV programs in which persons died or were killed. She commented that earlier that week, on hearing one such program, her son Howard had said that such programs were not good for him. That was one of the first times that Howard had openly said anything to either parent regarding his fears. She had no idea why he had done so now. When she questioned him about this fear, he said that he was afraid that he might sometimes lose his parents. Mrs. Ross commented that she was quite overwhelmed at the depth of feeling that even a young child could have; she had not realized that children ever thought of such things, especially since her older daughter did not seem to be as sensitive about such matters. Mrs. Bernheim questioned Mrs. Ross as to how she knew her daughter was not sensitive to the very same things that her son was. Mrs. Ross said that she was basing it on the fact that her daughter had never shown fears of death and she did not feel that her daughter ever had any such fears. Mrs. Bernheim doubted this. When questioned by the leader, she went on to explain that she felt that all children were concerned about death and the loss of their parents some time or another; that despite the fact that Mrs. Ross's daughter did not display such fears, it did not mean that she was free of them.

Mrs. Ross asked why the children were different in this respect and Mrs. Bernheim wondered how old the children were when Mr.

Ross had become ill. Mrs. Ross said that her husband had become (chronically) ill shortly after Howard's birth when her daughter was about five or six years of age. Mrs. Bernheim suggested that in view of this Howard had been surrounded by illness most of his life. Thoughts of possible death of his father were part of him, which his sister had not experienced. She was, therefore, not as fearful of death as her brother.

Mrs. Charles agreed that children responded pretty much to the experiences to which they had been subjected and that one child may respond differently than another to the same situation. She went on to say that the ideas that children had about matters frequently fashioned their thoughts and reactions. She cited her daughter who frequently became upset when she observed Mrs. Charles and her husband having a quarrel. The girl feared that her parents would get a divorce, an idea the girl had gotten from overhearing a conversation about divorce by parents of a friend of hers. Thus quarreling and divorce became synonymous to her and it was necessary for the mother to explain to the girl that this was not the case; parents did quarrel with one another without it resulting in a divorce. Mrs. Ross again registered amazement at the "depths of a child's feelings" and the confusions of their ideas. She spoke as though she had never realized that children reacted to situations so seriously and with feeling.

The leader wondered what the women thought the child's concerns were with regard to death or divorce of parents. Mrs. Bernheim and Mrs. Charles thought that a child may be concerned about being left alone and have fears as to what would happen to him since he was so small and helpless. The leader agreed with this, commenting further that children sometimes felt that it was their fault if the parents became ill, died, quarreled or were divorced. This frightened them a great deal; and when these situations did occur and such feelings were expressed it was necessary to help the child to understand that he was not responsible for them and was not to blame. The mothers present nodded their heads in agreement.

Mrs. Ross then asked how one explained death to a child, relating that her son once had asked about death and what happened to a person when he died. The mothers had difficulty in handling this. Mrs. Bernheim and Mrs. Charles said that their children had just grown to accept this and even though they were aware that the children thought about death they tended to treat the question casually. Mrs. Charles prepared her daughters for the eventual death of their pet fish and turtles by emphasizing that they were pretty old and may pass away soon. She stressed the naturalness of it. Her children seemed to accept this quite easily and from time to time commented that a fish or a turtle looked as if it was getting very old and would soon die.

The leader cautioned against lengthy discussions with children around death and its meaning and spoke of it as being a long rest from which people who were very, very tired never got up, and they just rested forever. The leader said that frequently the questions around death concerned the child in that they were fearful of pain and the uncertainty as to what might happen. Mrs. Ross commented that this seemed to be a very nice way of telling a child about death. She felt that perhaps it might be acceptable to Howard, too, when the question arose again.

At the end of the session Mrs. Ross commented that she had been getting more help at these meetings with the handling of her children than she had ever gotten in individual treatment. Of course, she said, she had never wanted to come in for her individual appointments, but she looked forward to the group meetings eagerly (see Chapter X).

Because the leader, a male in this instance, makes the mistake of acquiescing in the idea that a child should not make a decision whether or not he is to go to a doctor, he set off the women to talk about death, fear of death and the children's anxieties around the subject. The apparent naturalness of the conversation caused the leader to fall into the trap. In encouraging this content for the group's discussion the leader led the women to analyze their children's feelings and at the same time activate their own anxieties. Witness, for example, Mrs. Ross's feeling of relief after the discussion which she verbalizes at the end of the session. This, however, will not help her in meeting the situation in her family.

The discussion did not settle anything for them, nor did they get a satisfactory or workable method of handling the children's pre-occupations. In fact the advice given them that death be explained as a prolonged rest is entirely unsuitable, for it is not true.

Another area of children's fear, divorce, is brought out. Here again little constructive guidance can be given the members because of its emotional components. The question cannot be discussed in a guidance group without activating anxiety which would have to be dealt with therapeutically.

Had the leader asked Mrs. Ross to describe a specific conflict about going to a doctor, it would have been possible to suggest ways of preparing a child for the ordeal instead of arbitrarily telling him as she did a few minutes before the visit that she was taking him to see a physician. Adequate preparation a day or two in advance and an explanation of the reason for the visit, and what would transpire there, eliminates anticipatory fear. With little children role playing of doctor and patient between the mother and child has the same effect. Through this stratagem the leader would have made the session of permanent value to the mothers in their future dealings with the children. It would, in addition, prevent raising the question of death.

The matter of children's attitudes toward divorce was entirely gratuitous. Mrs. Charles was fully aware of this judging by her analysis of her daughter's fears and one could expect that as she became freer and less guilty through the help of the group, she would have evaded violent conflicts with her husband in the presence of children.

At one of the early sessions Mrs. Salkin (5)[1] stated that her son Harris behaved in a "vicious way." He had teased and provoked her, giggled, pushed her around, pulled at her skirt and made a face at her, finally accusing her of not loving him. As this continued for a prolonged period of time the mother finally lost her temper and struck the boy. A discussion ensued as to the validity of beating children during which the leader stated that sometimes it was permissible to strike a child when he became hilarious and was unable to bring himself under control. The leader expressed the opinion that the child under such circumstances would in fact feel grateful

1 For the meaning of the numbers, see Chapter V.

to the parent for helping him gain control of himself. Mrs. Salkin's face assumed an expression of surprise, though she verbally stated that it made sense to her. The mothers in the group reacted variously to this. Mrs. Friedman (2) said she was glad to discover that it was permissible to beat a child. Though she now seldom strikes Morris, she never strikes him when she is angry. Her need to strike him has decreased. She talks to him instead.

Mrs. Cross's (6) reaction was that, though she and her husband used to beat Sol all the time, she never touched him physically any more. She thought that it was wrong to strike a child, and she felt badly because of the lashings they had administered to him in the past. Mrs. James (3) averred that a child must know that at times he could not have what he wanted and a mother might have to use force to impress him with the fact. She found that sometimes she had to strike her children. Mrs. Kling (4) agreed with Mrs. James. "Children have to be hit sometimes," she said with emphasis. Mrs. Salkin (5), who introduced the subject said that she felt very guilty about it because it gave Harris a strong feeling of inferiority, especially when she punished or scolded him, but at the time referred to she felt that he was acting in a disrespectful way and she could not lose her "status" by allowing it to go on.

The leader had fallen into a trap here by approving beating of children which is never necessary, unless there has been an accumulation of errors on the part of the parents in the treatment of the child as a result of which the parent had lost status and control. Under such conditions he employs physical force as a last resort mostly because of feelings of impotence and guilt. To countenance physical beatings on the part of a leader in these groups who occupies the position of authority on such matters is a grave error. It plays into the parents' negative needs and removes conflict or guilt that may exist against a practice that at first frightens the child and later brutalizes him. In fact, the leader's statement aroused conflict in some of the mothers present and even surprised Mrs. Salkin. It certainly did not convince her. The leader's error is even graver when later in the discussion which is described below she stated that she recognized in Harris's behavior the fact that he was "in a state of sexual excitation." If this were the case, which was probably true, a beating was certainly not appropriate. This is one way in which sexual and psychological masochism is encouraged.

At one of the sessions Mrs. Cross (6) mentioned in discussing a situation of Mrs. Friedman's (2) son, that he may have been sexually aroused. Her point was that a boy might have sexual feelings because he was on the way of becoming a man. In response to this the leader made the error of saying in relation to Mrs. Salkin's boy that it was possible that he had such feelings though he was ten years old. Judging by the way he played with Mrs. Salkin, the leader said, Harris might have been sexually stimulated. Mrs. Salkin (5) responded by saying "the suggestion was interesting." She had not frustrated him at the time nor could she think of any other reason for his strange behavior. That must have been it, she said. She could not find any other reason.

Mrs. Friedman (2) reacted to this also by saying that the idea was "an interesting one," but what she would like to have the group do for her was to help her figure out how to get her son to attend the "club" (therapy group) of which he was a member. Apparently, Mrs. Friedman (2) became anxious, for the discussion touched closely on her difficulty, which we shall see presently, and diverted the stream of the conversation.

However, despite the almost instinctive avoidance by the group members of this topic, the leader fell into the error of initiating again a discussion around this sensitive area at one of the early sessions of the group. It occurred in the following manner as decribed in the report of that session from which an abstract is here reproduced:

I came back to Mrs. James's (3) point around the fact that Stanley when he was seven and one-half years old wanted the privacy of his bath. I wondered what that really meant in a child's development. Mrs. James said she could not understand why he should be bashful when up to then she had handled him as if he were just a little son of hers; a child of hers, she added. She is quite certain that Stanley considered himself until then as a boy and saw his mother as a mother. He never saw her in the nude. Mrs. Salkin (5) said that she did not know why at seven and a half and some children even younger should become self-conscious. Here she referred to her little six-year-old who does not want mother in the bathroom any more; and she does not insist. She developed the point that maybe Stanley at that age had begun to feel the difference between male and female and saw his mother as a woman and not just as a mother.

Mrs. James's (3) attitude changed a bit. She became more relaxed, smiled, and said she had a "little funny feeling" about it but maybe that would give her the answer to her difficulties with Stanley. For instance, this morning, he went into her bed for five minutes, under the blanket, just curled up next to her. She considered this babyish, thought it was cute, did nothing about it, giggled with him and then he ran away and got dressed. He does this every now and then but she considers this as only the baby in him. Mrs. Friedman (2) said that Morris sometimes kissed her on the lips as if he were a man and she often used to get upset about this, feeling that he was overly stimulated. She knows now, since our last discussion, that actually he is seeing mother as a woman and she should not permit such kissing. Mrs. Salkin (5) then talked more about her six-year-old as well as about Harris, who is not yet ten, and who also gets sexually stimulated. She described how the other day she was dressed up to go out with her husband and Harris said that he could make "whoopee" with her the way she looked just then; she thanked him for the compliment. At that moment she did not see him as a nine-year-old boy but as a nine-year-old boy with sexual alertness, but was not upset as she might have been before.

Mrs. Cross (6), with a family of two boys and a girl, now described how her girl ran into her father's bed and the boys ran into her bed. They never thought anything of it. They still do not, but she is now thinking more about the meaning of getting into bed with mother, especially with her twelve-year-old boy. Her difficulty is figuring out how not to continue to permit this without hurting their feelings. Mrs. Cross said that when they did this she considered them little children, much younger than their age. She cannot recall feeling, as Mrs. Friedman had said, upset about it. Mrs. Friedman said she really felt stimulated by her son's kisses as if her husband were kissing her on the lips.

Mrs. Kling (4), who had come late and who was quiet for a while, talked up at this point about the importance of not encouraging body contact with a boy that age. For her part, she does everything possible not to expose herself in any way before the boys, but her problem is helping the oldest, especially, to "cover up." Sometimes she thinks because she has a household of boys that they have much more freedom, but she is not stimulated by them. She tries to talk to them nicely, e.g., what would happen if a friend came in and what they would think of her if she permitted this. It has been better this winter.

There was a pause here and the leader took the opportunity to talk briefly about how confusing it can be for a mother to observe her child growing independent in one area and still remaining dependent on her for other things. Especially is it so in the sexual area where a boy like Stanley or Morris (mentioning the other children who are ten, eleven and twelve years old), who are rapidly growing up sexually and are stimulated by mother as a woman, actually the first woman the boy-child reacts to. Here she stated that the child's sexual development starts way back at mother's breast and certainly at the age of four or five when it begins to see mother as a parent of the opposite sex. Mrs. Kling (4) smiled and said the women teachers also stimulated the boys. The boys come home talking about what the teacher wore, how she smiled at them, etc. She wished teachers were like mothers who would understand the children. Mrs. Friedman (2) and Mrs. Ash (1) said: "Well, we can't expect so much from teachers. After all, they have too many children." Mrs. Ash wished that her boy had a better teacher altogether, but then teachers need special training. Mrs. Kling persisted in talking about how the teachers should be trained to understand not only how to teach but how to handle growing boys. She said that Jacob's teacher last year had been very understanding but that it was difficult for him this year.

The leader felt that the group ought to bring the discussion back to the uneven growth in the latency period, the topic initiated by Mrs. James. She suggested that possibly night wetting was an indication that the child was sexually stimulated and might be a way out of tension. Mrs. Kling (4) talked about the erections that her boys had and that this could even happen at the age of six years. Mrs. Salkin (5) concurred, describing her little six-year-old. She does not know why she did not observe Harris, her older boy, with an erection, but maybe he covered it up. She referred to his past masturbation which he did in hiding so she would not know. She is more at ease now so that maybe the six-year-old gives himself privileges and therefore she could observe his reaction. Mrs. James (3) was puzzled. Referring to Stanley's enuresis, she wondered whether it could be that Stanley was trying to have an erection and a night emission and that it wasn't as if he were an infant who couldn't get up in the night to go to the bathroom. "You mean, it was not just urination?" she asked with great emphasis.

Mrs. Ash (1) talked about her four-year-old who has erections and she always considered it rather cute but did not recognize this in terms of sexual stimulation. She wanted to know more about what an infant knew about sexual strivings. Mrs. Salkin (5) then talked about how "they just feel like you feel hungry, you feel something sexual around the genital area." Mrs. James (3) smiled and blushed. She asked: "Does that mean that a little boy of four wants to have intercourse with his mother?" Mrs. Ash said, "Maybe it is like being an animal. After all, animals do have feelings about sex and they do have intercourse at any time they have such an urge regardless of age."

There was more talk among the women about how their boys made them blush. Mrs. Cross's (6) younger boy of ten hugs her as if he were a lover, but then she has always attributed this kind of behavior to the movies and TV. The other day, Sol told her that she looked "ravenously beautiful" and she blushed. She did not know why, but she sees now that he stimulated her. At times, her husband says this to her and she feels very pleased, but she did not have the same feeling when Sol said it. Mrs. Salkin (5) said Harris wanted her at the TV at times, just to hold hands with her. She wonders if this is good; whether she would be playing into his sexual strivings if she held hands. Mrs. Friedman (2) described how when Morris saw a seminude woman on TV, he came over to see her, and asked her to stand in a certain position so that she could look the way the girl on TV did. She told him that he was crazy, that she was no actress. He said, "But you have a bosom like this girl." (She blushed even as she was talking.) Mrs. Kling (4) said that her husband sometimes was right. For instance, she hugged her little boy (who is nine years old) the other day and held him tight. It was for something he did that she thought was "sweet." Her husband later told her it was wrong because it was stimulating him sexually. She then referred to her big bosom which certainly could have easily affected him.

Mrs. James (3) said she wondered if it was good for Stanley to kiss his older brother. The older brother does not like it, but Stanley continually runs up and kisses him when he comes home "as if he was a woman." She remarked that this was one of the most valuable sessions of all that she has attended. What she got from this is how you can be mixed up with a growing child. She can now understand better some of Stanley's behavior as being part of the sexual development which she has not been aware of before. She treated him as an infant and not like a growing boy who has other urges. "You can count on me to come regularly now," she added. (She had explained earlier that she had to be absent because of her husband's illness.)

This discussion was continued in the next session two weeks later, *at the leader's behest*. We read in the record:

After a pause, Mrs. James (3) was the first to speak. (It is to be noted that she now feels comfortable and secure enough to do so and is now friendly with the women in a way she had not been before.) She remarked that she had observed in the last few days that when she and her husband kissed in Stanley's presence, he smiled, looked coy, and she could see the blush on his face. She noted that the preceding evening when her oldest son and daughter-in-law were visiting for supper and they kissed each other, Stanley reacted in the same way. She remarked that he blushed very much like she did, but she did not know why he should smile almost as if he were embarrassed. "Why should he be embarrassed? He is not doing the kissing," she added.

Mrs. Salkin (5) remarked that her boy, too, used to be that way but she thought it was because he was aware of sex—that affection to him was sexually stimulating. She also wondered why it should stimulate him. It would be different if he were kissing her or another woman, but he was not. It was she and her husband that were kissing. Like Mrs. James, she said, they just do not go around kissing each other, but when her husband comes home or sometimes during the evening there is an occasion when they kiss each other not being aware that the children are about. Mrs. Cross (6) remarked that it was possible that the boys felt ashamed because it was as if they were doing the kissing. They like it; she is sure Sol would like to kiss her on the lips the way her husband does, but maybe he knows he should not. The leader picked this up and said, "You mean that the boy feels he is kissing mother as if he were her husband?" All agreed to this and said it had not occurred to them that this was probably what made a boy like Stanley ashamed, blush and turn away.

Mrs. Salkin (5) said, "This is what we mean by the Oedipus, don't we? A boy wants his mother the way his father does." Mrs. James (3) said she did not understand this language. What did it mean? Mrs. Salkin responded by saying that Stanley really wanted to kiss his mother the way her husband was kissing her. Mrs. James said she could not understand how a little boy like that should want to be her husband. Mrs. Cross reacted to this by saying that this was something she had learned, namely that just because a child did not speak of his feelings, it did not mean that he did not have them. He has feelings like his father, but does not know it; that's the thing. He only knows he would like to be in the position of the father. She wouldn't know whether you call it Oedipus or not, but that's what it evidently is.

Mrs. James (3) came back with more questions and seemed very pleased with the discussion. She remarked she did not remember observing this behavior in her older boy and she could not imagine that little boys wanted to be like fathers, but maybe that was so. She would not be the one to know. She can now recall though how he would kiss his brother as if one of them was a girl, she cannot tell which. Sometimes Stanley for no good reason would kiss his brother in the back of the neck, sometimes just on the forehead. Some-times if the brother gets mad at Stanley, the latter will try to make up to him by kissing him even on the hand, like a little dog wanting his master's love, but she can only see that as an expression of a child who wants to be forgiven. That it should be sexual did not occur to her, but maybe that is what it is.

The leader mentioned that the matter of sex was not some-thing we observed only at this time. It gets started even at the breast, pointing to the fact how little children in the mother's lap when comfortable with the bottle or at the breast will begin to play with their penis or ears or go through some other activity, which is sexual in nature although it does not mean the child wants sexual intercourse. (The latter was stressed because of what Mrs. James had mentioned earlier in relation to the child wanting intercourse.)

Mrs. Salkin (5) then talked about how she recalled Harris pull-ing at his ear. After that, he began pulling at his penis and she sometimes used to take his hand away. She is glad she did not slap him, because she knows one woman who made her child very nervous because of it. It gives the children a feeling there is something wrong with what they are doing. Somehow, for her, thumb sucking was worse. She used to pull his thumb out of his mouth. When he got through sucking the bottle, he always wanted his thumb. She wished she had been smart then. It possibly meant he wanted more food and she did not give it to him, because the doctor had said this was as much as he should get and no more.

Mrs. James (3) said she always kept the children's diapers on them, but she must admit now she used to take their hands away, sometimes even slap their hands. She does not know if Stanley masturbates or not; she never noticed it. Maybe he does under the bedcovers, but she does not think she would be worried about it, unless it was done to a great degree.

Mrs. James said she has not yet really figured out how she was going to begin to change things for herself and Stanley. She knows now, however, that she has been considering him a baby and for that reason he acted like one. She must be the one to change, but how could she do this now and fast. Mrs. Salkin (5) said she should start with not kissing Stanley so much. She gave an example of her own situation, how she used to hug and kiss her kids even when they did not want it. Mrs. Cross (6) then recalled what had been said the session before about body contact disturbing a boy. It would be better if Mrs. Salkin just did not initiate kissing but just sort of patted the boy good night and then gradually stopped the patting too. Mrs. James (3) smiled and said, then she really should not even kiss the boy in between times. She did so, not only when he left for school and came back, but invariably just when she felt like having him near her. She then talked very volubly about how because there is a seven-year difference between Stanley and the older child, all of them babied him; she particularly. She did too much for him but loved it. He's her baby. "Ah," Mrs. Salkin (5) said, "you see, you let it slip. You still think of him as a baby." Mrs. James thanked the others very profusely and said she was going to change tonight—even if it hurt—and she would report on developments next time.

Despite the undesirable nature of the discussion, some benefits have accrued from it because it related to immediate, everyday affairs. This we learn from the conversation at the next session:

Mrs. Friedman (2) giggled and said that her boy had grown so independent that he now had a job after school which he started during the holiday week. He did deliveries. Previously she would have been horrified to think that her boy was running up and down stairs and earning a few pennies that way. Now she feels that it is good for him. When the leader wondered what she meant by "good," she said he was beginning to show in other ways as well that he was assuming responsibilities in a manner she would never have thought possible. Smiling rather sheepishly, she added, he even stopped wetting many days during the week. She explained that she must have been really "on his neck" all these years. He was ready to grow up long ago, only she held on, she was not sure he could make it. She now sees how her boy made good use of even the little freedom she gave him. "It's confidence," she smiled to Mrs. Cross who had discussed this subject in a previous session.

Mrs. Salkin (5), after a pause, said she'd like very much to know how Mrs. James worked out what she was going to do following our last meeting. Mrs. James (3), with much animation, said she had done her "homework" and it was already showing good results. She kissed her boy only once in the intervening two weeks and that was one day when he was going off to school and asked for it. For her, she thinks, this has been the most important change in her relationship to Stanley and vice versa. He didn't wet his bed for two days, "And that is unbelievable, but then he went back and wet again." She is very hopeful that this situation will change. To the leader's question what she thought was changing, Mrs. James said she thought what she had done to him was to keep him an infant and "mix him up." She developed the point that he was mixed up in not knowing whether he should be grown up or remain little and she made demands on him without realizing that she had been confusing him. She knows better now what we have been saying about the mothers' responsibility in helping a child grow. This is it. She has still far to go. She needs to learn more. She turned to the leader and said, "Is it all right for me to go on kissing my husband good night or good morning, whatever, without kissing Stanley?"

After a pause, Mrs. Salkin (5) said children had to know that the relationship between father and mother was one thing and the relationship between mother and son another. She therefore recommended that Mrs. James go on kissing her husband the way she did and she was sure that Stanley would not be jealous. Mrs. James (3) laughed briefly and said she must describe how Stanley and she kissed each other constantly and how her husband used to ridicule what went on between them. She and her boy were playing kissing games the way Mrs. Cross was playing geography games with her boy when the latter wanted mother around bedtime. Mrs. Ash (1) said that she had given real, serious thought to this business of kissing her boys and she was not as "vociferous" now as she had been; just a peck was enough when she tucked them in and here she described tucking in particularly of one of her boys who asked her to do it.

Mrs. Salkin (5) said that sounded as if she were babying him, tucking him in like an infant. Mrs. Ash said, "Well, I thought of that, too, and that's what I wanted to figure out, when to stop that tucking in." Mrs. James (3) suggested she stop right now; it had been going on too long already. However, she wondered if there was any jealousy between the Ash boy and his brother because if his brother got tucked in, maybe the other wanted it too. Mrs. Ash said yes, the competition between them was so keen that she would not want to stop unless she was sure it was good for the boy.

Mrs. Salkin (5) turned to Mrs. Ash to tell her that she could talk to her son and tell him that he was a grown boy and that tucking in was something for a little boy and maybe he would understand that she respected him and loved him without tucking him in. She then gave a description of her own way of handling her boy. Mrs. James (3) said the mothers never knew how much "to give" their boys. Here she gave her boy, she thought, so much love and expected better results, but instead it had the opposite effect. As to the Ash boy, she said, he had less and so he too was not developing. She turned to Mrs. Cross and asked what she did. Mrs. Cross (6) said that for her the problem of demonstrating love was not of great concern because she did not express it by kissing. For her it was a question of helping her boys to achieve, but she must admit that she did find it hard to convey to Sol that she loved him because she had been so critical of him, but less so with the younger one. In her case less criticism meant greater love to him.

Mrs. Friedman (2) smiled and added that she used to make a ritual of kissing her boy at bedtime, but stopped it when we first began talking about reducing physical contact. However, her husband took over the kissing ritual instead and that too has recently stopped. This was better for all of them. She, however, explained to Morris that she would stop. Mrs. Salkin (5) described how she had moved slowly from having been very close with Harris, even getting into bed with him at his request until he would fall asleep, to holding his hand, then gradually only tucking him in and giving him a kiss. Now it is just a good-by wave which is acceptable to everyone concerned. Mrs. Ash (1) giggled and said she used to go to bed with her older boy before she came to the group. Now she is at the point of only tucking him in so she thinks she is just one step behind Mrs. Salkin. Everyone laughed.

Enlightening parents on "sex education" and alerting them to the pitfalls in their relations with their children in this area is one of the aims of Child-Centered Group Guidance, but this must be done without engendering confusion, guilt or anxiety. The results obtained through the discussion summarized above could have been achieved through direct suggestions from the leader or a directed group discussion without mentioning sexual feelings and reactions. The awareness of the boys' sexual (genital) intent toward their mothers and of the latters' libidinized responses to their sons cannot but seriously damage parent-child relations of the ordinary unenlightened parents. The self-consciousness and guilt-evoking behavior on their part will be the cause of tension and discomfort between them and their children in the future. The rapidity with which the women took steps to correct their behavior with their sons may be an indication of guilt which they sought to allay. Had the therapist stuck to exploring actual behavior and suggesting the methods of changing the relations without entering into the catacombs of human sexuality, much anxiety would have been prevented. Some of the mothers would have remained unaware of their sexual feelings toward their boys, the recognition of which must have been a great threat to these rather uneducated and culturally unenlightened women, and their aroused self-consciousness vitiated their relations with their sons.

Other group leaders, including myself, have dealt with such questions in the manner suggested. A direct statement made quietly and objectively that children reach a stage in their development at which physical contact with them should be as sparing as possible or given up altogether, seemed to suffice. Apparently, the parents' own unconscious doubts and guilts in this regard needed only reinforcement by the leader (authority) without plumbing the depths of incestuous trends.

Mrs. Friedman, for example, evaded her own guilt feelings by introducing a rather dangerous situation: she reported that her husband took over the routine of kissing the boy instead of her—which may have represented a possible homoerotic act, or a means of defying his wife. (Fortunately this statement was passed without comment in the group.)

One of the almost fatal errors leaders of child-centered parent guidance groups can make is to react to the members' discussing their mates. It is inevitable for husbands and wives, especially those who have difficulties with their children, to feel either resentful or hostile toward each other or wish, as a defensive measure, to shift the blame to the other. To permit discussing these intramarital tensions and resentments would set up anxiety in both the narrator and auditors which cannot be dealt with in these groups. Expressing anxiety, tracing its source, and helping in its dissolution are processes for analytic therapy groups for which the criteria of selection of patients and of grouping are quite different from those in the groups under discussion here. In addition, the role of a group psychotherapist is at great variance with that of a leader in a guidance group. The leader must, therefore, be on the alert to prevent continuance of such discussions by either diverting it, going passive, or by retracing or recalling techniques.

One guidance group leader very directly told one of the women who introduced such a topic that only children are considered in the group, not husbands. This she did without a trace of annoyance, authoritarianism or reprimand. She said it rather gently and matter-of-factly and it was accepted. By this statement the leader laid the foundation for the primary group code, as do also the other techniques suggested. It can be done in this direct manner, though less direct and more subtle means are preferable, since they prevent the possibility of misinterpretation by those group members who may be keenly sensitive to authority and react negatively to what may seem to them an arbitrary attitude. When difficulties with children stem from relations with mates, the children cannot be helped without first affecting that relation which can be done by altering the intrafamilial forces (see Chapter VII). Such parents are unsuitable for child-centered guidance groups (see Chapter IX).

Another error that the leader can commit is to stimulate or to allow prolonged discussions of relationships with the members' own parents for they can engender a great deal of anxiety that would require therapeutic intervention rather than guidance. The following rather rare interchange occurred among women in the third session of their group.

Mrs. Gelfman and Mrs. Benson were talking about defiance in children. Mrs. Gelfman said that as a little girl she had been stubborn and would not wash dishes for her mother. Her mother was very lenient about it, but her father was strict and stubborn. People used to think that Mrs. Gelfman would never grow up to be a good housekeeper, yet she is very meticulous in her home. "When you want to be a good housekeeper, you are, even if you haven't had training in your home," she said. Neither did she want to go to sleep until very late when she was a child just like her son does now. Her father was very stubborn about that, too, and he "put the law down." She had decided she would never be as stubborn with her own children; and she is not. Yet she must admit that she gets very annoyed when Ray does not go to bed at a reasonable time; that is, what she would call reasonable. In this situation she acts more like her father and her husband more like her mother. He is more lenient and that is where the trouble lay. She and her husband do not get together, just as her mother and father did not get together on such matters, and Mrs. Gelfman got away with things as a child.

Mrs. Benson said that her problem was not her husband; she and he agreed. Her difficulty was her mother and she described a situation in which her son was pampered and overprotected by her mother. Now he is acting like a little boy wanting to continue to be indulged. At the same time he also wants to be grown up. She and her mother have had many arguments about this; they sometimes nearly come to blows. When this occurs, she lets her feelings out on her son because he is the cause of it all. Her mother still thinks that the boy should be more indulged and that too much was expected of him, whereas Mrs. Benson tells her mother that she should lay off and let her, Mrs. Benson, handle her son.

A third member of the group entered into the Gelfman-Benson discussion, pointing out how she had had to "talk up" to her mother, too, and briefed Mrs. Benson as to how to deal with that problem. She said that because she recognized that her home situation would never be cleared up for her children and for herself, she decided to give up her day job and now worked evenings. Her mother is thereby relieved of being the sole housekeeper and the children do not have to obey her. She decided she wanted to be the children's mother and so she is working harder, but she is finding it easier with the children. As for defiance, Mrs. Tarsy said, she was very happy when her boy could talk up to her. Her problem had been the reverse. The boy kept everything to himself, revealing his feelings only on his angry face and his readiness to scream, but "if only he would scream." She had had talks with her mother, some of them bordering on quarrels, but she thinks that is the only way to get things straightened out. She wished she had been like this when she was a little girl, not bottled up the way she had been and her son is now. It is her understanding that bottling up is also a form of repressed defiance. She said she understood that even appendicitis can be caused by emotional disturbance; she had that experience with one of her children. Her son is now beginning to show some progress because she, herself, is not as defensive about her views and is showing more interest in his ideas and feelings about things. She is still learning and still wants to know what she has done wrong and how to rectify it; but maybe "We don't have to go backward too far, maybe we could just go from day to day," she said. She liked what the group was doing, she added.

This episode in itself was not too disturbing, though some anxiety is evident. The recognition of the parallelism between Mrs. Benson with her husband and that of her parents, and her childhood patterns with those of her son, may have caused the discussion to turn to early problems and emotional trauma. In this case it did not activate such memories and feelings but they could have been so activated by even a slight indiscretion from the leader.

At one of the groups the leader allowed the women to indulge in a rather prolonged narration of their children's dreams. Most of the dreams were, as could be expected, of the anxiety type and some were nightmares. As a natural outcome of this some of the participants reported their own dreams which led to association with some actual situations in their lives. At the following session they suggested to the leader that they discuss *themselves* rather than their children. It seems that the activation by the dreams of their unconscious, their early memories and current fears made them desire to proceed into a therapeutic relation that would relieve them of these anxieties.

A typical pitfall against which leaders of child-centered parent guidance groups must guard is being drawn into a discussion of the many ramifications of sex beyond factual information. This is particularly important where the sex of the leader is different from that of the members. While factual information is useful and sometimes necessary to give parents in groups, elaboration of it in a way that may arouse anxiety must be avoided. The material has to be derived from, and focused on, the biological rather than the psychological aspects, and pathology must be definitely avoided.

A situation arose in a group of women where the leader was a rather attractive young man. This emphasized the difficulty since, as can be expected, the members of the group were unaccepting of their mates and the male leader, in a very subtle way, became the desired mate.

At a session of the group Mrs. Ross introduced the problem of giving children instruction in matters of sex. She wanted to know how the subject should be treated if the children should ever ask her. She was concerned with the fact that her older daughter who was approaching puberty had not broached the question and wondered whether she was completely ignorant of the subject. Mrs. Charles stated that children are not ignorant of such matters, even though they may not ask questions. She believed they knew more about it than parents suspected. When children do not speak to parents about sex, they have probably garnered the information from other sources. Her own pubertal daughter, she felt, was not free enough to discuss the subject with Mrs. Charles because she herself was unsure in this regard. Mrs. Ross who listened with interest again wanted to know what kind of questions to expect from her children in this area and asked how she should answer them; she wished to deal with the situation properly so as not to confuse them. Other members of the group joined into this discussion.

Finally, the leader asked the group whether they had any idea of the type of questions that children asked concerning sex. The women suggested that the children would be interested in birth;

how the baby got into the mother's body, how it started to grow, how it grew to be big, and how it emerged. The leader took the cue from them and explained that they could tell the children that there was an opening in the mother between her legs, in which a seed is planted and the baby grew inside the mother's stomach until it was ready to be born. "The baby then lets the mother know when it was ready to be born." The opening between the mother's legs then becomes enlarged and the baby comes out.

The leader reported that "the women were quite amazed at the simplicity of this explanation. They were impressed by the fact that this explanation was devoid of any complicated adult feelings and that it did not arouse anxiety in them and therefore felt it would not arouse any anxiety in the children either." He stated that at the end of the session, all the women were laughing and commenting that they could not wait for the time when their children would ask them for the information so that they could give it to them in the way in which the leader had done, but somehow, they did not feel entirely secure and expressed the wish *that the leader were there* when they were giving this information to their children.

At the next session, two weeks later, Mrs. Ross started off with the discussion of the preceding session. She again broached the question of sex education. She felt that she had bungled matters very badly because she announced to her children after the group meeting that she was ready to answer any questions on the subject. She felt that she did not do very well with her daughter who had made inquiries. She went on to say that her son "was certainly making use of her offer" to discuss sex matters, for he had asked her a great many questions. She felt more secure with her son because, being "only a child," his questions were elementary, but she was upset by her daughter who asked her about menstruation as well as "more intimate details on sexual matters." Mrs. Ross said she did not feel at ease and as a result referred her to a book. She felt a little depressed about this because she had failed.

At this point Mrs. Charles reported that her daughter too had begun to speak more freely regarding sex since the last session. Her daughter's curiosity related to her fears of pain during menstruation and her horror concerning the menstrual discharge (blood). It was she who recommended to Mrs. Ross the book for the latter's daughter, but now she felt that using a book was not a good idea. Mrs. Boris who had been absent from the previous session said that "parents must first feel comfortable in their own minds about these matters before they can discuss them with their children." It was only under these conditions that the children can receive reassurance and overcome the secretiveness concerning sex. The leader supported Mrs. Boris in this and further commented that children learned things much more quickly through verbal instruction than through reading.

Mrs. Ross wondered how she could talk about menstruation with her daughter and overcome the latter's fear about it in view of the fact that she herself is frequently bedridden with pain during the menstrual period. She related that on such occasions her daughter was concerned about Mrs. Ross's condition and probably expected to experience the same pain when she, too, would begin to menstruate. On one such occasion, Mrs. Ross said she had reassured her daughter that menstruation was not always accompanied by pain, that hers was a special condition. Mrs. Ross again returned to her complaint that she had bungled the matter with her children.

Mrs. Arthur now brought forth the subject of masturbation that children engaged in. She had learned from a previous discussion that masturbation was more or less common among children and that it passed away if no fuss was made about it. A situation had arisen with regard to her boy and she handled it by telling him that it was "all right to masturbate; all children do that" and that if he wished it, he should do it in private rather than in the presence of his sisters since people may not approve and might scold him for it. Mrs. Charles and Mrs. Ross evinced keen interest in this, but said that they had never observed masturbation in their own children

Mrs. Arthur proceeded to say that she believed that all children masturbated and her youngest child, a girl, even as an infant would occasionally play with her genitals. "There must be some pleasure attached to it," she said. Mrs. Ross wondered if this would not be "harmful to a child and should it not be prohibited?" Mrs. Arthur disagreed, commenting that she felt it was natural for a child to play with himself and that her son (with whom this was a serious problem) was improving in this respect since she no longer chastised and punished him for it. Mrs. Ross, however, insisted that it was possible that masturbation would make a child "nervous."

The leader picked this up and asked the other mothers what they thought about it, and since there were no comments he elaborated on the topic, stating that "nervousness comes from too frequent and excessive masturbation on the part of the child," and not from moderate indulgence.

The length to which the women in this group had gone in discussing sex has more meaning than their desire to acquire the knowledge and skill of dealing with their children. There was in evidence a sexual provocation on the part of the women toward the male leader. In a sense, he now was in possession of a harem. He was advised to steer away from the subject in future interviews and, as a result, the topic was very quickly dropped.

We are refraining from discussing the errors in the interpretation and advice given by the women to each other and by the leader, since this is not the aim of the present volume. It is also evident that the women had not employed the information they had acquired in the group properly or constructively. Such discussion in groups and the information contained therein has to be graded to the readiness of the members to accept it objectively and utilize it properly.

CHAPTER

IX

Criteria for Selection

We have already emphasized that the most important single condition for the success of Child-Centered Group Guidance of Parents is the proper choice of members who can gain from this method. It is my conviction, derived from examination and treatment of several thousand patients, that the predominant number of failures in all psychotherapies is largely due to the inflexible application of one method in a blanket fashion. Techniques should be suited to the specific needs of each patient. The high incidence of improvement in our practice of group psychotherapy is almost entirely due to the fact that we have devised different methods of treatment for different types of patients, and the elimination of those who required other methods.[1] The type of group described in this volume is an outcome of this fundamental recognition. Because this method was developed in a clinical setting (though it was first initiated by me in 1947 with a group of parents whose children did not present clinical problems), many of the parents had been placed in guidance groups after they had been found to be inaccessible or otherwise unsuitable for individual treatment. Chapter X consists of a detailed description of such a case.

It must always be kept in mind, however, that criteria for selection are at best tenuous; they are never entirely reliable. My own experience with criteria for categorizing human beings is that none

[1] See S. R. Slavson: Criteria for Selection and Rejection of Patients for Different Types of Group Psychotherapy. *International Journal of Group Psychotherapy*, Vol. V, No. 1, 1955.

is completely applicable because of the infinite variability in personalities. Clinical indications can be, and frequently are, offset by some individual peculiarities or latent character traits, while counter-indications are often disproved by experience with patients who have compensatory ego strengths and resources that could not have been determined in advance by any known clinical tools. Errors in selection and grouping are, therefore, inevitable, but one must always strive to reduce these to a minimum.

In this chapter we shall make an effort to list some communicable criteria for selection of parents for Child-Centered Group Guidance, but the reader is asked to keep in mind that these are tentative; they are only *indications* requiring elaborative consideration and intuitive judgment supported by experience. The procedure we shall employ here will be to describe briefly cases of success and failure from which an effort will be made to draw conclusions as to suitability or unsuitability for membership in these groups.

Our first case is that of Mrs. Suskin[2] and her son Saul, ten and a half years old. He was very jealous of a brother four years his junior, clung to his mother, constantly inquiring if she loved him, was uninterested in school and resisted going to classes. He was generally very unhappy and once attempted what he claimed to be a try at suicide; he was found by his father when he tried to tighten a noose made of a towel around his neck.

Mrs. Suskin was a very attractive person, very well groomed, colorfully but tastefully dressed. She was a rather intelligent woman, speaking rapidly and volubly, with a great deal of anxiety. She appeared tense and "neurotic." Previous to Saul's birth, a girl was born to Mrs. Suskin. The baby suffered a brain damage at birth, was later institutionalized and died at eighteen months of age. This was followed by a miscarriage. Saul was born soon after, prematurely, and was "near death the first three months of his life." He had dysentery and other illnesses. The mother was "shocked" at giving birth to a boy instead of a girl and her attitude toward him was negative from the start. Another boy was born four years later, with two miscarriages intervening.

The mother was the youngest of six children, four sisters and one

2 Not to be confused with Mrs. Salkin, mother of Harris.

brother. The oldest sister was eleven years her senior and she was actually brought up by her two older sisters. She was an unwanted child, born "accidentally" when her parents were advanced in years. The father was a sickly man, ineffectual, and died when Mrs. Suskin was sixteen years old. However, a grandfather who had lived in the home and pampered her, seemed to be a father substitute throughout her childhood and adolescence. She described her only brother as being "just like one of the girls. He had no backbone." He was effeminate, at least so Mrs. Suskin described him. She had fears of separation from her mother but claimed she outgrew that dependence and could not understand why her son should continue to be dependent on her. Mrs. Suskin had strong guilt feelings around Saul. She was aware that she had openly rejected him and that her son felt it was wrong for her to be unkind to him. She too had the feeling that she had been wrong in displaying her hostility so openly, but did not know how she could help herself because of her strong "nervous tension."

She did not want to involve her husband, who had only recently entered on a new business venture. In fact, she felt that he would not be interested in coming for help, that he was too preoccupied with his business, and, anyway, he had completely turned over to her the rearing of the children.

The boy was assigned to activity group therapy where he had made very good progress.

The intake worker stated that Mrs. Suskin would require individual treatment because of her "intense feelings about the boy; the seemingly terrific amount of overt rejection and almost disgust with his continual demandingness; because of the impression she gave of being overwhelmed and bewildered by him, and because she had displayed such strong feelings around the first child who had died." There was evidence that she wished Saul to take the place of the dead girl. However, due to the unavailability of individual therapy for her at the time, and her insistence that she get some help under the threat of withdrawing Saul from treatment, she was placed a year later in a guidance group as a temporary measure and a stopgap. By that time it was determined through group treatment of the boy that he was far less disturbed than his mother described him, and much of what she had said about him were exaggerations. She had really wanted to paint the boy in as bad a light as possible.

In the group, where there were eight women in addition to herself, Mrs. Suskin was at first competitive with another member who outdid her in volume and intensity of speech. As a result, she was not sure after the first session whether she would continue since, she said, another mother had even worse problems than hers and did not give her an opportunity to speak. However, the other woman did not return to the group and Mrs. Suskin took over her role at the second session. She became forceful, dominating, and in a way assumed the leadership. Despite this behavior, the group leader recognized in Mrs. Suskin "a great deal of warmth which we did not observe before, and a real feeling of sociability with the other women." She was also able to elicit sympathetic reactions from them.

At first she appeared to the leader as "a weepy, dependent, clinging woman, very much like what she said her boy was; at the same time, fighting that dependence." What she was seeking was a relationship, though a dependent one, since for all intents and purposes she never had a mother. She was aware of the wrong she had done to Saul and the other women commended her for recognizing this. One of them had said: "Well, if you know this, why can't you correct it?"

In the third session, Mrs. Suskin talked less and listened more to the other women who presented their problems with their children which, in some instances, were very much like hers. This universality seemed to interest her, and she listened with striking objectivity "as though there were six Sauls and not just one." Soon she displayed a generalized interest in the needs of children. She began to recognize that her difficulties did not stem only from her; there were extenuating circumstances such as the difficulties that were imposed on her in the past, her need to travel from one Army camp to another during the war with Saul while Mr. Suskin was in the Service, denying him the security of place that he needed. As her situation was externalized she became more relaxed and more objective. She gave up pressing Saul to go to school and do things and decided not to force him to go out to the street to play when he did not want to do it. Instead, she helped him feel comfortable in the home. If he wanted to be loved by her, and inquired if she loved him, which he frequently did, or demand things from her, she gave him affection and did not argue with him at every step as though he were an adult.

Her fellow members helped her adopt these new patterns. She accepted the fact that she had to control herself, but she complained that she did not always succeed. She found that when she did not press or oppose her son and showed "just a spark of love, of interest," he was able to go along for days without creating difficulties and do well in school, but the minute she lost her temper and her confidence in him, he regressed, stayed in the house, did not want to go to school. Again, she had to resort to force. Many a time the leader doubted whether Mrs. Suskin would continue in the group, but Mrs. Suskin came regularly, and listened attentively. She became interested in the wider world of children.

At the seventh session, she reported notable progress which pleased her. Because of the reduction of guilt through universalization and security and the acceptance by and support from the other mothers and the leader, she was able to control herself better, and, as she said, she began to "count not to ten but to twenty" before she took steps with her son. When the time came for registering for camp, she did not press Saul. She left the decision entirely to him. After a considerable period of vacillation, he decided to go and had a very constructive experience that summer.

Another situation which Mrs. Suskin handled well was after Saul had his second bicycle stolen because of his negligence. While waiting for the insurance payment to come through, Saul wanted his mother to advance him money to buy a third vehicle. She did not accede to his demand and explained to him that he could not have things the minute he wanted them. One must wait. Before that she would have scolded him, because, she said, "That's the way I am. The minute I have something to say, I must say it. If I don't—I burn up; I tear up." She further suggested to Saul that he could in the meantime look for another bicycle so that when the money came through he would know where to get the kind of bicycle he wanted. The group had discussed the situation and suggested this procedure.

When the bicycle was finally bought, mother and son together worked out a plan of how to prevent a repetition of the incident.

She did not say to him: "Now don't you dare lose it again!" Instead the group helped her in recognizing that there are other than authoritarian ways to help children take care of their possessions. Mrs. Suskin said to Saul once: "You know, when you're riding a bike, you can't think of baseball. Bring the bike home and then go down and play baseball, because otherwise, you'll have what you had last time. You put it up against a tree, you play baseball, and you don't know who is going to pick it up. Anyone has the right to do it. You don't even have a chain. You had a chain, but you kept it in your pocket. So, if you want this bicycle, and you want to hold onto it, there are ways in which you can do so." In every other situation she reacted reflectively and in a more relaxed fashion; she timed things. "I am no longer rushing into things," she once said.

The "follow-up" caseworker whose responsibility it was to observe Saul's progress summarized his impression as follows: "Since Mrs. Suskin joined the guidance group, I have seen her several times. After the third session in the group, she stopped in my office to tell me, in a very demanding, insistent way, that she wasn't being helped, that she needed individual treatment. In the group she could not talk all the time because it was not fair to take the time from the other mothers. She demanded help. After a brief interview, she agreed to stay in the group until such time as we could assign her to a caseworker, commenting, "Well, it's better than nothing." When I saw Mrs. Suskin again after the tenth session, I observed a dramatic change in her. She appeared different physically. Instead of the most harried looks that I had ever seen on a woman, and her emotionalism and tenseness and panic, she seemed now self-possessed with an inner calm. She walked into the office calmly, sat down quietly and evaluated the group. She said that she still needed more than the group was giving her, namely, her marital situation needed to be straightened out, but she felt she could not properly bring it up in the group. She talked about the group with pride and pleasure, and obvious satisfaction. She told how she had been given an 'experience in success'; for the first time things she had tried were working with Saul. In the past, whenever he wanted something, he would nag her and she could never carry through her efforts at firmness, and in the end she would always give in, but would then be resentful because he had won out.

"She then described several situations. (One of these was the one with the bicycle which she felt she had handled well.) She described another incident when she took both boys to buy sneakers for the summer. When they got into the store, Saul saw something else, I think some type of baseball equipment that he wanted very much. The mother said that in the past, a 'terrible scene' would have ensued between her and the boy right in the store of which she would later have been terribly ashamed. She would have 'lost her head.' This time she just told Saul, 'Look, we are here to get sneakers, and that's all. I have no money for anything else. Now, if you don't want the sneakers we won't get them.' The boy, somewhat sullenly at first refused the sneakers, but then said he would have them, but he was quite mad and on the way home kept commenting resentfully about it. She said she tried very hard to control herself and succeeded in not reacting to it, though she was 'ready to explode.' When they reached home, she did not mention a word about the incident. Later Saul came to her and said, 'I'm sorry I acted the way I did in the store.' This represented to her a complete triumph and I, too, think it is rather remarkable."

In addition to the effects which the relationships and the group's encouragement toward success has had upon Mrs. Suskin, it was felt that a major cause of the change in attitude was the leader's quiet firmness. In the group Mrs. Suskin repeated the competitive pattern that dominated first her own family—sisters and a weak brother— and was later re-enacted with her children. She had forever dickered with her boy; there was a sort of clash of wills in which he usually won out, largely because of his perseverance and capacity to nag. When she saw the "follow-up" caseworker before she was placed in the group, she openly stated: "You are taking care of Saul. He is having a good time in his club, but you do nothing for me." The worker had seen her a number of times during the year and her son once before she was assigned to the group. Several times she requested the interviews and the worker was impressed with the "childish nature of her demandingness."

In the group as well, Mrs. Suskin would argue with the other women frequently with the intention to win rather than to seek out the truth. Quite often when the conversation would become tangential, or inconsequential, the leader would pull it back either to the original or a relevant subject or to something more meaningful that some member of the group had said as long as a half hour before. This was done quietly and firmly which served two ends as far as Mrs. Suskin was concerned.

One was that the leader was interested in her; the other was a demonstration of quiet authority. The leader acted out the appropriate role of a parent that requires being firm as well as tolerant and kindly. Thus, the leader serves as a living demonstration of the role parents have to assume in the family. We are convinced that Mrs. Suskin has, to a large degree, imitated the leader and re-enacted her demeanor. This firmness, without talking about it or explanation, shows parents how to remain the deciding factor in issues, without appearing weak or losing face through arguments or punishment. The incident with the sneakers is a good illustration of this. Here the boy was able to accept her authority because she did not waver; also because she accepted his hostility and expressions of feelings without becoming angry or irritable—all of which the leader demonstrated in the group.

Contrariwise, Mrs. Suskin was able to accept the boy better because he accepted her firmness. Both her son and Mrs. Suskin had the same family backgrounds; neither had a strong or consistent parental figure in his life. She had never experienced benevolent control herself, so she could not give it to her children. Now that she experienced a little of it with the new family group, she was able to pass it on to her boy.

Basically, Mrs. Suskin is a phallic woman. She rejected Saul because he was a boy, she strove to outdo her brother and has kept her husband out of the picture because she wanted to be the head of the household and yet be a woman and a mother figure. In view of these conflicts as to her own identity, it is questionable whether she can hold the improvement and whether guidance without deeper psychotherapy will be sufficient in this case. We do know that she has grown more relaxed, that she was able to befriend the women in the group whose "sort of little girl" she has become, as she had been with her sisters. She went home with them, they discussed things and made plans together. Mrs. Suskin had established ties that were very meaningful to her and gave her a great deal of security; and her treatment of both her children has greatly improved which helped them a great deal. She never discussed either her husband or her early background in the group. Even if Mrs. Suskin did not sustain a fundamental change, her relaxed state and changed treatment of Saul aided and abetted our therapeutic efforts with him.[3]

Mrs. Allen, forty-two years old, had been a widow for eight years and was both mother and father to her family. She was the only one in the group of eight who had had individual treatment for about a year and a half before joining the group. Her son, more than eleven years old, was also receiving individual therapy. Her difficulty was that she restricted the boy, was meticulously clean and orderly, insisted on perfect behavior in school and took over the entire responsibility for him and a girl two years older. The daughter, however, was less restricted and somewhat rebellious against her mother's domination. The boy slept in the same bed with his sister until treatment was initiated. When he was separated from her, he insisted on sleeping with his mother.

Mrs. Allen was found inaccessible to individual treatment beyond gaining a limited amount of understanding of how she was creating sexual difficulties for her boy and perpetuating his dependence on her.

The boy and his mother had been treated by the same therapist which was later found inadvisable. They were, therefore, separated, the boy continuing with the caseworker and the mother, because of her limited capacity to improve, was placed in a mothers' guidance group to which she responded better.

Though her son was of average intelligence, Mrs. Allen demanded from him scholastic achievement beyond his capacities. She fancied him a very bright child that would gain great heights and eventually take care of her. When her son was an infant, her own father was ailing, and being devoted to her parents, she spent a great deal of her time helping her mother in caring for him. The father

---

[3] Mrs. Suskin was assigned to individual treatment and later to a therapy group.

died and soon after her own husband became ill and was hospitalized for a long period for a complication of illnesses. When he returned home, she took care of him, but he passed away when the boy was four years old. Thus, the son was denied his mother's attention through most of his early childhood. Although she tried to provide him with good physical care, he was shifted from one relative to another. After her husband's death, she went to work and placed him in a day nursery. When she left him in the nursery he would cry bitterly and would cling to the nurse through the day. She therefore decided to stop work, obtained a widow's pension and looked after her children. The boy has clung to her tenaciously ever since.

Mrs. Allen was raised in a small community in New England and was very devoted to her mother. She was the third child in a family of nine siblings, but the first girl, and had always assumed the role of mother's helper. She helped care for the whole family. Mrs. Allen, her mother, and a number of Mrs. Allen's sisters lived near each other, but Mrs. Allen spent more time with her mother than did the others.

Mrs. Allen was described as an intelligent person, very reserved, quiet and soft-spoken, who had always been a conforming person, making no demands, "giving more of herself than she asked from others." She was always tidy and well-dressed and expected from her children modesty, neatness, conformity, and submission. She was not given to self-pity or depressed moods. The leader had the impression that Mrs. Allen knew a good deal, and wanted to know more and strove to a level of life beyond her means.

In the group, she talked sparingly, but listened attentively. Neither the other mothers nor the leader pressed her to speak. At the third or fourth session, one woman asked her: "Don't you have any problems?" Mrs. Allen replied: "I have, but I've been waiting to hear about the other women's problems." The other urged: "Well, maybe you should take the initiative." Mrs. Allen replied that she would wait her turn. At that session one of the women talked about school difficulties and wondered whether one should sympathize with a child knowing how bad the teacher was and whether one could do anything through the principal. Mrs. Allen felt that most of her son's difficulties were around school and she fully participated in the ensuing discussion.

In several subsequent sessions Mrs. Allen talked about how she had always overprotected her son and had always talked to teachers at the beginning of each term to lay the groundwork of sympathy for him on the score that he had no father and that she was alone and trying to do the best for him. She related that he would sit on her lap and kiss her, as if he were a baby instead of an eleven-and-a-half-year-old boy, and that she had to feed him like a little child. She asked the teachers to please cooperate with her and give him the love that he had never had. Most of the teachers went along with her and he would take full advantage of the situation. She always got him out of scrapes for he never got along well with children, never wanted to be with them; he only wanted to be her baby.

Mrs. Allen conveyed a picture of a mother who indulged her child out of guilt for the neglect during the first years of his life when she could not take care of him properly. She even took over the father role and acted as though she was responsible for the death of the father. She felt that her daughter had done better because she had seen more of her father and had a "healthier beginning," as Mrs. Allen formulated it.

While Mrs. Allen was in the group, one of the teachers refused to fall into her pattern. This was a man, the first her boy had ever had in school. This Mrs. Allen could not take, but the teacher insisted that the boy have extra tutoring to bring him up to the grade. The mother rebelled. It was not up to her to do this work. It was the teacher's job, she said. This resulted in continual conflict between the two. Finally, one of the mothers said: "Say, how long are you going to go on getting him out of scrapes?" But another supported Mrs. Allen when she said, "This is a tough teacher. He has no business being in that school. You should go to the principal and talk it over with him to see if the boy should be transferred." Mrs. Allen said that she had him transferred before in another grade, that if one teacher did not suit her she had always been able to get another because she aroused the sympathy of the principal.

At this point, the leader took an active part questioning how the boy could grow into manhood if his mother went on doing these things for him. She asked what Mrs. Allen meant when she talked of the boy's growing up. The other members of the group lapsed into a discussion of the impending confirmations of their boys and their entering into the estate of responsibility and independence. This contrast to her own attitude led Mrs. Allen to ask: "What should I do about the teacher?" She, however, rejected the advice to go to the principal because that might get her boy into even worse trouble. She did not intend to see the teacher any more; she did not like him anyway. She now doubted if she would repeat her previous maneuvers. Perhaps it was better that the boy learn that he has to improve his behavior, she said. His work was not too bad; it was fair. It was his conduct: he clowned in the classroom and disturbed the teachers as well as the children. They all hated him because he always tried to outsmart everyone else, act more foolishly than anybody; displace everyone in the group and even usurp the teachers' authority. He was as difficult in school as he was at home; "just like a child looking for power."

This was the first time Mrs. Allen saw as clearly and somewhat objectively her boy's behavior. Encouraged by the others in the group she decided that she would "talk to him" about the situation and ask him point blank how long he expected her to fight his battles now that he was twelve years old. This she did and after sending a note to the teacher that she was doing all she could and would do no more to manage her boy's affairs, she left matters in his hands. She stopped "pressing and pushing him around" and has left it all to him.

As far as her own adjustment was concerned, Mrs. Allen became increasingly more a part of the group. She began initiating discussions, responded better, and the women, in turn, reacted better to her. She had come out of her shell, as it were. She no longer felt she had to conform and she took as much time as she wished to discuss her situation and to occupy the center of attention. She had become firmer with her son and generally more assertive.

Her persistent demands upon the children had greatly abated. She no longer pressured the boy about school, nor about his going out to play, and left it to him to spend his allowance as he saw fit. In the past when she had given him his allowance, she would outline for him how he should spend it, telling him what he needed, such as pencils or a copy book, or urged him to save his money. The other women in the group discussed this with Mrs. Allen thoroughly urging her to leave it to the boy to decide. "You should not interfere with him," they told her. She believed that by doing this she "taught" him responsibility. Mrs. Allen had changed many of her earlier patterns that were considered "compulsive" which completely changed the home atmosphere. As a result, the staff of the summer camp to which the boy went reported a good adjustment on his part.

Mrs. Allen was diagnosed as anal-compulsive, a diagnosis that seemed to us unjustified from the start. While her neatness, meticulousness and orderliness would seem to lead to this diagnosis, they actually were conditioned by cultural patterns and her need to please her mother was not necessarily on an anal but on a sibling rivalry basis. There was here also an admixture of strong hostility toward her mother with submissiveness, a hostility which she acted out toward authority figures as teachers, the little use she made of the leader in the group and her inability to utilize individual psychotherapy. She could not develop a transference toward a mother figure, but was able to do so to the impersonal climate of the group. The leader also reported that at times Mrs. Allen tried to displace her.

Having assumed an overmature role in her parental home as a child by taking on the responsibilities there at a young age, she misunderstood the meaning of responsibility and has learned unsuitable ways of discharging them, namely, by unending control and assertiveness. There is little doubt that Mrs. Allen identified in this strongly with her own mother. We know that she considered herself of superior cultural background and married a man with a higher education. Her own standards of deportment and personal appearance which she sought to impose on her children were a part of this selfimage rather than a compulsive character or neurosis. This is confirmed by the ease with which she was able to give them up through the guidance group.

Mrs. Allen was about ten years older than the other women in the group. She was the older sister here, as it were, which helped her overcome her earlier diffidence and recessive role, a role she had assumed as a result of her submissiveness to her domineering mother whom she emulated in relation to her children. Mrs. Allen can, therefore, be considered as having a character disorder with strongly repressed hostility, but she also had sufficient intelligence and an urge toward a wholesome adjustment that was supported by the group. Her pattern that appeared to be compulsive on the surface was accessible to examination by her ego, the strength of which she utilized in curbing her habit patterns and in altering them.

While Mrs. Allen carried over some of her hostility toward her mother into the group and acted it out in a disguised form toward the leader which was accepted, she drew strength from the group through several channels. One is the fact that the group allayed her guilt through universalization. It also supported her in her unconscious desire to detach herself from her son, which she was unable to do before because of her guilt. In the fellow members she had objects of identification other than her mother, and the group served as focus for extending interests beyond her family. The acceptance and warm human relations diminished her feelings of isolation and aloneness which always destroy one's inner strength.

One man had to be withdrawn from a group after three sessions. His family had been carried by the clinic: his son was in an activity therapy group, and his wife, in a guidance group. His behavior in the three sessions was openly hostile, resentful and competitive in relation to the group leader. He almost completely monopolized the stage by incessant talking in a very forceful, defensive and aggressive manner. At the very first session, when plans were being made, he suggested that the group meet once a month or less frequently. He went further and said that the men did not have to come to the meetings, but instead could take their children out somewhere. By this he challenged and sought to eliminate the leader. He seemed obsessed with the theme that the only thing his family needed was a change in physical environment; if they could only move to the country or could live on the first floor where he or his wife could watch the boy at play on the street, and the boy could see them, all their difficulties would vanish. The boy, who was eleven years old, was afraid to go down, he said, because there was no one to watch him.

Another theme that Mr. Barshay constantly reiterated was that it really did not bother him that his son was way off the pace of other children, and that he was behind his younger brother in development. "It don't bother me. I just let it pass. So what?" he would say with utmost resentment and hostility toward his son. Mr. Barshay had a very disquieting effect on the other men who participated little in his presence. The absence from the sessions of three members of the group could be directly attributed to Mr. Barshay's influence. These three returned after Mr. Barshay was removed.

After the third session when his aggressions mounted in intensity, and he continued to monopolize the sessions by his constant talk and his insistence that the group meet elsewhere, the leader asked Mr. Barshay to see him. It was suggested to him that perhaps he was uncomfortable in the group. He first denied it, but when the leader said that he had a hunch that "his arm was twisted' and he was made to come, he flushed and after some time acknowledged that his wife forced him to come. He really did not see any need for it, though claiming he would cooperate in any way he could.

In the interview Mr. Barshay spoke warmly of his mother, and avoided discussing his father whom he described as old-fashioned and as having had very little contact with his children. He himself rarely saw his father, and there was very little community of interest between them. When he was interviewed prior to placement in the group, Mr. Barshay stressed that in a sense his life had been a failure. He was headed toward a political and legal career, had been president of his high school class, and it was always assumed that he had a bright future politically. Somehow things did not work out for him, he said. He was now a traveling salesman and, in a sense, removed himself from his family as his father had done from his.

In Mr. Barshay we have a man who re-enacted his very strong rebelliousness and hostility toward his father, toward the leader of the group, thereby blocking the group process and preventing its possible benefits to the others.

Another father with whom we had difficulty was Mr. Sands who severely rejected his son by being continually critical and impotenizing toward him. The boy had an organic handicap, a slight brain damage he sustained at birth, and had therefore always trailed behind other children. He was poor at school, could not hold his own athletically or socially, was rejected and was a "lone wolf," spending most of his time in the house. Mr. Sands repeatedly compared his boy unfavorably with a daughter who was about six years the boy's junior and would comment in his presence how much brighter the girl was. The boy rocked himself to sleep at night, an activity that made the father "very angry." He would come into the boy's room and strike him to get him to stop. In individual follow-up interviews on his son prior to his assignment to the group, Mr. Sands displayed resentment to authority, especially when he talked of teachers and school principals. He would recount with biting sarcasm that teachers were always trying to tell him what to do or implied that he and his wife were responsible in some way for their son's inadequacies. He repeated this several times, both in individual interviews and in the group.

During the early years of his marriage, when he was past thirty, Mr. Sands had an affair with a sixteen-year-old girl, which lasted for several years. This was finally broken up with his wife claiming that there was never the slightest bit of hard feeling about this on her part.

The most salient characteristic of Mr. Sands was his defensiveness and his general anxiety and tension. Just being in the group seemed to intensify his anxieties and guilts that made the sessions almost unbearable to him. One had the feeling that at times he would be struggling and trying to accomplish something through the group: he would acknowledge that he had a poor relationship with his son, that somehow he could not seem to tolerate the boy. But one was impressed with the quality of his feelings and their intensity and that group guidance could not impinge on him because the boy represented to Mr. Sands, himself, his own immaturity, his lack of masculinity and infantile characteristics, and his own failures and inadequacies.

Mrs. Green, diagnosed as borderline psychotic, had been in individual treatment for some time with no progress. The therapist felt that she could not be reached, and in the interest of her child Mrs. Green was placed in a guidance group on a trial basis. In the group as well, Mrs. Green was unable to talk about her child, though she participated in discussions of children of the other group members. When she did talk about her own child once, she broke down, wept copiously and cried that she could not go on. (She continued in individual treatment and came to the group which met on alternate weeks.)

Mrs. Green frequently complained of her inability to talk, though she felt she understood other people's problems, which was very true. She was perceptive, had a way of drawing out the other women and to see through their behavior. She was anxiety-ridden in relation to her own child, and did not make any progress either in individual treatment or in group guidance. Though she felt she has benefited some from listening to the other mothers, this was not reflected in her behavior. Because of her disturbed state, we found it advisable to close her in the group and provide her with individual guidance rather than psychotherapy.

Mrs. Ginn, a very disturbed woman with depressions, was the mother of a ten-year-old boy. In the group she talked about having wanted to be a man when she was a youngster and having run away from home to prove that she was as capable as the other girls in her family. She talked freely of the fact that she and her husband were badly mated. She had left their bedroom and slept in her son's room. She considered her son superior to his father and took his part against the latter. Both she and her son deprecated him. She considered herself the boy's slave and actually fed him because he wished it. The boy dominated her and "twisted her around his little finger."

After a period it became evident that her deeply rooted personality disturbance prevented her from incorporating any benefits from the group. In fact, we felt that she was damaged by that experience because it increased her conflicts with which she did not have the psychologic wherewithal to deal. She was accordingly assigned to an individual caseworker who also found her very difficult. Despite the help that was offered her she was unable to affect a separation from her boy and had manipulated his psychotherapeutic career whimsically and inconsistently, rendering this total case rather hopeless.

Mrs. Jacobs was another woman who was unable to separate herself from her son. She was threatened by the treatment he was receiving at the clinic lest the caseworker displace her in his life and repeatedly withdrew him from therapy, returning him as soon as she found she could not manage him. She would urge him to come to the clinic, then just as suddenly would decide that it was more important for him to go to the family doctor every week "to have his weight checked." She reacted to her own psycho-therapy with hysterical conversions. When her anxieties would over-whelm her, she would become ill. This also served as a dependency mechanism as well as a means to evade treatment whenever her basic problems were touched on. One of her urgent desires was to be a male.

She reacted to the group with a need to prove its members wrong; thus, whenever she accepted suggestions from the others, it was with the intention of proving that they were unsound. However, from time to time she would report that her six-year-old girl taught her how to deal with her boy. It seemed that by saying this she would try to show that her little girl was wiser than anyone in the group. This was part of her hostility and a rejection of the ideas she could not accept.

Among the boy's difficulties was bed wetting, which was a source of great torment to her. He was constantly demanding her attention and time. This she could not understand. In addition, he was "filthy in his body habits" and she had to wash his feet with a wet washcloth after he fell asleep. On the one hand she babied him, and on the other expected him to be grown up.

Mrs. Jacobs continued in a guidance group for a whole season and at the end complained that things were worse than ever before, and that she had grown increasingly more anxious. Both she and her husband now bit their nails and both were at their wits' end.

Before treatment was initiated, she said, they did not feel so guilty about the way they treated the children. Now they did the same things but felt guilty; and when they refrained, they felt "nervous." A significant statement she made to the leader was: "I try to do what the women tell me and control myself, but I get so tense that I shake all over and get a terrific headache and have to lie down." It was agreed that she could not benefit from the group, and was returned to individual therapy, which she had been receiving for a brief period before.

Mrs. Jacobs did not do well in that arrangement either. The therapist reported that she was insatiable in her demands. The whole world was evil and everyone was her enemy. The only friend she had, according to her, was her little girl who guided her as to how to deal with her son. When summer camp was suggested for the boy (as a means of separating him from his mother), she could not accept it because, as she said, he could not take care of himself and she could not trust the counselors. Individual guidance was continued, however, as a means of assuring that she would allow the boy to continue in treatment.

The father, though a more positive and more wholesome person, came to one session of a group and discontinued. It was evidently too threatening for him as well. Because the boy was in combined individual and group treatment the "follow-up" caseworker occasionally saw both the father and the mother in this case. The parents, though married twelve or thirteen years, seemed still to be having a "honeymoon" which the two children were interrupting.[4] For example, the father said: "My main responsibility is to my wife. I have to be with her and help her and have to give her my affection. The children definitely come second. Since my wife means so much to me, naturally all my attention goes to my wife."

Mr. and Mrs. Jacobs appeared like two children living together who resented the presence of the "other" two children. Neither parent could accept the fact that they may have had something to do with their children's difficulties. The mother saw the boy's behavior as motivated entirely against herself and could not conceive

4 See "Parental Phalanx" in S. R. Slavson, *Child Psychotherapy*, New York: Columbia University Press, 1952, p. 90.

that she was in any way responsible for it. It was our feeling that although the father may not have been consciously aware of it, he perceived his wife's pathology and played into it, this being the reason why they got along so well. He seemed to know how to feed her needs.

This mother evidently saw her son as a part or extension of herself and could not accept his individuality and autonomy. She wanted to be a boy and her son was an actualization of her own yearnings to be a man. He was the fulfillment of this dream. We cannot expect any appreciable change in her through psychotherapy on a once a week basis. It is a serious problem of self-image and body image, with a psychotic tinge, and her involvement with the boy as part of herself could not be affected by Child-Centered Parent Group Guidance. The father had to reject the group for fear that it might affect his attitude toward and his treatment of his wife which would have disrupted whatever stability there was in this family.[5]

From the sampling of parents in this chapter as well as those that were mentioned or described in other parts of this volume, some criteria can be gleaned as to prognostic indications for Child-Centered Group Guidance. First let us consider the concept "readiness for parenthood" that was suggested (see p. 44) and attempt to understand this generic concept and the elements that go into making one ready for parenthood. An examination of it would show that the elements involved are (1) physical stamina, (2) capacity for instinct gratifications, (3) comparative freedom from oedipal involvement, (4) ego strength, (5) correct sexual identification, (6) absence of neurotic involvement with children.

1. No one who has had the experience of parenthood is unaware of the heavy call that it makes upon one's physical resources. The demands of a baby at all hours of day and night that interfere with proper rest, sleep and relaxation, especially in the mother and to a lesser extent also in the father require considerable physical

[5] See "Equilibrium Under Tension" in S. R. Slavson, *Child Psychotherapy, loc. cit.*, pp. 68-70.

stamina and recuperative powers that some people do not have either because of constitutional factors or emotional tensions. The absence of these physical reserves generates or increases fatigue which, in turn, intensifies irritability and sets back the threshold or organic-emotional integration and, therefore, loss of ego controls. Irritability always results in behavior that, whether so intended or not, gives the infant or child feelings of insecurity and of being rejected. We must recognize that modern artificial living conditions, in addition to emotional factors, cannot but induce tensions and fatigue which must be dealt with if we wish to lay the foundation for and maintain a wholesome climate in the home. In all my work with parents, therefore, I have emphasized the importance of health measures and adequate rest for the mother, particularly, sometimes even at the expense of some favorable routine for the child. It was my conviction that minor omissions in the care of the child are less injurious than a tired and irritable mother.

2. Parenthood requires that the individual should be comparatively free of the inhibitive and restrictive forces in his character that prevent average instinct gratifications. He should be free of rigidities and compulsions that prevent enjoyment of the ordinary pleasures of life such as indulging in humor, in having fun, enjoying food without faddism or too apparent preferences or aversions, sociability and acceptable discharge of aggression and hostility as well as kindliness and friendship. Above all, satisfying sexual adjustment between the parents is an essential precondition for a calm climate in the home that is of utmost importance to a healthy childhood. Lacking this mutuality, parents live under tension which is conveyed to the child in very subtle nuances by their appearance and behavior. Proper sexual identification, which is described in greater detail later in this chapter, is another requirement of the healthy living out of the basic instinctual trends essential for adequate parental function, for no one is ready for parenthood who is unready for matehood.

3. To be able to function adequately as a parent, one must have achieved a sufficient freedom from one's own parents. The depend-

encies and ties characteristic of child-parent relations impede one's capacities for a parent-child relation later in life. The irrationality of human emotions and the fact that they can be displaced from a true to a substitute object cause parents to act toward their children in a manner that frightens and confuses them. Parents who have not been freed of earlier ties sufficiently displace their antagonism and dependency onto their children. In addition, being tied to one's parents retards maturity, impedes the development of the sense of reality, and the capacity to deal with reality. Readiness for parenthood, therefore, requires freedom from infantile ties and cravings. In this connection, one must note that relations with other members of one's family such as siblings must be also considered, because attitudes toward them are also transferable to one's own children.

A father in one of the groups has given evidence of confusing his son with his younger brother. Both had the same name and similar difficulties. He had two sons, one eleven and the other ten years of age. The father repeatedly returned to the same theme in relation to the two boys, namely that the younger of the two always outdid the older. The father was strongly affected by this because he thought that the older boy must be terribly upset by this. At the same time in actual situations it was apparent that he caused the older to fail in relation to the younger. This was a replica of his own relation in his earlier family.

In the guidance group, he would distort the discussion ever so slightly, but significantly enough to gain a neurotically determined end. He described in one session, for example, how the older boy had bought a bag of peanuts from the younger for fifty-five cents. He intended to sell them two for a penny, but was unable to dispose of his wares. The boy then phoned all of his aunts and uncles to induce them to buy his peanuts. The father then said: "Well, I got quite mad. Had this happened some time ago, I probably would have punished him in some way but I remember (addressing the leader directly) you once saying something that because of the thirty year difference between us and our children, we do not always understand them which makes parents treat them harshly. I never forgot that. Therefore, I decided to see if I could help the boy out.

So I thought about it and what I did was to persuade my younger son to buy the peanuts back. I then gave the younger boy a quarter extra, for buying them back."

It would seem that his intention to help his older son was well meant, as was the fact that he did not punish him, but his inherent neurotic pattern derived from his relation to his brother caused him to work out the situation in such a manner that the older boy was defeated by the younger. He could have helped the boy to sell the peanuts, for example, or he could have bought them himself instead of persuading the younger boy in the presence of the older to take them back. He thus helped the younger boy to emerge as the stronger.

A further study of the relations in this family uncovered the fact that this man was in strong competition with his wife. In the group, he attempted to involve the leader in a competitive relation with caseworkers. He would say, for example, "My boy's social worker [or my wife] said that this should be done. What do you think?" He attempted to pit one authority against the other. Obviously, because of the neurotic nature of this man's competitive needs of which his son was an integral part, group guidance was not indicated for him.

4. There must be minimal ego strength to deal with inner tensions and outer pressures, without feeling a sense of defeat, panic or failure. This particular lack has been demonstrated by a number of parents described in preceding pages, especially the borderline women and the men with character disorders.

5. The conditions described under the generic title of "readiness for parenthood"[6] make men and women accessible to group guidance because their emotional involvement is not too intense and being comparatively objective, they can alter attitudes and behavior in accordance with a newer understanding. This is not the case when the subjective involvement is too intense, such as

[6] I have given a rather detailed description of specific characteristics of mothers and fathers that produce specific problems in their children in my *Child Psychotherapy, loc. cit.*

when faulty sexual identification and the inability to accept with equanimity one's biologic destiny exist. We have seen from the examples already cited the difficulties women experienced in assuming the maternal role because of their envy of males, their desire to displace their husbands and jealousy of their sons. Similarly, some of the men cited assumed subordinate places in the families thus confusing their children as to their own identifications.

The ideology of the modern woman, the changing image of womanhood within herself and in the culture generally, and her male-patterned strivings greatly interfere with and distort the maternal instinct. This is one of the most serious and race-degenerative by-products of a technological social order. Because it supplies ready satisfactions of her competitive strivings in relation to males, the basic masochistic nature of woman as it expresses itself in motherhood is weakened and in many entirely eradicated. While women cannot shed organic urges and biologic cravings to be mothers, the capacity for sacrifice and self-denial that rearing children entails have been greatly diminished (see Chapter I). As a result, those who do have children, treat them with impatience and irritation.

6. The basic requirement for inclusion of parents in child-centered guidance is that the child must not be a part of the parent's neurotic syndrome; that is, where the pattern of dealing with the child does not stem from the neurotically determined compelling need, for as we know the repetition compulsion of the neurotic is only partially under the control of his ego or "will." Whether it is strictness or laxity, domination or neglect, infantilization or acceleration of maturity, rejection or pampering, if they are compelling needs as a result of a parent's neurotic constellation, they are not accessible to the ego and therefore cannot be affected by re-educative guidance. Most of the parents with whom we had been successful in these groups were those whose behavior with their children stemmed rather from culturally determined attitudes and values. An even more reliable indication of success is where there is misunderstanding of the parental role in the growth and development of a child. As already seen, in our culture it means force and authority and

shaping the child in accord with tradition and societal mores. The pattern of abject obedience is particularly imbedded in the ideology of parents. When these attitudes and values have superficial roots, they are accessible to the ego and can be controlled under guidance; when they stem from a neurosis other means have to be sought.

Among our parents there were those who, having come from different cultures, such as the Near East and East Europe, and from Americans of lower economic levels, could not accept the idea of undesirable sleeping arrangements, for example. This was not because of any pathological state or incestuous wishes, but because they have themselves grown up in congested quarters where no heed was given to the subject, and they were surprised or distrustful of the "overmodernized" ideas. Where such arrangements reflect their backgrounds rather than being a response to emotional needs, the parents could accept suggestions for changes. When they are, however, based on an unconscious need of the parent, guidance may help them change a particular situation, but their subjective needs will cause them to do something else in line with those needs with even more destructive consequences.

Parents with self-effacing and masochistic strivings that originated in early family relations gain greatly from these groups. This, of course, is true in instances of psychic or "moral" rather than sexual masochism. The status and acceptance by the leader and the group correct faulty self-image and counteract self-effacing, submissive and fearful reactions. For parents who do not assume their rightful place in the family constellation because they are too different or because they misunderstand their roles, these groups are eminently valuable. This is particularly applicable to certain types of men. We have had many men who because of identification with their own passive or withdrawn fathers, or because of the values of their particular cultural group, turned over the rearing of their children to their wives. In many instances, as amply demonstrated by the case material in this volume, their wives wished that their husbands would assert themselves and felt relieved when they were activated in their paternal roles through the groups.

Many fathers, as shown in the group discussions summarized in preceding chapters, are actually not aware of their place in their children's personality development and mental health and quickly respond when this awareness is aroused. The reader will also recall instances where fathers could not be so activated or made aware because of deep intrapsychic disturbances or highly charged relations with their wives, children, or their own parents and siblings.

The mutually supportive and ego-strengthening guidance groups are of special value to parents with dependent characters. The group in these instances becomes the good mother upon whom many of the parents look for support and guidance. Thus, very frequently a mother or father would not act even in a very provoking situation with their children without "first talking it over with the group." But unlike their real parents, the groups do not foster dependence; they rather expect and encourage each to come to his own decisions, or at least to participate in arriving at them. When any one of the members tends to dominate it or to make decisions for the others, the leader has to fend for them so as to prevent developing the repetition of a domineering parental figure.

The need and the experience to assert oneself in the group causes much anxiety in some of the less secure and frightened men and women. They can remain silent and inactive for as long as need be until such time when their fears are dissipated, a process that in some instances requires the leader's help. A good example of the value of such groups to dependent persons is Mrs. Friedman (see Chapter V), who overprotected her boy and watched over him to the extent of stealthily following him in the adjoining cars of the elevated trains in which he traveled to his activity therapy group because of her own intense dependence on her mother. She complained of her husband's lack of masculine assertiveness. As already indicated, she was confused as to her sexual identifications and had castration anxieties. She gained from the group a great deal as far as her handling of the children was concerned, however, because, among other things, her dependence upon her mother and sisters was diminished. This diminution of dependence made it less necessary to make her children dependent on her. This is the mother, as the reader will recall, who could not understand why her pubertal son objected to her walking in on him when he was in the bathroom. "He is my son," she averred, "why shouldn't I walk in when he is dressing?" Not having attained a sufficient degree of individuation, she was not able to allow individuation in her children. The group helped Mrs. Friedman diminish her dependent strivings because neither the leader (mother) nor the other members (sisters) have fostered or exploited them. However, as already stated in relation to this woman, the more involved psychodynamic difficulties in her personality remained with her. Only her function as a parent had been improved.

By and large, therefore, the positive indications for inclusion of men and women in child-centered guidance groups fall into two categories: (1) culturally or ideologically determined behavior, and (2) some types of simple character deviations. We have seen, however, that quite a large number of mothers with more serious neurotic involvements have improved through these groups, at least as far as their treatment of their children was concerned. A number of borderline women as well have made impressive and even remarkable changes in their behavioral patterns.

This can be explained on the basis of the satisfactions they have derived from belonging with others, the comparatively intimate interchange, the identifications they established and the need to please, and be like the others.[7] We cannot claim without further investigation that basic changes had been affected by these groups, but it is certain that the children have had a breathing spell during which they were able to make strides in their development.

One of the group leaders who is also a group therapist described it thus: ". . . group settings have provided a health-nurturing milieu for the alleviation of tension and unhappiness. The presence of others in similar difficulty banishes guilt, shame and feelings of stigma; the individual no longer feels isolated with his troubles. In the group, man's primitive, age-old longings to be with his fellows are satisfied. The therapist, in his pervasively non-critical and accepting role, creates an atmosphere in which trust and confidence progressively supersede suspicion, rendering the group safe for the individual to be himself. Such a setting induces growth, encourages

[7] For elaboration of these points, see Chapter XI.

human exchange and mutual assistance. Fundamentally, it provides a realistic laboratory in which man can learn to live with others around him."[8]

In selecting parents for therapy groups we have assumed that the overassertive masculine women could not be affected. This hypothesis was made on the grounds that behavior and reactions stemming from serious character deviations are not within the ego's control. The function of the personality as a whole involves the ego as one of its major component parts. It is as a result unable to deal with intrapsychic reactions. We have, therefore, assumed that such women would not be suitable subjects for Child-Centered Group Guidance. Quite inadvertently, a woman who, by ordinary standards, could be considered as extreme in her masculine behavior was placed in such a group and she responded with eminent success and surprising rapidity to such guidance. We have had a rather large number of women with pronounced masculine identifications who responded favorably to the group experience.

On the other hand, a counterindication to assignment to such groups are women and men with depressions since their hostilities and self-devaluative tendencies may be easily enhanced by the discussions in the group. As a general rule we have eschewed accepting psychotic women but have found that some have responded quite well to the "group ego" and that they have carried out suggested routines in their homes with greater willingness than they did through individual treatment.[9]

A definite counterindication for child-centered group guidance is intense marital discord. When the relation with the children on the part of the parents proceeds from or is a reaction to their negative or antagonistic, and in rare instances overpositive, feelings (as in the case of Mr. and Mrs. Jacobs), efforts at our type of guidance would obviously be doomed to failure. Since the parent-child relation syndrome is an irradiation or a reflection of the relationships between the parents and rooted in them, we have to address our efforts to correcting that relation first. This is not the intent of these groups;

[8] Leslie Rosenthal, Group Therapy for Problem Children and Their Parents. *Federal Probation*, Dec. 1956.
[9] See case study in Chapter X.

it is rather in the realm of psychotherapy and in less involved instances of marital or family counseling.

Parents with children who are in any way atypical should be excluded from these groups. Special groups for parents of such children are necessary. When children have sustained brain injuries or suffer from any other type of organic defects, such as mental retardation, glandular deficiency, muscular atrophy, cretinism, abnormal physical growth, blindness, crippled states and other forms of organic inferiority and deficiency, special groups are necessary for they cannot follow plans made for children without handicaps. This rule is self-evident. Ways of dealing with children suggested or decided by the group for the ordinary or "average" may be undesirable and destructive where handicaps are present. Little or no ground for mutuality exists among parents of children without handicaps and pathology and those whose offspring possess such disadvantages. Such children require special handling for which training and guidance for parents should be given by specialists in these fields.

Discussions of the problems of handicapped children with the inevitable guilt and anxieties set up in the parents add to the strain that infect the other members which would impede and probably prevent them from solving their own difficulties. An added counter-indication arises from the fact that learnings and understandings arrived at in relation to ordinary children would not be suitable to the exceptional child which, if applied to him, may only make his lot even more difficult. Where handicap and stigmatization exist, plans for dealing with the child in accordance with his special needs have to be evolved. These differ in most essential respects from those recommended in ordinary situations.

It has been the practice by some psychotherapists to work in groups with parents of children with one specific handicap. Methods for carrying out this work effectively have not yet been sufficiently developed and nearly all of the work in this field is of a hit-and-miss nature. Perhaps one illustration will demonstrate this point.

In the course of my work, I am consulted by workers in various efforts in group psychotherapy, guidance and counseling. One of these conducted groups for parents of premature babies who were born blind. After a period with these groups she sought out help because she found that the parents had grown increasingly disturbed. In fact, so intense was the reaction that one of the mothers of such a blind baby fell ill, another became hysterical at one of the sessions, still another attempted suicide. Finally, one of the members of the group, a father of a blind baby, called on the leader and told her that he felt that the group discussions were harmful and the parents would be better off without them.

The leader was taken back by this frank evaluation, but could not understand why this should be the case. She then asked for a consultation to clarify the difficulty. When asked what the group discussions consisted of and what her aim in holding them was, the leader replied that she sought to have the parents "accept the children's blindness without conflict" and she, therefore, repeatedly stressed the fact that they were blind. She would then advise them how to deal with their handicapped and deficient offspring. While her method seemed entirely *logical,* what the leader was not aware of was that in repeating and emphasizing the fact that their children were blind, she was scratching at the parents' wounds, as it were, without giving them a chance to form a scab and heal. She kept their wounds open and did not permit the natural defensive processes of absolescence, rationalization, and adaptation to take place. The result was that the parents' guilts, instead of slowly receding, were kept at a high pitch and in some cases increased. Where this occurred, their defenses broke down and violent reactions resulted.

Though no valid technique for dealing with such cases has yet been evolved, it would seem, on the face of it, that the leader's gross and unsubtle emphasis on the children's blindiness only served to increase the parents' concern rather than allowing the accommodative processes that are continually going on in the human psyche to take hold. The leader's preoccupation with the subject and her repeated confrontation of the parents with it was an implied accusation as well, which intensified their guilts, self-blame and their tragic sense. Their situation loomed even more devasting than it actually was. The leader was told that instead of placing so much emphasis upon the children's defect, the leader would have been more helpful if she had accepted the blindness as a precondition of her work, namely, as the primary group code. Her own attitude of indifference or, better still, acceptance of the inevitable, would have been taken on by the parents by the process of induction.

Once she had succeeded in conveying by her own attitude that the children's blindness was not a "problem" but a condition of their lives, she would have helped the parents to view it with lesser self-defeat and guilt. This could have been accomplished by proceeding to suggest to the parents how to treat babies and children (not *blind* babies and children) and in a practical way arouse or activate compensatory senses in the child's organism. All this can be done without even mentioning the fact of blindness.

In these groups as well, the procedure should be one of member participation and free exchange. The parents should be encouraged to communicate to their fellow members incidents in the life of the blind or otherwise handicapped children, their awakening responses, reactions and perceptions and the ways in which the parents dealt with the new manifestations of the growing organism and psyche of the child. Here, too, explicit and minute details of feeding, bathing, playing, introduction of toys, pets, playmates and similar experiences in the child's life should form the body of the group conversations. All this can be done without emphasizing the children's handicaps.

No parent should be encouraged to escape facing the fact of his child's handicap or stigma. Denial of it will only postpone a more intense impact of it in the future. He must accept these as a condition of a life in which specific adjustments will have to be made and for which the child has to be prepared or trained. Parents can be helped to accept these realities with greater equanimity, however, as they acquire techniques and tools for dealing with their handicapped children in a constructive way rather than dwelling on the handicaps. Guidance or training groups for parents of children with handicaps, therefore, must be directed toward positive, functional aspects and conducted by leaders thoroughly versed in the nature of, and the most up-to-date enlightened methods of dealing with them.

Parents of psychotic children also are not suitable candidates for child-centered guidance groups for reasons given in the cases of the physically handicapped and the stigmatized. Such children require different treatment than do the ordinary, and decisions arrived at through group sessions as to ways of dealing with the latter may be imperatively counterindicated for the psychotic. This is also true of children with latent schizophrenia who may not present overt bizarre behavior and reactions. While in most instances parents of such children have an uneasy feeling about them and wonder whether there is something radically wrong, they have not come to the realization of their children's condition. This is due to the fact that apart from some irregularities in reactions, the children appear "normal." Despite this misleading appearance, however, such children require treatment different from those whose basic ego potentials are adequate to deal with reality under ordinary conditions. The schizophrenic does not have this strength and to make demands on him as one would on the average child would exacerbate the condition or bring on an active break.

Parents of children with latent psychoses, especially schizophrenia, are vaguely aware of the inapplicability of much that is said in guidance groups for parents with children in the behavior and character disorder categories and the neuroses, but they are not always able to formulate or verbalize their reservations. All they say is, "This won't work with my child," or words to that effect. If, on the other hand, they do follow some of the suggestions made by group members, their children become worse.

The practice of organizing special groups for parents of schizophrenic children only, may therefore be a valid one, provided they are conducted along appropriate lines. The advantage of having such homogeneous groups is that the children's behavior reported by all the parents have the same inherent nature and quality. The basis for the interchange is a common one and the conclusions, guided by a trained and thoroughly experienced psychotherapist who should preferably be a psychiatrist, would be applicable and constructive. Classifying such parents' group as "group psychotherapy," as is now the practice, is incorrect, however, unless the parents are treated *as patients* and their own intrapsychic problems corrected. The aim of the guidance groups is not the treatment of the parents but rather to equip them to deal with their atypical children in a way that does not intensify their difficulties.

One could expect that in some cases at least, one of the parents of a schizophrenic child would have the same disturbance and would require group or individual psychotherapy, as the case may be. If this is so, criteria for selection and grouping suitable to psychotherapy should be applied and the group interviews be directed toward the parents' own difficulties. Under the circumstances, there is no need, and in fact it may be impossible, to select them on the basis of their children's illnesses. If they are considered patients in their own right, they would rather have to be selected and grouped in accordance with the commonness of their pathology or psychologic syndrome.[10] When groups for parents, as parents not as patients, are organized, the assumption is that the common denominator of its members is the nature of their children's illness. When this is the case, the groups, by definition, cannot be referred to as therapy groups.

From the above characterization of these groups, it should not be construed that the discussions must take on the form of psychiatric lectures or seminars. While the parents should know and accept the fact that their children are schizophrenic, it is not necessary to dwell on this unduly. The nature of schizophrenia has to be explained to them clinically, dynamically and sociologically. They should also know of the potentialities and limitations of a schizophrenic child for his future adjustment, realistically, but also hopefully. The effect of environment upon the abatement and intensification of the condition must be thoroughly impressed upon them and the importance of interpersonal relations and ego support brought to their attention. Beyond that, the discussion in these groups ought to be carried on in the same manner as are the other child-centered parents' guidance groups described in this book, but with the different frame of reference in mind, namely, the children's ego deficiencies and deviant psychic organization.

The procedure of intake to child-centered group guidance of parents has not yet been solved. Hospitals and clinics have central intake, i.e., a caseworker interviews the applicants, obtains the case

---

[10] See S. R. Slavson: *Analytic Group Psychotherapy*. New York: Columbia University Press, 1952; and Criteria for Selection and Rejection for Different Types of Group Psychotherapy. *International Journal of Group Psychotherapy*, Vol. V, No. 1, 1955.

histories and other pertinent information. These form the basis for a consultation with a psychiatrist or someone charged with the responsibility of referring applicants to appropriate services. In child guidance clinics, also, this procedure is prevalent. The child is either assigned to an appropriate treatment facility or is referred to another agency or hospital where the needed services are available. In recent years, parents of the children have been considered for treatment as part of the routine practice, since it has become increasingly clear that preadolescent children cannot gain from treatment and hold the improvement when they do acquire it without some behavioral changes in the parents, usually the mother. To achieve this parents are referred to individual treatment or counseling or guidance. Group psychotherapy for parents has been introduced later which, for the purpose it was intended, was considerably more effective and certainly more economical, for not only did it save time for the therapist, but the therapeutic process was greatly accelerated through mutual catalysis. In the last ten years we have been experimenting, in addition, in a child guidance setting with the type of group that forms the subject of this volume.

To assign patients in accordance with their best needs to individual psychotherapy, individual guidance, group psychotherapy, or group guidance requires an exhaustive knowledge of their problems, backgrounds and psychopathology which cannot always be obtained from a single intake interview; more often the full picture is gleaned after a series of interviews. This presents us with a dilemma which I have so far been unable to solve. We have relied upon the single intake interviews in some cases, in others on descriptions of the personality of the candidates by individual therapists, but found that these were inadequate or unsuitable. Detailed exploration of background and personal history before assignment to guidance groups, on the other hand, set an "anticipatory attitude" for self-revelation and self-analysis in the candidates, which, while suitable for psychotherapeutic groups, is counterindicated for guidance groups. Another defect of the single interview method was that while we were able to glean the clinical picture of the candidate, his personality traits and characteristics that make him suitable or unsuitable for group participation were not revealed. Therapists whose experience is limited to individual work only are not always reliable judges as to suitability of their patients for groups. Lacking the experience, they are not aware that their patients possess mannerisms and patterns that make them unacceptable to groups. They also do not have the clinical judgment as to what patients can or cannot gain from groups, a fact that has plagued us now for more than twenty years in group psychotherapy.

Our policy has been to avoid the leader's seeing the group members individually before they met as a group. This policy was based on theoretic grounds since we wanted the guidance to emanate from the group rather than from an individual for reasons already given. It was, therefore, thought that individual contact with the leader would lay the foundation, the anticipatory attitude, for an authoritative role for him in the group. As a compromise, a next-to-the-best, intake procedure was adopted. This consisted of supplementing the one intake interview for new candidates or the referral summary by individual therapists on cases under treatment by a brief interview with the guidance group leader who, in addition to the information in hand, judges the characterological suitability of the candidate for a group. Such an interview, even of brief duration, reveals to some extent the intensity of anxiety, compulsive talkativeness, defensiveness, degree of blaming others (projection), rebelliousness toward authority, neurotic mechanisms in behavior and other attributes that may make a person unsuitable for this type of group guidance.

To obtain the necessary information the following suggestive outline was placed in the hands of intake workers, caseworkers and group guidance leaders. This information was the basis for judgment in selection.

1. Child's Personality and Problems.
2. The Parent's Background.
3. Family Relations.
4. The Parent's Attitude Toward and Treatment of the Child.

In our evaluations of the members' progress in group guidance the following factors are considered:

1. The Parent's Personality as Revealed in the Group.
2. Reaction to the Group.
3. The Nature of Participation.
4. Changes in the Parent's Personality.
5. Changes in Family Relations.
6. Changes in the Parent's Attitude Toward and Treatment of the Child.

CHAPTER

X

An Atypical Case

In a child guidance clinic it may become necessary at times to place a patient in a guidance group despite counterindications in terms of clinical suitability, as indicated in the preceding chapter. This is sometimes necessary when the treatment of the child is ineffective without some modification in the parents' handling of him, such as overintense pressures and demands, overprotection and overinfantilization of punitiveness. We have already mentioned a number of such instances in other parts of this volume.

One such instance was that of Mrs. Ross (see pp. 207-210) whose son was referred to the child guidance clinic at the age of seven. Since the age of four years, he had suffered from nightmares and sleeping difficulties, was afraid of remaining alone, and would not let the parents go out in the evening. There were fears of animals, especially bears, tigers, and of the dark; he would go to sleep only when there was a light in an adjoining room. He was enuretic and his mother still diapered him at night, a procedure to which a ritual was attached. The boy, even at the age of seven years, would bring her diapers, rubber panties and his pajamas which the mother would put on him as though he were a baby. She would then spread a rubber sheet on his bed and put him to sleep. One of the concomitant acts on the part of the boy was to direct his mother's hand toward his genitals, which she said she "tried to ignore."

The boy's nightmares had somewhat abated, but his conduct during the day had grown worse. He screamed at his mother when he wanted something and there was constant friction with a sister,

266

three and one-half years his senior. The latter teased him and he responded with screaming and striking her and digging his nails into her arms. He did not play with children, claiming that he could not stand fights or noise.

Since the age of two he was allergic to pollen, dust, wheat, garlic and eggs. Just before the nightmares started, he was given a series of allergy tests and ever since has been afraid of "needles." He responded to frustration with temper outbursts and crying and disobeyed his mother.

Mrs. Ross displayed intense hypochondriacal preoccupations with her children. Against the advice of several physicians, she forced on her daughter a brace for a slight inequality in the alignment of her shoulders, which was unnoticeable. Being set on "correcting" her daughter's posture, Mrs. Ross went to see one doctor after another until she finally came upon one who fell in with her plan, since, he said, he, too, had his daughter wear a brace for a "less serious condition."

Mrs. Ross fussed a great deal about her children's food, making them aware of the values of certain foods and the importance of proper combinations. She constantly dwelt on matters of health and harangued the children, especially the daughter, in this connection. Being in rather poor financial circumstances, Mrs. Ross had to skimp on necessities to provide her daughter with the rather expensive appliance which the latter wore under protest, resenting it very keenly. Mother and daughter were at constant loggerheads, though Mrs. Ross described her as "a very sweet little girl."

The father, aged thirty-two, was a clergyman, seriously ill with rheumatic fever, and spent some time in a hospital. He was described as affectionate, good-natured and honest, but also as hot-tempered and at times harsh with the boy. The mother, aged twenty-nine, was more lenient with Howard but appeared to be at a loss as to how to deal with him and gave in to him through fear that his nightmares and sleeping difficulties would be aggravated.

The nightmares and the many fears seemed to point to developing psychoneurosis, anxiety hysteria, with conduct and habit disorders in the boy. In line with her hypochondriacal trends, the mother was extremely anxious that treatment begin as soon as possible; she seemed to be vaguely aware of her own and the family's role in the child's difficulties. She had real warmth and concern for the child, but there was a "vagueness in the material about her ways of handling him." More information was needed as to how Mrs. Ross handled the child and how she responded to his difficulties.

Mrs. Ross was described as a rather attractive young woman who maintained an air of distance and seemed to radiate bitterness and hostile suspiciousness. She came from a very orthodox background and the youngest of twelve children, only four of whom were currently alive. At the age of seven she and her family came to the United States from Poland. She remembered her own childhood as very unhappy, because she had to help her mother, a chronically ill woman, a great deal and bear responsibilities at an early age, thus having little freedom or time to play. Mrs. Ross felt deprived because of her mother's constant illness. Her attitude in early interviews in individual treatment had been one of extreme guardedness; she tended to talk only about current situations and avoided revealing information about her past life. It was notable that except in the intake interview, she had never mentioned her father.

Mrs. Ross married her husband when she was nineteen years old. At that time, she stated, she knew that she was not in love with him. She married him because of her parents' insistence. "He was even more orthodox than they were," Mrs. Ross said, and her mother was very happy about that. Mrs. Ross felt that through the years she had grown to love her husband more and more. She spoke of him in glowing terms except that frequently there would break through marked hostile feelings toward him, especially as a reaction to his temper outbursts.

Mrs. Ross had an air of martyrdom which was especially evident when her husband was ill and she traveled to the hospital two and three times a day to bring him kosher food. She complained of "neuritis" with pain in her back and feet. Her attitude toward Howard was that she had "failed him somewhere," though she also projected a great deal of blame on her husband. She felt that Howard "may have inherited something mentally wrong from the father's family."

Both the child and the mother were assigned to a psychiatrist in training for treatment. The psychiatrist found the mother resistive. She was described as "extremely tense, anxious, nervous, overconcerned about her son and daughter." She hardly spoke about herself, her family, or her background so that very little was known of her history. After nine months of treatment when the psychiatrist left, he wrote the following: "Prognosis has to be guarded in view of Mrs. Ross's extreme resistance to therapy. She seems to come most often when she is overwhelmed by her anxiety, or when she can utilize the therapist for what she considers her realistic needs. The problem of contact with the boy on a 'catch-as-catch-can' basis has been the most prominent one and it is hoped that as therapy progresses with the mother this can be ironed out."

The case was "divided," the mother being referred to individual treatment by an experienced and skillful caseworker, and the boy to another caseworker. Treatment with the mother continued for approximately a year with the new therapist who reported similar resistance to entering into a therapeutic relation or to reveal problems or background material. As with the psychiatrist, Mrs. Ross persisted in continually inquiring as to what to do with the children, demanding direct answers to these questions and evading consistently the therapist's effort to have her enter into a therapeutic relation. Mrs. Ross steadfastly evaded speaking about her problems that would lead to the origin of her difficulties. The therapist, who had had many years of experience, described this woman as "the most difficult case I have ever had."

Despite the fact that Mrs. Ross constantly sought direct instruction, she continued during this period to infantilize the boy and to be seductive with him. The nightly routine of his bringing in his diaper, rubber panties and pajamas for the mother to put on him continued. This was not given up throughout the two years of effort in individual treatment. Mrs. Ross also continued to force the girl to eat, despite her refusal and resistance, so that every meal was a battle between the mother and daughter. Many of the conflicts Mrs. Ross related evidenced the girl's hostility toward her mother. In the interviews the latter stressed how much she cooked and baked in order to have "good, healthy food" for her children, but when she served the food and told her daughter how good and healthy it was, urging her to eat it so that she would be "healthy," her daughter would never even touch it. "After I work and bake and cook and slave so hard, she wouldn't even eat it!" Mrs. Ross would wail. What did she eat? She ate all the things that Mrs. Ross branded as "unhealthy." The girl preferred bread and other starches and "all those kinds of things." The therapist got the feeling that the mother was convinced each time the girl reached out for a slice of bread she was deliberately defying her. She saw it as an act of hostility and spite.

In reviewing the case, it was decided that the mother's hostility to her own mother was so great that she was not able to establish a transference relation with an individual therapist. It was also thought that because of this incapacity to relate, she would not fit into a therapy group although in such groups transference is diluted. As a last resort, in order to help the treatment of the boy, it was decided to try Mrs. Ross in a child-centered guidance group, the leader of which was a man. The group had been meeting for some time before she joined it.

The leader's remark concerning her at the first session is rather significant: "It was my impression," he wrote "that Mrs. Ross was the most overtly anxious woman in the group and if not too severely attacked by the other members may gain most from the experience. She appears to have a genuine, intense desire to understand her child and to work out her problem with him."

At first Mrs. Ross challenged the group, asked many question as to its function, what the group was for and how it was conducted, then asked the leader by what professional authority he was conducting the group. The leader recognized her challenges as stemming from intense anxiety and a wish to be reassured that the group would be of help to her. Her questions were answered by another woman who had been in the group for several sessions before. This woman who had had considerable experience in parents' group discussions in schools and child study groups responded to Mrs. Ross by saying they were there to "sensitize ourselves to the child for a better understanding between mother and child." She further informed Mrs. Ross that the leader did not give direct replies to questions, but whatever questions were raised were discussed by the women among themselves. She noted with a smile that "for the most part, Mr. A—was like a sphinx." It was for them to discuss questions on their own.

When the women discussed the matter of forcing children to wear particular clothes, the opinion was expressed by most of those present that a child should have a choice of what clothes he wore as long as they would protect him. Mrs. Ross was dubious. She wondered if a child did not need more "direct guidance" from a parent rather than freedom of choice. In her case, she told her children which clothes to wear, but when an impasse was reached she would allow the children to make their own choice.

A discussion between guiding and authority ensued and Mrs. Ross again returned to the question of clothes in regard to her son who disliked to get dressed up when they went out visiting. At one time, she had a real struggle to force him to change his dungarees when they were going to a wedding. Here she felt that her point was demonstrated in that a parent must use "direct guidance," which ended in her having to punish him and force him to change his attire. When she stated that her son would rather not go visiting than change his garments, another woman suggested: "Maybe your son does not want to go and does not want you and your husband to go and this is the way in which he tries to stop you. This must be so since, as you say, he always succeeded in doing it." Another member of the group remarked that perhaps that was the way in which the boy controlled Mrs. Ross, and by preventing her from doing the things which she would like to do he punished her. The only way in which this situation could be handled, this woman suggested, was for Mrs. Ross to carry out her plans anyway. At this point Mrs. Ross became sufficiently aware of her situation to say that because her husband was frequently ill she had to give him a great deal of attention, thus depriving her children of their share as well as having to keep them quiet so that her husband could rest.

The leader diverted the discussion from illness on to the children, but still another member of the group tried to explain Mrs. Ross's children's behavior as a reaction to anxiety which they probably felt over their father's illness and that perhaps Mrs. Ross was neglecting the children for her husband. Children do not understand these practical matters and want attention, no matter what; if Mrs. Ross were really reconciled to her husband's illness, it would not interfere with her handling of the children. Mrs. Ross reacted with considerable anxiety to this.

The leader felt at this point that her disturbance was too threatening to her and suggested that illness of one parent was a real problem for the parent who was well and that parents after all were only human and had just so much to give to everyone around, especially when one was tired and weary of the many tasks that impinged upon one. The leader recorded the following reactions to this statement: "Mrs. Ross visibly relaxed and smiled at me in agreement. She appeared to feel better at the thought of having some of the other women in the group appreciate the fact that illness in the family could disturb a mother as well as the children a great deal."

As a result of this relaxed state, Mrs. Ross in the discussion that followed was able to accept the fact that parents sometimes did take out on their children feelings which they had toward others. The women were quite sympathetic in this regard, commenting that perhaps where there was such a difficult situation, one had to stop for a while before lashing out at a child or punishing him. One should try to understand what was going on in the child's mind, and what it was that he wanted. They felt, too, that it was important to separate anger against one person or situation from another, especially a child. The women suggested that by doing this perhaps Mrs. Ross would be able to think more clearly about what was happening. When she did approach the children, she would understand their feelings better and could let them know that she really cared for them and wanted them to be happy, even though she was unable to give them all the attention they might want. All felt it was practical also for the child to know that illness in a family did deprive him of some things that he might feel were his due, but that this was not being done purposely and deliberately.

The women also suggested that despite the amount of work Mrs. Ross had to do, it might help the boy as well as her if she could find some special time that she could devote exclusively to him.

About six weeks later, Mrs. Ross reported on the difficulties she had with her daughter's eating. She felt that her daughter had to eat certain foods "because it was healthy for her." She complained that she always cooked food that was "good for the children," but the girl would not eat anything except bread. One of the other women in the group suggested that possibly the girl ate bread because it was one item of food the mother did not handle. After a prolonged discussion all agreed that Mrs. Ross should simply put the food before the child and say nothing. When she does not eat the mother should say that the food would be in the refrigerator whenever the girl wished to have it.

The following session Mrs. Ross came in quite pleased, exclaiming: "It's amazing!" "What's amazing, Mrs. Ross?" the leader asked. "Well, I prepared for the Friday evening meal. I prepared a meal with some of the things which I knew she never liked, but I prepared them anyway. I put it on the table. She began to make faces at me; she did not want it. I told her: 'Look, if you don't want it, you don't have to eat it. It will be here for you if you should.' She looked at me as if I was crazy and tried me out by not eating anything." Mrs. Ross continued to recount how difficult it was for her to see her daughter pass up the meal, but "I controlled myself," she added triumphantly. The following day at the noonday meal, she had put food on the table, made no fuss about it and her daughter ate! Since that time there has been no difficulty whatever with her in the matter of food. She no longer lays stress on food and she can see that her child gets along just as well whether she eats "all these healthy foods or wants to miss a meal occasionally," and that "it does not do any harm at all." Mrs. Ross appeared very happy about this development.

The other women then discussed training in food habits, and Mrs. Ross again questioned with some concern the rights of children to make decisions on their own and again asserted that she did not feel that children had the right to decide certain things for themselves. One of these, for example, was going to the doctor. This was explored by the group and guidance given by the leader as to how to prepare a child for a visit to a doctor.

When the group discussed the reaction of the children of one of its members to death and divorce of parents, Mrs. Ross reacted with some amazement and said that she had never realized "the depth of children's feelings and their confusions." The leader had described Mrs. Ross in the past as one who had never recognized that children ever responded to situations seriously and with feeling. At the end of that session, which was the sixth for Mrs. Ross, she commented that she had been getting more help from the group with handling of her children than she had ever gotten in individual treatment. Of course, she added, she had never wanted to go for treatment, but now "eagerly" looked forward to each group session.

At the following session, three weeks later, in this instance, Mrs. Ross talked of her son's bed wetting, which he had never stopped since birth, and he was more than nine years old at the time. She now openly described how he brought his diapers and rubber panties and pajamas and she would diaper him each night. Everyone in the group became uncomfortable. After a moment of silence the women recovered from the shock and one of them said: "There is something about this that is not quite right." Why should there be all this to do about bed wetting? Why couldn't the boy just wear a pair of pajamas and have a rubber matting on the bed? Why couldn't he put on his own pajamas? These and similar questions came at a rapid rate from a number of the group members.

Mrs. Ross offered all kinds of excuses: the mattress would get wet, the boy would catch cold, the house would smell. The others insisted, however, that that was not the case and that Mrs. Ross was making too much out of a simple situation. The boy had no incentive for growing up under the circumstances. He was getting too much pleasure out of all this. "Why should he give up bed wetting if you make it so pleasant for him?" one asked. "If you treat him like a grown-up and less of a problem child and give him less cause for concentration on this business he will give it up," another insisted. Still another said: "It is easier for him to be a baby, and what you are doing is keeping him one. Then you complain that he does not grow up and makes demands on you and does not obey you."

Mrs. Ross listened attentively. (She was described by the leader as "the kind of woman who tries.") That very evening she took away the diapers and rubber panties and told her son that he was getting to be a big boy and he should put on his own pajamas. He did not have to come to her to put on "the whole business."

At the next session, however, she reported that it did not work. She still thinks it has to do with the amount of water he drinks. She also heard of a theory that there was something in milk that caused bed wetting. She, therefore, eliminated milk from the boy's diet. When asked by the leader about the results, Mrs. Ross said that the bed wetting had continued. The other members of the group insisted that she continue with the new regime, pointing out to her that after all she had practiced the ritual for seven years and tried the new approach only one week. "Keep trying," they encouraged her. Being pressed, Mrs. Ross promised to go on trying.

The following session, Mrs. Ross reported that the boy had stopped bed wetting for the first time in his life and had not wet for three days in a row. She had abandoned diapering him, but attributed the cessation of bed wetting to the fact that she had stopped giving him milk at bedtime. She then proceeded to say that she explained to the boy that he was no longer a baby and that in time he would stop bed wetting, indicating to him that this was nothing about which one should make "too great a fuss." She had told him she knew that he, too, was unhappy about his bed wetting, but she was not too concerned about it because she knew he would eventually stop.

One of the mothers asked Mrs. Ross what had happened on the fourth night when Howard had wet the bed again. Mrs. Ross said there was nothing special that she could think of except that they had been very excited about his having stopped his bed wetting and promised him money if he continued dry. The mothers picked this up. They thought that Mrs. Ross should not have promised him money because that implied "concern and attention to the bed wetting, but in another form." They thought that the "less attention and less fuss and concern" was displayed the sooner the boy would stop wetting.

The following session, the third at which this subject was discussed, Mrs. Ross reported that Howard was dry almost a whole week and that "there were no bets laid on it." The boy wore only pajamas now which he put on himself.

In a later session, Mrs. Ross said that she now realized that it was her own consistent attitude that made it possible for Howard to accomplish this feat. When she was "wishy-washy and uncertain" the boy could not achieve it. She expressed her gratitude to the group for helping her "to find the strength" to deal with her children more securely. In the ensuing discussion, in which a newcomer to the group talked about her concern over her son's using "four-letter words" and the fact that children could not be forced to do things without first winning them over, Mrs. Ross commented that this was the attitude which she had adopted with regard to the eating problem of her daughter and the situation was "working out beautifully."

Mrs. Ross responded well to group discussions and there was a very evident change not only in her dealing with the children but in her total personality. While in the past she used to be withdrawn and frequently quite depressed, she now presented a lively appearance; there was color in her cheeks and her eyes shined brightly. In fact, the transformation in her appearance was so great that her former therapist who once met Mrs. Ross in the building remarked that she could not "believe her eyes, there was such a complete change in the woman's personality." During this encounter Mrs. Ross told the caseworker that "this group is what I needed all my life. I just can't talk to anyone individually about the things that I am talking about in the group."

Because Mr. Ross was greatly impressed by his wife's change of attitude, the improved management of the children, and the alteration in her personality, he became more aware of his own inadequate functioning as a father. He had been rather impatient with the children to the point of irascibility, and very punitive with his son whom he struck frequently. The improvement in his wife's conduct set off his own behavior by contrast sufficiently for him to seek help for himself in the same child guidance clinic where his son and wife had been treated. Mr. Ross made good progress in individual treatment despite the many difficulties in his personal adjustment and in his family. One of the traumata the Ross family sustained was the suicide of Mr. Ross's brother who had "a serious mental illness." The nature of this illness was not known to us, though we did know that he had received shock treatment. There was also a sister of Mr. Ross who was reported to have been psychotic.

One of the important elements in this situation was Mrs. Ross's attitude toward her husband's psychotic brother. This brother required a great deal of attention from Mr. Ross who had to drive him around in his car to various psychiatrists and hospitals as well as for diversion and change of scene. Mrs. Ross was disturbed by this and complained bitterly against her husband's giving time and attention to his brother, and tried to prevent it in every way possible.

During this period, Mr. Ross had gone through a rather difficult conflict between loyalty to his brother and his affection and feeling of responsibility toward his wife. When the brother committed suicide, Mrs. Ross became very guilty, was very disturbed, cried a great deal and showed every sign of a "breakdown." In her depressed state she turned to her son's caseworker who had seen her a number of times.

The group leader was not able to continue with the group after the ensuing summer vacation. After a lapse of about six months, Mrs. Ross's group was reassembled by a woman leader. When she learned of the change, she became depressed and sought help from her son's caseworker, at which time she bemoaned the loss of the former group leader. The following appears in the record of these discussions:

"Mrs. Ross felt neglected and deprived by her mother early in life. The same situation occurred again in her relationship to the clinic. She had formed an attachment to Mr. A—, the group leader, and when he left she became depressed and came to see the present caseworker. She related her depression to her feeling that no one was interested in her, that she might 'go crazy' and there would be no one to take care of her children. She expressed strong feelings about being deserted by the previous therapists. She talked exclusively about her husband, but now her anger toward him and her feeling that she had made a poor marriage came out. She expressed resentment at the attention he paid to members of his own family. When his brother committed suicide, she was guilty because she had not wanted her husband to pay attention to this brother. After the feeling about the brother-in-law's suicide subsided, she again concentrated on the marital difficulties and her hostility toward her husband and especially toward her husband's mother. This was obviously related to her feelings toward her own mother which she could not verbalize at the time."

Despite the reactivation of her original difficulty, self-deprecation and current deprivations, she had retained her more orderly and more effective appearance. The exacerbation of her intrapsychic problems did not break down her controls over the management of her daily affairs. She did not revert to diapering the boy or pressing her daughter in the area of food or wearing the appliance.

When she was placed in the new group, Mrs. Ross did not get along too well. She again withdrew, seemed very tense and disturbed at the sessions. The new leader felt that Mrs. Ross was too disturbed for a guidance group and thought that she should be assigned to individual treatment. On her own part, Mrs. Ross complained to her son's and husband's caseworker that she was getting nothing out of the group, that she did not like it and was not able to talk about her problems as she did with the former group leader. Her tensions and anxieties were so great that the husband's and son's caseworker found it necessary to see Mrs. Ross rather frequently in order to supply her with some avenue of release.

We find the following entry in the caseworker's record during this period:

"I had to handle with Mrs. Ross the fact that Mr. A— would no longer be in charge of the group. She had become quite attached to him. She told me that she used to come here and see Mrs. K— [caseworker]; actually, she said, she came infrequently because she did not feel she had been helped at all. It wasn't until she started with Mr. A— that she was helped. The group was always very good and she learned a lot. She had heard there was going to be a fathers' group.[1] She wondered whether her husband should join it.

---

[1] This group was to be conducted by Mr. A—, the leader of her group to whom she was so attached.

I elicited her feelings on the subject and at first she said that it would be good for him to have a group with Mr. A—, especially if Mr. A— was going to have the fathers' group. Later she thought that her husband would not talk in a group. She said she talked easily and could talk better in a group; her husband, on the other hand, was 'very introspective' and had confidence in me. She thought he talked more easily to me than he would in a group, that he probably would never say anything there. She hoped we would not put him in a group because he was being helped by individual treatment with me. Actually she feels Mr. A— and I are competent and that the family has been helped since the group started last year. This was in contrast to her first years when she was in individual treatment when nothing was accomplished.

"When I tried to explore her feelings about the change in the group, she said that if I told her Miss B— [the new group leader] was a competent woman she would believe me. When I tried to find out how she felt about being with a woman leader since things had worked out so well with Mr. A—, she said that she did not think it had anything to do with the fact that the leader was a woman. After all, she said, she can get on very well with me: in fact our short discussions had been very helpful. She had wanted to see me more frequently. However, she knows when the group begins she will be able to handle her problem there. I said it must have been somewhat upsetting to her that her husband and boy had been coming in regularly and that I had been able to see her only occasionally. I tried to evoke some of her feelings around this. She said she thought that the clinic had shown poor taste in not initiating the group soon after the summer and having delayed it so long. After all, she can come and see me when she wanted but there are some women who had to wait just for the group. She said if Miss B— were as competent as I am, things would go along all right.

"In the last interview during this period, I saw Mrs. Ross the day after the group had started meeting. Mrs. Ross was dissatisfied with what had happened the day before at the group session. This was partly because there were only a few women present, she said, but largely because when she asked the leader why Howard was so sensitive and reacted to everything with tears, the leader could not tell her. Mrs. Ross registered several other complaints about the group and the leader, and expressed disapproval even of the previous years' group because it had grown too large. She liked it when it was small. She was jealous. After all, she said, she came here to get help for herself and did not care to listen to other people's difficulties. She did not think the new group leader could understand all that was happening in her family since I saw both her boy and her husband."

Because of Mrs. Ross's disturbed state, she was referred again to individual therapy.

It would be of interest to speculate why Mrs. Ross was so resistive in individual treatment with two different therapists, one male, the other female, but responded so well in a guidance group. Although this case had been reviewed by two psychiatrists, it seems that the basic psychotic structure of Mrs. Ross was not recognized. Both individual therapists had treated her as a neurotic, a procedure unsuitable for her due to her unconscious fear of a break. Part of Mrs. Ross's ego was healthy while the other part was pathologic. The healthy part of the ego predominated in her case which not only kept her in contact with reality and sufficiently under control to carry on, but also protected her against the unraveling in treatment of her unconscious. She instinctively avoided the analytic interviews and kept them on reality levels, the immediate problems with which she was confronted in conducting her home and managing her children. Her constant repetition that so annoyed the therapists and her continued asking for advice was her way of controlling them on the one hand, and of establishing identification with them that would strengthen her ego on the other. In a sense she sought to internalize or incorporate the therapists' egos, a fact they did not perceive.

It was evident to us at the very first examination of the material that the failure of seeing the basic psychotic structure in this patient and the consequent unsuitable treatment approach defeated the therapeutic effort. Her psychotic structure was evidenced by her extreme preoccupation with orality as manifested in her attitude toward her daughter's eating; by her hypochondriacal tendencies as revealed in her own complaints and the preoccupation with her daughter's fancied deformity; the fact that she permitted herself to diaper her son until he was nine years old; her intense anxiety; her "vagueness" and her striking hostility and suspiciousness. Her anxiety served as a signal against overstraining her ego resources which were of a low level.

At the beginning the treatment of this patient had to avoid uncovering her unconscious; it rather had to be direct and somewhat authoritarian so that she would be supported and her ego gradually strengthened through identification with and incorporation of the therapist. The content of the interviews needed to be focused on reality which would have helped her diminish her psychosis. Not having received this kind of ego reinforcement from the therapists, she was unable (or afraid) to enter into a therapeutic relation with them. This she found in the collective personality of the group as well as in the leader, both of whom directly reacted to her confusions, feelings of inadequacy and fear, and gave her not only support but a *plan of action* which she could utilize through identification with the group. Thus, the group became her ego ideal as well as a source for ego support and an instrumentality for a better ego organization.

Her attachment to the leader which sustained her so effectively originated in the episode when he understood that she could not bear the severity of the women's attack on her at her first session and "rescued" her, as it were, by universalizing the situation and minimizing Mrs. Ross's guilt and inadequacy feelings. Her gratification was plainly and dramatically demonstrated by the appreciative and pleasurable expression on her face, which was vividly described by the leader. This was the *critical event*[2] in establishing the relation. From this point on her identification with the leader, who was in every respect different from her mother and father, became complete and the loss of him inevitably threw her into a depression.

The major service of psychotherapy for a woman like Mrs. Ross

2 See S. R. Slavson: *Introduction to Group Therapy*. New York: International Universities Press, 1952, pp. 124 f.

is the fact that she has an object of identification in the person of the therapist whose ego is intact and strong, which she can internalize. Patients like her attempt to model themselves after the therapist; because of their keen and sensitive unconscious, they act during the interview situation as well as outside of it in a manner as though they were the therapist. Through their keen perceptiveness they judge what the therapist's role would be if he found himself in their situation, and act upon it in a similar way. In a sense, the patient becomes one with the therapist and is, at the same time, a reflection of him.

The skillful therapist utilizes this identification to strengthen the patient's ego through the support, acceptance and approval by him and by helping him to dissolve the fantasies, thus dissolving the psychotic content and substituting reality for it. This requires a prolonged relationship with the *same* therapist since the process takes a long time and it is difficult for a schizophrenic to develop relationships. The basic oral dependence of the latent and borderline schizophrenic patients makes "abandonment" by a therapist a serious deprivation. This was the case with Mrs. Ross. Three successive therapists have left at short intervals which was traumatic for her and resulted in a depression. In this state she turned to her husband's and son's caseworker as the next closest person to whom she bitterly complained of having been abandoned and neglected.

The error that was made in the treatment of this woman was assignment to an interne who could not have remained with her for more than eight or nine months and when he left she was unable to relate to another therapist. The change was made even more difficult for her because a woman therapist was assigned to her who represented the mother figure. In the group, on the other hand, the therapist was a man and therefore more acceptable to her. In the group also she did not have to confide. The diluted transference was more acceptable to her and the fact that the major objects of identification were the other members of the group, or possibly the group as a whole, made it even less of a threat. However, the therapist still represented the good mother figure who accepted her without reserve.

The group presented Mrs. Ross with a situation that was less demanding and exerted fewer pressures, where she was also accepted and respected. Here she could relate to people within the limits of her capacity without being threatened or hurt, and the members of the group evinced a strong interest in her affairs and genuinely tried to help her. This was particularly important in this case. To be accepted (loved) without the threat of being monopolized and restricted (incorporated, eaten up), as had been the case with her mother and in individual treatment with a woman especially, made Mrs. Ross secure and she was able to attach herself to the group. This in turn made it possible for her to identify with the ideas, values, and expectations of the group rather than with any one person. It was the *collective personality* of the group rather than the individual personality of the therapist that she could accept and emulate.

It must be recognized that in terms of permanent change, a patient like Mrs. Ross is not very rewarding. One cannot basically *change* her personality by means so far available to us. She can, however, *improve* through support and guidance so that the impact of her influence would be reduced. Our objective, therefore, was to remove or diminish the pressures upon the children and give them a breathing spell, as it were, when they could reintegrate their psychotic forces and recover to some extent from the damage they had already sustained. As we have seen, one aim of child-centered guidance groups in a clinical setting is to give children under psychologic treatment the opportunity to change by warding off or reducing their parents' damaging pressures during the period of therapy.

The male therapist who subsequently treated Mrs. Ross individually reported that she was much more accessible to treatment than she had been described by the other therapists. It may be that the group experience has strengthened her ego which is exemplified by her improved treatment of the children and husband. It has also reduced her fears and increased her capacity for object relations and, therefore, also for a therapeutic relation.

It is therefore possible that child-centered guidance groups can be effective in treating borderline and latent psychotic patients when included with ordinary persons that meet the qualifications.

Membership in a friendly, family-substitutive group, unlike the one the patient had been exposed to in childhood; the permissive, accepting, friendly, and understanding leader; identification with a group; the emphasis upon reality and reality testing; and the free incorporation of the ideas and personalities of fellow members and leader made possible in such groups—all these may constitute the very setting in which latent and borderline schizophrenic patients can be treated.

The Dynamics of Child-Centered Group
Guidance of Parents

The reader will recall that a distinct contrast was drawn between psychotherapy and guidance (pp. 14-16), a contrast that is applicable also to group psychotherapy and group guidance. We have also suggested that in special cases the latter may be therapeutic (p. 283). This may appear at first glance to be conflicting statements. However, closer scrutiny will show the statements consistent, but before we launch upon the task of harmonizing them, it may be fruitful to bring into focus some of the basic dynamics that operate in child-centered guidance groups which yield the results reported in this volume with carefully selected adults. What follows are some of the formulations we were able to make at the present time. There is no doubt that further experience and study of this new technique will add others, perhaps of more relevant nature.

Buttressing positive trends. The group discussions reproduced at different points in this volume unmistakenly reveal the fact that the participants buttress each other's positive trends and constructive elements in their lives. The talks tend to counteract or dissolve hostile and destructive practices as reflected in critical, fault-finding, restrictive and rejecting responses toward themselves and their families. The outcome is clearly an optimistic, hopeful outlook displacing their pervasive hopelessness and sense of defeat. The group members with the aid of the leader guide one another toward discovering effective ways of dealing with hitherto frustrating situations, thereby eliminating or reducing their sense of failure and defeat.

The prevalent expectations of failure are diminished and hopes for success and comfort enhanced. In more fundamental terms these groups ally themselves with the life urge rather than the negative or destructive impulses. The principle of love and understanding is substituted for hate and irritation. This is partially achieved through the leader's positive, constructive and helpful attitude and intent which is inevitably communicated to the members of the groups. His attitude reinforces the latent love instinct that had been overwhelmed or subordinated through the overpowering suffering and negative experiences of the past and the hopelessness that these beget.

The mutualistic pattern and clear and honest intent to be helpful and to understand that pervade these groups generate new feeling-responses in the sibling-like setting, alien to the past relations of these men and women. A new awareness of self-other-self-relatedness emerges; new and formerly unknown emotional reactions are activated. Here are people (as exemplified by the leader) who are not propelled to be critical and disapproving; rather they share their difficulties, preoccupations and problems; they sympathetically seek to help, are interested in each other's welfare and genuinely aim to be of service. This mutuality and oneness of purpose and the warmth stir new and hitherto unknown and unexperienced constructive feelings that enhance the love impulse with the consequent diminution of hostile, destructive reactions. The new-found feelings give the personality mellowness, tolerance, flexibility, and capacity for empathy and understanding that cannot but overflow to all relations, especially those with mates and children.

Empathy with children. The groups dissipate rigidities toward children and expectations that they live up to idealized images and adult-approved standards. The interpretation of the child's unavoidable, in fact inherent fears, confusions and immaturity predisposes parents to a *willingness* to understand and accept his basic differences from themselves, and to respond to children's needs, rather than demand conduct which they are not yet capable of achieving. As a result parents react to their children empathically and sympathetically rather than demandingly, punitively and rejectingly.

Self-acceptance. Because the parents in the groups experience for the first time in their lives acceptance, that is, they themselves are not criticized, humiliated and made guilty, they are able through imitation as well as through newly acquired inner relaxation to accept themselves with less criticism and resentment. Having had the experience of being accepted, they are on the road of accepting themselves in a more sanguine light; and when this occurs they are also able to accept with greater tolerance limitations and foibles in others. They are rendered more disposed to take a positive view of and to empathize with the struggles a child has in adapting himself to the adult world and to the demands made upon him.

Mirror reaction. Parents do not normally stop to examine the validity of their ways of dealing with their children; being emotionally involved, they are not aware of the effects of their conduct and of their part in children's difficulties and anomalies. In these groups such matters are mulled over and over until awareness finally emerges. This awareness is greatly accelerated and enhanced through seeing one's self mirrored in the acts of others. While a parent in isolation may succeed through his defensive mechanisms and fear of guilt in blocking out and in denying or ignoring his undesirable behavior, this is not as easily accomplished when faced with similar behavior in others. Unless the defenses are too rigid, in which case the parent would not be acceptable for our guidance groups, his identification tendencies cannot but lead him to recognize reactions in himself similar to those presented by fellow members. Such mirroring of one's mechanisms and acts is one of the important dynamics in loosening up the crustification of convictions, behavior patterns and defenses and in laying the foundation for emotional detachment, objectivity and flexibility.

Universalization. Time and again members of child-centered parent guidance groups expressed their relief at finding that others, too, had problems with their children. Reduction of feelings of uniqueness and of being alone with one's guilt and discomfort diminishes tension in guidance groups as it does in therapy groups. The discovery that one is not alone in an undesirable trait or in failure allays guilt and bolsters self-esteem. Failure, even if it is not consciously admitted or verbalized, leads to self-devaluation and feelings of unworthiness. On the other hand, the discovery that others, too, are subject to similar inadequacies and errors and are comrades in distress decreases onus and stigma, setting one up in a better light. Universalization is inherent in guidance groups with all the salutary results of relaxing the individual and thus making him accessible to learning and evolving new patterns of behavior.

A psychotherapist who referred a father of one of her child patients reported that the man told her he enjoyed going to the group because there he met people who also had problems with their children similar to his own. She felt that this experience had helped this father to overcome his uncontrollable feeling that his child was "abnormal." He began to recognize that his concept of normality was not true to life and that variant behavior did not necessarily mean abnormality or mental illness. This recognition, she felt, as well as the father's decreased feeling of isolation with his troubles made him more accessible to her therapeutic efforts.

Mutuality. Due to the fact that all participants have substantially the same difficulties and are preoccupied with similar problems, as well as the fact that a spirit of intimacy, sharing and mutual helpfulness reign, there emerges a feeling in groups which we describe as *mutuality.* Our guidance group leaders felt that this was of prime value in enlisting the parents in making an effort to deal with their children more appropriately. It was as though they attempted to please the group, gain its approval and be accepted by it. This can best be observed in the group itself, which was described by one of the leaders as follows: "On the basis of my experience in both children's activity therapy groups and the fathers' guidance groups, I have the feeling that the *group itself* seems to have as much meaning for them as it has for the children. The fathers seems to have a great need and a great hunger for group association as such. One becomes aware of an actual physical enjoyment on the part of the parents in being with others, which is sometimes translated into language. The men would sometimes make a comment, such as: 'It's peaceful here.' On the evening of the last session of the group season there was a very severe storm with heavy rain. I did not expect that any of the men would come, instead eight of the nine fathers turned up."

It is understandable that when persons with disturbing difficulties are offered a setting in which feelings of isolation are reduced and the sense of being a failure diminished, they would seek out and enjoy such a setting. The men and women in our groups do not, by and large, have warm or close relationships; they feel more isolated and lonely than the average. Being with others in a relation of mutual acceptance and sharing cannot but give them a feeling of inner warmth, pleasure and security. In fact, friendly relations often extend beyond the group. Members drive each other home in their cars, for example; they help one another to find parking space for their cars; offer one another discarded children's toys and equipment. The reader will recall the instance where one of the fathers offered a hamster cage for the latter's son. They also proffer advice to each other not only on matters of dealing with their children, but also as to suitable pets for children of different ages and sexes and ways of caring for them. In one instance a member of a group placed his son in a scout troop led by another.[1]

In large urban communities where individuals tend to get lost and feel isolated and lonely, a small group such as a guidance group with its atmosphere of friendliness and intimacy fulfills a need for belonging. Another reason for the enjoyment of membership in these groups is that parents of young children have little opportunity to meet with others because they are occupied with their numerous and pressing duties and have to stay home with their children. This limits their circle of social contacts which these groups extend.

There is also the possibility that the emotional experience of mutual relationships such as our groups supply causes the parents to recognize the constructive value of human interdependence, which is a component part of mutuality. This recognition tends to make them more tolerant, more understanding and more appreciative of the value of their children's dependence on them, which in turn

[1] It may be interesting to note in this connection that the man became interested in working with children as a direct result of his membership in a child-centered guidance group.

enhances their capacities for empathy and responsiveness. As they accept their normal dependence upon others, they are not as disturbed at the manifestations of these feelings in their children. The leader's attitude toward their foibles in these respects brings home to them the conviction that nonpunitiveness is a more effective and a more constructive way of dealing with situations. The group's mutuality serves to reduce their rivalries and competition outside of the group and is manifested in improved relations with siblings, parents and mates.

Mutuality, and the security it yields, serves to reduce the defensive aggressiveness in some and diffidence and withdrawal in others. Just as the frightened and the diffident children in activity therapy groups gain courage to act assertively and with confidence, so do the adults in this permissive environment grow in this direction. Many of the fathers and mothers who have been initially cautious, silent and fearful have gradually become active participants, and some of them later proved to be the more perceptive and the more thoughtful among their fellow group members. As we shall attempt to show later, this is only one of the number of similarities between activity group therapy for children in latency and guidance groups for parents.

Identification with wholesome parent figure. In view of the fact that the leader accepts the members of the group unconditionally, is tolerant and permissive, and respects them and their ideas, he serves as a pattern on which parents model their treatment of children. We have seen how aggressive, intolerant, quarrelsome men and women have curbed themselves. Having been accepted without criticism or castigation, their defensiveness had been diminished, their attitudes altered, and conduct improved. They grew more tolerant and more accepting as they identified with the good parent figure, the leader. In a real sense these groups are replica of the family, for in families where parents are tolerant, accepting and kindly, the siblings are in comparative harmony with one another both because they identify with the parents and because sibling rivalries are at their lowest ebb under such conditions.

By virtue of his position, the leader is a model of identification and of ego functioning whom the members emulate in relation to one another in the group and later toward their mates and children. Mrs. Cross, for example, made the statement that through the group she had learned that she could talk matters over not only with her children, but also with her husband. In the past she assumed that her function was to make decisions and that everyone in her family had to obey her (p. 167). Having experienced comforting and gratifying equalitarian relationships and participation in give-and-take discussions, she grew sufficiently relaxed to accept the leader as a model whom in the past she would have rejected and opposed as she did her parents. This new pattern she then incorporated in her family relations.

Acquisition of knowledge. The positive effects of guidance groups on parents is not solely derived from unconscious and emotional sources. The records of group sessions have shown that at appropriate times the leader amplifies the discussions by specific information on a subject at hand, giving it body and substance and preventing the spread of unfounded or little corroborated opinions. Parents with little educational background and scanty or no psychological insights frequently go off the "deep end" on subjects of child rearing, child development, human relations and personality growth. Many of the ideas are antiquated and the information misleading and incorrect. The leader has to be prepared to supply scientifically valid facts and the most reliable and best founded information available. He supplies factual information on matters that may puzzle the group members or where their conclusions are unsound. There is no dearth of information in the field on child nature and sequential development, but care must be taken that the discussions do not degenerate into academic lectures or abstruse peroration. The conversations must be on a level of empiricism and operational use in dealing with children. Information should be given sparingly and only to buttress or clarify points under discussion.

Reduction of ego load. Parents suffer from basic and unavoidable guilt, because of their awareness of failure, of incompetence in dealing with their children, of lack of knowledge of child nature and needs. These factors impose a great load upon their egos. It is the ego that is called upon to carry the burden of anxiety, conflict, guilt and confusion, to control hostile, aggressive and otherwise negative impulses, to arrive at compromises and find solutions, to establish and operate defenses. When a parent has to carry all these, and many more tensions and burdens, the ego becomes *overloaded* which results in irrational and disadvantageous behavior. Tempers overflow, aggressions are acted out in unsuitable punishment, unwholesome relations ensue and the total family atmosphere becomes vitiated and unsuitable for both children and their parents.

When this is the situation in the family, reduction of the ego load is indicated. The individual requires help, which in some instances may be forthcoming from his mate, parent, friend, minister or therapist. Communicating one's burdens and adversities, that is, sharing them with another person, halves the weight of trouble. It is this sharing of ego burdens that persons seek when they talk. Talk has been correctly characterized as "unburdening," for bearing pain and tension in loneliness is a great strain, indeed, upon the ego and the total organism.

For this reason, "sharing," to which frequent reference has been made before, is so important. It is even more valuable when one unburdens himself to kindred souls, to persons who can understand and empathize because of similarity of difficulties and life situations, as is the case in our guidance groups. "Sharing" in this sense means distributing the load the ego is carrying so that it is freed for other functions and demands. General improvement observed in members of these groups is the result.[2] The striking improvement in physical appearance, gleam of the eyes, color of the cheeks, general alertness, mood and intellectual functions are derived from freeing ego energies hitherto absorbed in holding down or resolving guilt and conflict. The energies thus freed are automatically employed toward personality integration and expansion. Physical improvement of parents in child-centered groups has been commented on by all leaders and a few were recorded in this volume, notably Mrs. Ross.

Increased ego reserves for daily function derived from the elimi-

2 See S. R. Slavson: *Child Psychotherapy*. New York: Columbia University Press, 1952, pp. 145-153

nation of intrapsychic tensions that absorbed them before are employed in more constructive dealing with children. Parents now have the energy to hold down dissatisfactions, irritations and aggressions. Their "boiling point" is higher. They can call upon new strengths that have been inaccessible before because they had to be spent in maintaining a tenable emotional equilibrium. The feeling that one is able to deal with a problem and is not helpless generates a state of relaxation and detachment, which in turn make one accessible to reason. They also beget appropriate response.

Encouraging ego versus impulse function. A corollary of the preceding section is the phenomenon of increased ego function (self-control) and a corresponding decrease in id function (impulsiveness). This change in dynamic relation is an inevitable outcome of the shift of ego reserves described. The discussions at the group session enhance this change. The content of the discussions is directed toward better treatment of children that involves also a better understanding of behavior and needs. It is, therefore, inevitable that the parents should become aware of their unreasonableness and impulsive reactions; also of the need for a more controlled, more thoughtful way of responding to and dealing with children's conduct. This in itself, aside from the changes already described, tends to strengthen the role of the ego or reality principle as against the id, or the pleasure principle.

The trend is amply reflected in the behavior of the parents who had been participants in child-centered guidance groups. It is also reflected in some of their verbalizations. For example, one mother stated that: "I find that I have to count till twenty." In another group when Mr. Daws says in discouragement: "Is there any answer to this?" another answers, "Brother, you'll have to count not till ten but till fifty."

The groups discourage regressive trends and, in a way, expect each to act in an appropriate adult manner toward his children. Members are "pulled up," as it were, by the others when they describe their impulsiveness and uncontrollability (id reactions) by pointing out their ineffectiveness and inadequacy. The implication is that the group expects them to act with greater appropriateness (ego level). The group in this sense becomes a parental figure, usually the mother figure, but at other times it is the image of the father. When members seek approval, protection and gratification, the group represents in the unconscious the mother; when it expects or demands mature behavior, it takes on the role of the father. There is in a definite sense ego reinforcement that results in a more adequate ego function.

Reduction of guilt. Since the dominant emotion of parents is guilt, it must become the center of attention of everyone who is attempting to help or re-educate them. The most effective single dynamic involved in this is universalization. The others, in order of their importance, are objectification, release through verbalization, and increased knowledge. Parents have repeatedly expressed relief at finding others similarly "afflicted." Not to be alone in failure, or what they consider to be failure, cannot but have a salutary effect. In the past the men and women have warded off the depressing and anxiety-evoking recognition of their real and fancied responsibilities for children's ailments, suffering and maladjustment. Many of these are unavoidable and transitory, part of the growing process—a fact that many parents do not recognize. They feel unjustified guilt because of the painful struggle the child has in adjusting to and mastering the progressive realities incident to maturing. They feel guilty about the necessary exercise of authority on their part in training and inhibiting and applying punishment, as well as for the unconscious undesirable wishes they entertain toward their children; they feel uncomfortable and guilty over their envy and jealousy of their offspring and for the increasing difficulties the latter encounter as they grow older.

But in addition to these fancied and inevitable sources of guilt, there are realistic causes for it as well. Parents do overexercise their authority; they frustrate their children and deny them when giving and permissiveness would be more appropriate and more constructive; they do act out their unconscious wishes which they are unable to inhibit and impede; they act more cruelly than necessary, and they do have little respect for the child's individuality and rights as a person.

In a guidance group parents discover, through their own efforts, that while they have acted inappropriately in the past, much of what they considered to be particular and special in themselves is inherent in human nature and is universal. This discovery serves to relieve a great deal of guilt in addition to the general relaxation as a result of release, ego support, enhanced knowledge, acceptance of the inevitable, and other dynamics already described. Such discoveries, differentiations and clarity relieves parents of much of their realistic as well as fancied guilts.

Buttressing parental instincts and ideals. The effect of the nature of the discussions in child-centered parents' guidance groups is to strengthen the ever-weakening parental instincts in the modern adult. We have already indicated that while biologically this instinct is present and is as intense as ever, unfavorable social conditions and psychologic resistances to it are on the upgrade. This dichotomy of forces begets conflict and tension. Because the discussions in the groups are centered on children and the members' sole preoccupation is with them, the inevitable effect is strengthening the desire to be good parents and reducing the conflict between the biological and psychological forces that operate in this syndrome.

Many who have come to our groups did not fully accept parenthood, but dwelling on children in group discussions, searching for better parent-child relations and striving to function more adequately as parents, enhanced their acceptance of their role. They revised their images of themselves in which parenthood became an integral part and have evolved new objectives, that is, to be good parents, something which some had sought to evade or minimize. Others who have taken it too seriously and charged parenthood with excessive affect (cathexis) were able to relax and function more appropriately.

Support of cultural values. The ideal of being a "good parent" ranks in our culture as high as being a "good person." Bad parenthood is a social stigma; it arouses criticism and disapproval, and punishments of various intensity are meted out by society for neglect or mistreatment of children. In recent years some of the more enlightened jurists have extended the concept of neglect to include an unfavorable emotional climate in the home and the absence of love and affection for the child on the part of parents.

The obvious intention of child-centered guidance groups coincides, therefore, with the communal ideal of parenthood, and reinforces it. Our groups help parents to acquire status and the ability to live up to the social ideal where they failed to do so in the past because of lack of knowledge. It is, therefore, understandable that where no serious intrapersonal conflicts are present, parents readily adopt new ways for dealing with their children, for in addition to other satisfactions and advantages, they feel society's approval.

Widening fields of operation. As in the case of group therapy, we have found that guidance groups for parents also serve to widen the scope of interests and social participation. Some parents, especially mothers, are so immersed in the affairs of the family, absorbed and pressed by everyday demands that they exclude most or all other interests. This preoccupation and unilateral interest limits the parent's social participation and causes boredom and irritation. We, therefore, have here a situation that in some ways reverses the family process. While parents usually restrain and inhibit children, here conversely the children, and the total family setting impede the personality expansion of parents. In some cases children increase this through excessive demands and other devious devices that tie the parent down and force concentrated attention on the child.

Many are overwhelmed by the responsibilities and actual work required to maintain family routines and discharge the numerous and variegated functions in congested living quarters; others, because of personality characteristics, tend to overstress details and as a result become overburdened; still others have always been limited in social contacts and, therefore, do not feel the need for extrafamilial group associations.

Whatever the reason, families and children are negatively affected by such absorption on the part of parents and the result is impoverished intellectual and emotional development. Children gain when parents share ideas, activities and experiences with them and bring to the home a fresh point of view and an enriched personality. Without these outside stimuli the atmosphere in the home becomes stale and barren, for the attitudes and spirit of joyfulness, spontaneity and friendliness are destroyed by monotony and monotonous burdens and routines. In such families there are limited educational and cultural opportunities for widening experiences; neither is the urge to seek them present. The guidance groups, in addition to other advantages, supply to a limited extent variety to lives that are in most instances drab and monotonous. Though the exchange in these groups is largely confined to children and ways of dealing with them, the social contact adds diversity to the parents' lives and supplies, in some measure, at least, expansive opportunities and experiences. One can also hope that the groups serve as incentives to seek out other associations and that they are only first steps in the direction of expanding intellectual and social interests.

While we were not able to institute planned studies of the effect of these groups on the expansion of horizons of their members, evidence exists of these possibilities. During the group conversations parents mentioned from time to time their joining an art class or a community educational or pressure group. One definite development is noted in a father who had become a boy scout leader following the discussions in a child-centered guidance group. A number of the women referred to their being "den mothers" of junior scout troops.

Supervised practice in parenthood. If parenthood is to be considered a skill and not entirely a series of instinctive responses as it is in other animals, then obviously training for it is essential. This fact was made palpable by the questions and discussions in the material reproduced in this volume. No practice of a craft or a skill can be acquired by theoretic learning only. Skills and ways of carrying them out can be acquired exclusively by doing and by example. This is true of all professions and trades. Medical and nursing training includes inservice practice under supervision. Graduation in engineering is considered only a preliminary professional step. Training in architecture is predominantly of a practical nature and the problems the students are asked to solve are in every respect similar to those they will meet in the actual practice of their profession. This is equally applicable to all mechanical skills and trades. Empirical training on the job is the only road to skill.[3]

There is no reason why the same principle does not apply to the skills of parenthood. Book knowledge of child psychology and development seldom leads to appropriate action. Appropriate action can be learned only through guided action which these child-centered parent groups supply.

[3] A fuller discussion of the need for this is contained in Chapter II.

XII

The Relation of Group Guidance to Group Psychotherapy

The relation of group guidance and analytic group psychotherapy. We have already indicated that child-centered group guidance is different in every essential respect from group psychotherapy. A systematic comparison of the dynamics of the two makes this clear. The five dynamics of psychotherapy: transference, catharsis, insight sublimation and reality testing,[1] are either absent or substantially different in guidance groups. The nature of the transference in these groups is still unclear. It can be assumed, however, that transference feelings are different in different individuals according to their conditioned memories and feelings toward men and women and toward persons with more advanced knowledge and authority which the leader represents. Whatever they are, they are not in evidence or "worked through" in the group, for no free association around feelings is permitted, memories and earlier unrational reactions are not recalled, their association with current feelings and behavior is not established and their significance is not interpreted. The primary code of guidance does not encompass this procedure. This is reserved for psychotherapy.

The libidinal aspect of transference is not activated by the type of discussions either. Since unconscious sexual strivings are not touched upon in any way, we must assume that the sexual libido re-

[1] See *Analytic Group Psychotherapy, loc. cit.,* Chapters II to V and *Child Psychotherapy,* Chapter VI.

mains in the same state of equilibrium with which the group members come. No disturbance in this equilibrium occurs, therefore no change takes place. This does not mean that the libido, sexual and nonsexual, is not operative, or that it does not affect the positive or negative reactions of the group members or the total group climate. All reactions to all persons on the part of everyone have an inevitable sexual component, even though they may be rationalized or denied. In guidance groups with which we deal here they are at a minimum. All the leaders of these groups have observed this. There were definite evidences of a man becoming attached to one of the members and perceptive observation, as well as knowledge of his history, made it quite clear that the relationship was an offshoot of unconscious homoerotic tendency. It was also clear that the assertiveness and domination of some of the women stemmed from their phallic drives. Submissiveness and compliance of some and domination and rebelliousness of others could be easily traced to psychic and sexual masochism and sadism.

The intensity of unconscious strivings, however, cannot exceed normal limits in these groups since no interpretation or insight occurs; by "normal" is meant the quantum of these trends found in usual, stable relations. Excess of it in any member renders him unsuitable for guidance groups. As in the case of any other group the quantum of hostility, tension and social pathology that a guidance group can tolerate has its limits and these limits are much narrower than in therapy groups.[2]

Catharsis is limited in these groups to associative thinking.[3] Free association is not permitted and one of the important skills of the leader is to prevent it. Because free-associative catharsis uncovers anxiety-inducing memories, acts and situations, it cannot be permitted in group discussions intended to deal with "top realities" only, and with a limited set of them at that, namely, the understanding of the behavior and specific acts of children and ways of dealing with them. Since anxiety is a state of disequilibrium, it propels the individual to seek relief from it. In a therapeutic situation he

[2] See S. R. Slavson: Common Sources of Errors and Confusion in Group Psychotherapy. *International Journal of Group Psychotherapy*, Vol. III, No. 1, 1953.
[3] *Analytic Group Psychotherapy, loc. cit.*, p. 189.

achieves this by talking about the anxiety-arousing situation and the associated circumstances and feelings which result in release and insight. These in turn result in emotional freedom from cathected areas and persons as they are brought out into the conscious and the light of mature understanding is thrown on them.

It is clear that to allow this to go on in a group, the selection of the patients and grouping them for therapeutic ends require criteria quite different from those indicated for our guidance groups. Revelation of painful and otherwise emotionally charged material activates anxiety in all by the dynamics of induction, intensification and identification. A group, in a state of anxiety, requires that the therapist assume a different role from that of the leader of a guidance group as described in this volume. The aim of these groups is to prevent intensifying anxiety. It is certainly at a much lower level in guidance groups. The content of the discussions which avoids affect-charged subjects and the direction of the leader is aimed to prevent anxiety. Interchange that would arouse strong guilts and tensions are scrupulously avoided in child-centered guidance groups.

The "level of insight" that can be acquired in these groups is limited. In fact, by definition, the aim of child-centered guidance groups is not to acquire insight, but rather to sensitize parents to their children and help them understand their needs.[4] Insight can be achieved through freeing oneself from emotional rigidities and unreasonable ego defenses, which are not the aims of guidance groups. Instead of intellectually recognizing and emotionally accepting latent, covert and repressed impulses and strivings which is the aim in psychotherapy, in child-centered guidance groups our purpose is to throw the light of knowledge and understanding upon children's needs and their manifestations and to acquire the means for dealing with them appropriately. Whatever empathy and feeling tones are derived therefrom result partially from identification with the leader and partly through the reduction of guilt feelings and consequently in a lessening of resentment and of punitiveness.

The question of sublimation as it relates to the groups under discussion is a moot one and requires further study. Whatever

---

[4] For a differentiation between "insight" and "understanding" see, *Child Psychotherapy, loc. cit.*

material on the subject can be offered at this time must be at best tentative. Just what occurs to the hostile and aggressive feelings of the parents when they cease to discharge them against their children is in the realm of speculation. It is hoped that they are not displaced on other persons; at least our observations lead us to eliminate this possibility. Nor do we have evidence that substitute channels of socially approved nature have appeared in their stead. We must, therefore, assume that because we choose specific individuals, these impulses are only temporary noxious entities, emanating from tensions brought on by, and serving to release, an accumulation of anxiety, guilt and ignorance. When these are eliminated through the more relaxed feelings resulting from the group discussions no need exists for discharging them on others. Note should be taken, however, that parents develop new interests and participate in activities which may serve in some instances at least as sublimation channels.

In one dynamic only are analytic psychotherapy and child-centered guidance groups similar: they both rely on reality testing, but they differ in degree in this regard since reality testing *in situo* is of lesser importance in analytic psychotherapy. It enters into the therapeutic process as far as patients test reality, and themselves against reality, outside the therapeutic situation itself. In child-centered guidance groups, however, the sole concern is the reality of the child-parent relation and the actuality of their current acts and behavior. It is with these that the members of our groups are preoccupied, that is, the "top reality" of a specific and limited nature—child-parent reactions—which constitutes the focus of the group discussions.

Despite sharp contrasts between analytic group psychotherapy and child-centered group guidance, our observation leads us to the unexpected conclusion that guidance groups, too, have a limited therapeutic effect. It was noted in a few instances in preceding pages and can be justified on theoretic grounds.

The relation of group guidance and activity group therapy. A careful study of the type of parent that gained from child-centered guidance groups revealed a striking similarity with the children whom we succeeded in helping through activity therapy groups. In the latter, also, we had to eliminate the seriously disturbed and psychoneurotic children, the psychopathic, the psychotic[5] and the organically or constitutionally deficient. We found through extensive experimentation, prolonged observation, and evaluative studies that children in latency with ego involvements and some specific character disorders invariably improved. Follow-up studies as long as six years after termination of treatment showed that they held that improvement. We found that, to gain from activity groups, children had to have a measure of ego strength and a fairly good superego development. Such groups could not offer children who had been arrested in their development at too early a stage the setting for growth which can be attained only in a relationship with important adults, usually the parents. This principle applies also to the development of a healthy superego. A certain degree of strength of both the ego and superego is essential, for upon this strength the group can build, strengthen or extend. In fact, one of the requirements for suitability for activity therapy groups is that the child must have had a positive relationship in his life, even if a brief one, with some important adult. This relationship may have degenerated or been disrupted later, but the fact of having experienced it, had laid the foundation for "social hunger," which serves as a motive for change and the desire to become acceptable to the therapy group first, and later to others.

A close scrutiny of the criteria for acceptance of adults to child-centered guidance groups as outlined in the proceeding chapters, reveals a striking parallel between these and the criteria that obtain for the children's activity groups. Here, too, intensely disturbed, high-strung, neurotic persons cannot but fail, and, further, prevent the improvement in others in the group. Psychotic and with some exceptions borderline adults, as is the case in the children's groups, are also counterindicated, though we have found that some mild latent schizophrenics have made a good and beneficial adjustment in the groups which was found to be the case also in children's activity therapy groups.[6] These groups, however, had to be mild and

[5] Some latent and borderline schizophrenic children have improved through activity groups. See Leo Nagelberg and Leslie Rosenthal, *International Journal of Group Psychotherapy*, Vol. V, No. 4, 1955.

[6] See footnote 5.

extremely nonthreatening. As in the case of adults, children with primary behavior disorders (rather than psychoneurotically determined compulsive reactions) could be included in the groups. The reader will recall that where adults acted out toward their children an unconscious, neurotic drive, they were excluded from the groups.

We find that a parallelism exists also in the dynamics of the two groups. The factor of mutuality, for example, which is so important in our guidance groups, is observable also in activity groups, at least in later stages of the group life. At first the children function almost as isolated individuals, but common interests, fleeting though they may be, sharing and compromise, slowly make their appearance. The factor of mutuality is not as strong or as important among latency children as it is among adults, which is understandable in the light of the differences in the psychologic and social development characteristic of their respective ages. Another important factor that operates in the guidance groups is also a major therapeutic element in activity groups. This is the factor of guilt diminution. The children feel less guilty about their destructive and annoying acts through the acceptance of them by the therapist and fellow members. We saw that the parents as well have benefited in the same ways. The element of ego support so prominent in activity groups is present also in the guidance groups which is clearly shown in the minutes of the group discussions.

An important contrast in the two groups is the medium of communication. In the one it is action, in the other language. This too can be attributed to the inherent difference in age. Action is the language of the child, but its meaning is frequently clearer and more forthright than is the verbal language of adults. In this respect child-centered parents' guidance groups fall between activity groups and analytic groups. The medium of communication is that of the latter, the level of that communication is similar to the former. Both deal with, and occur, in reality. To the child, the group is a tangible and imposing reality; the guidance groups serve also the adults as a medium for dealing with actuality in their homes. In both cases the groups deal with the present, leaving the past and the future covertly untouched, or nearly so. Preoccupations are with the immediate events and conditions. In the case of the children, the environment is that of the group setting, which includes the other members and the therapist. In the case of the adults, the environment is that of the home. Both are in the present time-space dimension.

I have pointed out in my various publications that the therapeutic gains achieved through activity groups are predominantly in the realm of the ego,[7] though due to the integral nature of the human organism certain changes in libido distribution also occur, and some other purely psychologic effects are produced. From this point of view, the guidance groups are also similar to the children's activity groups. The elements present in the former, which we have outlined in this chapter and in other parts of the book, concern themselves largely with the ego. "Reduction of ego load," "encouraging ego versus id function," "identification with wholesome parent figures," "widening the field of operation," and others, all address themselves to the ego. The improvement in function and in dealing with children can be explained on the basis of a strengthened ego and the resultant ego controls. The strength to restrain impulse-ridden behavior is derived from the dynamics already discussed and listed above. Such strengthened ego occurs also in activity groups with children, and in this respect the two types of groups are identical.

This brings us to the somewhat tenuous conclusions which at this stage of our work with child-centered parent guidance groups must be considered tentative. This is the formulation to which reference was made on two occasions, that these groups are in a sense therapeutic in their effect, even if they are not so in intent. The influence of the group experience, the reduction of feelings of guilt and anxiety, the support the self receives, and the improved ego functions cannot be understood in any other light. One must be on guard, however, not to confuse them with or employ them as psychotherapy. The areas of psychotherapy are (1) libido redistribution, (2) correcting of superego function, (3) ego strengthening, and (4) changing the self-image. In guidance groups we have

---

[7] The reader who is acquainted with the literature will know that my concept of ego functioning embraces organic and constitutional factors, identification, psychogenic and somatogenic anxiety, fear, guilt and numerous other elements that buttress or devitalize ego functions of an individual. My most complete treatment of this topic to date will be found in my *Child Psychotherapy, loc. cit.,* pp. 45-47 and 162-163.

evidences that only the ego functions can be affected and in a specific relation, that is, the family relation. We can also assume that the self-image is improved. We are unable to affect either the libido or the superego by these means since the interchange is limited only to the area of parent-child relations and all other topics are ruled out; nor do we have conclusive evidence at this time that even the total ego function is affected by this method beyond the specified area of attitudes toward children. This and many other possibilities remain open for future study and validation.

XIII

Implications for General Mental Health

Relative to implications for Child-Centered Group Guidance of Parents, it would be appropriate to quote the following which I have said in another connection:

> It is idle to talk about mental health for the individual without taking cognizance of the setting in which he lives and functions. Total health can be attained only when life and relations favor it. Man does not live in a vacuum, nor can he insulate himself from the impingement of his environment; whatever effort he invests in attaining personal well-being is fully or partially defeated, directly or indirectly, by too adverse circumstances and oversevere stress. One cannot view the mental health of the individual, therefore, as unrelated to conditions, environment and relations. The individual is inexorably entwined in his climatic, physical and emotional environment in which he strives to survive as a biological entity and a social atom. Whether he is aware of it or not, he constantly makes organic and social adaptations to tacit and active demands of his world. As a moral being he absorbs the values and codes of that world and internalizes them to form the inner authority that guides his life; they are also the root of his fears and anxieties. Whether he wills it or not, he must submit to the authority of his group and that of his society and modify himself in accord with their demands and codifications.[1]

Even though it is not an autonomous institution, no one can gainsay the fact that the family and the relationships in it are the

1 S. R. Slavson: *The Fields of Group Psychotherapy*. New York: International Universities Press, 1956, p. 273.

roots of mental health. The family reflects and derives its character from the larger social climate, but in our culture the earliest perceptions the child develops of himself, of others, and of the world generally, the feelings of being loved and of security, are indelibly stamped upon his personality through the treatment he receives, and from the attitude toward him by his parents and other members of his immediate family.

As we have seen in the preceding pages, much of the deleterious home influences are derived not from hostility and rejection, but rather from the lack of knowledge, understanding and awareness of children's needs, from the absence of skills to deal with them as growing and evolving personalities and the social mores. Hopelessness, fear and despair about children's vagaries and lack of faith in their potentialities, are attitudes that beget catastrophic outcomes in many instances, and are the cause of avoidable suffering and deprived or constricted lives in multitudes.

One of the major errors of our culture is the assumption that everyone who can bear children can *ipso facto* also rear them. Provision is made in some localities for ascertaining physical fitness for parenthood through legally required premarital medical examinations, and a concerted effort is made by governmental and private agencies to impart knowledge on the physical care and diets of babies. No such planned or widespread instrumentalities are available to alert present and prospective parents as to their children's mental health requirements. In the isolated instances where such efforts are made, the educational techniques employed are unsuitable for sound and telling results. The procedures employed are directed toward imparting *information* (as differentiated from knowledge, understanding and insight) about the sequence of children's physical growth, intellectual unfoldment and emotional needs. We have seen even from the limited number of illustrations cited in the earlier pages of this book that mere factual information does not assure its application. Abstract information is ephemeral and the human mind is unable to retain it for very long in some instances, and of recognizing its applicability to a given situation in most others. Interferences and blockings by parents' and teachers' own personalities in these matters also play an important part, for when one is involved in an interpersonal relation, his judgments and intellectual functioning are not at their highest levels. Unlike matters concerning physical health, dealing with the emotional and other psychological unfoldment of the child requires more than mere information or even knowledge. It requires *sensitivity* and *empathy* that do not, for reasons indicated in other parts of this volume, emerge in modern urban man without conscious sensitization and preparation.

The approach and techniques of Child-Centered Group Guidance of Parents have amply demonstrated its efficacy with persons already in the thrall of parenthood and whose children may or may not have presented unusual difficulties and problems. However, even a cursory examination of the process and the results obtained suggest that in this method lies the potential for an effective and dynamic preparation for parenthood. With parents, the grist of the educational (not teaching) process consists of the actual situations and tensions, which in preparation for parenthood, the same practical problems can be presented verbally and discussed *as though* they were actually experienced. This "case method" is employed with profit in the training of teachers, physicians, psychiatrists, clinical psychologists, caseworkers and psychotherapists, and can be employed with effectiveness for future parents as well. The closer to reality the "case presentation" of the situations offered for analysis and discussion, the more profitable the experience can be. Here, too, as do the parents, the young people, the future parents, may at first react with traditionally patterned clichés of discipline, punishment, obedience, and insistence on "parents' rights." The conductor of such groups has ample and unparalleled opportunities to "sensitize" the young prospective parents to the subtleties of baby and child reactions, the build-up toward difficulties later in life and the means for avoiding them.

The emotional fragility of babies and children and the emergence of their attitudes, feeling tones, values and behavior, can be made palpable and impressive when they are related to actual reports of situations, rather than through teaching and even discussions of abstract theories. If the discussions of actual situations on a case history plan are carried on long enough, a sensitivity and responsiveness is generated in the participants which will serve their still unborn children in good stead when they are brought into the world. Just as some high school girls are in some instances encouraged to be present when nurses bathe and feed babies, as part of demonstration, and are sometimes even given a chance to do it themselves (which is contrary to good baby mental health, by the way), they can also participate in or be present at discussions by young parents' groups of the emotional care of babies and children. Where such parents' groups are unavailable, typical situations such as have been described in this volume and appropriate films demonstrating good and bad emotional care of children can be presented for discussion and analysis by young people.

Were Child-Centered Guidance Groups for Parents to become an integral part of young and older women's and men's clubs and organizations and used extensively in high schools, young adult groups, college classes, neighborhood and church groups, the level of mental health in the community would in time rise immeasurably. One must be aware, however, that where massive personality problems exist in parents and prospective parents, they will assert themselves when these persons enter the parental estate, as they do in all other relations. No educational method, no matter how high its excellence, will suffice to correct these. Psychotherapy only will make them better people and better parents. But where such problems are minimal, which is the case with overwhelming numbers, the guidance technique as described in this volume would prove of value beyond compare.

Appendix

Sol came to the first session of the group accompanied by his father. They were the first to arrive. The father introduced himself and his son. Sol seemed to be a neat, rather short, dark-haired boy, with handsome features. He was well dressed and gave an appearance of cleanliness and attention to his person. As his father introduced him he smiled without saying anything, but the smile seemed forced and the boy shifted about restlessly. When his father left, promising to wait in the neighborhood until the group session was over, Sol was alone with the therapist. In the very short interval before the arrival of a second boy, Sol wandered aimlessly about the room, lightly touching and looking at some of the materials and tools that were available, without picking up anything.

As the other six boys who attended this session arrived, they were introduced to Sol and to each other by their first names. Sol would acknowledge the greeting with a quick glance and then turn away immediately to look somewhere else. He had nothing further to do with any of them. He later took courage from the example of some of the others and began to do some work, demonstrating ability to concentrate, some knowledge of tools and manual dexterity. He busied himself mainly by pasting shells on a plastic form and worked as if determined to finish his project by the end of the session. He approached the therapist two or three times during the two-hour session to ask simple informational questions such as where he could get some more iron glue or where he could put the pins and earrings he had made. His questions were put in a sort of whining undertone and as soon as Sol received a reply, he quickly left the therapist's side.

Although there was considerable hub-hub in the room, Sol did his work quietly and seemed impervious to his surroundings. Toward the end of the session he began to make ashtrays which needed to be hammered out on a form. This necessitated his making noise, which he seemed to keep down to a minimum. He had not said one word to any of the boys throughout the session, though there was considerable interaction among the other members of the group.

During the refreshment period at the end of the session Sol ate his cake and milk quietly, waiting for his turn and making no demands or suggestions as some of the others did. After the refreshments he left quietly, apparently to meet his father downstairs. He carefully collected the things he had made which he took with him, and said "good-by" politely as he left.

From his demeanor at this session one received the impression of a neat, clean, industrious child, under rigid controls, with a need to achieve and to finish projects, full of underlying fears and anxieties. He isolated himself throughout the session apparently unable to make contact with boys his own age.

His behavior at the second session a week later was very much the same. However, he came to this session alone, which he continued to do thereafter. Sol traveled home by bus on a route that none of the other boys used so that he came and went alone. He arrived early, waiting for the therapist outside the meeting room. Throughout, he was consistently among the early arrivals. He would wait for the therapist and then anxiously run ahead as if being propelled by a need to be the first to burst into the clubroom and pre-empt whatever was available.

In this second session he was again very industrious and displayed skill in the construction of a bench. He again worked alone but exchanged a few passing comments with some of the other boys. He neither asked for nor offered help, nor did he participate in the scuffling that broke out in the group from time to time. He seemed to become tense and to stiffen whenever the therapist approached him and seemed acutely aware of the latter's presence. However, unlike his isolation in the first session and though seemingly oblivious of the boys around him, Sol would now and then glance about quickly and furtively. The intention of this was more to see whether anyone was watching him rather than interest in what was going on. He continued to be quiet and polite during the refreshment period and displayed good table manners. His clothes were again neat and clean and somewhat on the dressed-up side. When he left the session they were still unruffled and well arranged. He politely said "good-by" and left alone, taking the bench he had made with him.

At the third session Sol was again waiting in front of the building and greeted the therapist with a tight little smile, but without saying a word. He bounded up the stairs with the other early arrival, who was a loud, obstreperous youngster. Running for the closet where the materials were stored, James, the other boy, quickly found the makings of a leather belt. Sol began to look anxiously for one, but could not find any. There were a few brief remarks of disappointment, uttered half to himself, half to ascertain James's attitude. The latter was determined to keep the materials for himself. Sol then turned directly to the therapist and asked if there were more of the leather and buckles and when told that there were none, he turnd away quietly, but with obvious disappointment. For some time Sol seemed to find little to occupy him.

Soon James lost interest in the belt project and shouted: "Who wants this?" Sol and Paul dashed up together. They decided to choose for it. Sol lost and seemed to feel keenly disappointed. He then proceeded to saw plastic rings on the electric saw, and unlike the first session, made a great deal of noise. He did not appear particularly interested in what he was doing, tossing the rings aside as soon as they were finished. Suddenly he took a cap pistol out of his pocket which he shot off at intervals. This attracted the rather admiring attention of other boys who made various remarks. While Sol did not respond to any of the remarks, he nevertheless appeared to enjoy the attention he was receiving. Throughout the rest of the session he would, from time to time, draw his pistol out of his pocket and fire it. Then as if conscience-stricken over not accomplishing some specific task, he set out to weave lanyards. When the therapist volunteered a commendatory remark about his work, Sol became very tense. Later he fired the pistol in a rather rowdy, aggressive manner, even at the refreshment table. Sol's behavior at this session represented quite a turn from the earlier sessions. He was fairly aggressive and noisy. He did not seem to feel the need for being industrious and neat and displayed greater awareness of the other boys.

Sol attended the next three sessions. He continued to come early and was the first to enter the clubroom, manifesting restlessness and an air of anticipatory anxiety to get into the room. However, his need to do definite work was gradually and markedly diminished. His concentration and aim-directed effort was much less and he seemed not to mind that at times he had nothing to take home from the group sessions. His clothes too showed a marked change. He came to the group less well dressed. He now wore dungarees and a lumberjacket, and no tie. He did not seem to mind when he soiled his clothes a little, though this was a very slow development. For a long time Sol sought to maintain a neat appearance after the sessions.

Sol gradually became much more vocal. In later sessions he would occasionally shout and he carried on bits of conversation with the other boys. However, it always seemed as if he did this with some strain; it did not seem natural or spontaneous. There was always the feeling that he was doing something improper for which he may be punished. For example, whenever he screamed or committed some aggressive act, he would anxiously and furtively look around to gauge his activity in relation to that of others. While some of the other boys used profanity, Sol was not able to bring himself to do so, though he was later able to join with the others in some boisterous and destructive behavior. He would pair off with another boy in this or join the entire group, but he was always the follower. All his associations were consistently short-lived. He had not developed close or lasting relations (supportive ego).

Wandering about aimlessly and becoming aware of a clay-pellet battle in progress, he would without a word join one side, investing great energy in the battle. At such times his face would glow and his eyes sparkle. After such an episode he would seem quiet for a while. Once, when one of the group members suggested that the locked cupboards belonging to other groups be jimmied and ransacked, Sol hung back, though obviously attracted and interested by this defiant project. Slowly he drew nearer and then feeling protected by the fact that almost all the other boys were participating, plunged in, too. The fact that he found some things of interest to him, particularly belt material, seemed to justify this plundering especially because the other boys, too, appropriated some of the equipment.

At the next, or fifth session, Sol was one of the first to suggest breaking into the lockers and in his haste seized a chisel and got to work on a hinge almost as soon as he got into the room. When the therapist suggested that this was the group's own locker and that he had the key for it, Sol, taken aback, at once went to work industriously to fix the hinge he had partially undone. At this session one of the boys was painting the walls of the clubroom with blue paint. Again, at first timidly, then with greater daring, Sol joined in painting wide streaks of blue on the wall. He appeared very excited and seemed thrilled; his face was flushed as the paint spread and oozed downwards. However, when some of the paint dropped on the tools lying nearby, Sol seemed frightened as if he were going too far. He quickly put down his brush and walked away.

At the sixth session the boys built a small fire on the floor of the room and jumped about with great excitement. Sol joined in. He too was greatly excited and with a flushed face darted back and forth to throw a scrap of paper on the fire. He seemed tense and excited, making remarks and suggestions in a high-pitched voice. While suggesting that a larger fire be built, he at the same time expressed fear that it might spread. When a boy suggested extinguishing the fire, Sol responded to it immediately. He ran to the sink and returned with a large can of water.

Unlike the other boys who sought to extinguish the flames quickly, Sol poured the water very slowly and carefully in a thin, even stream over the smoking heap and even though it was no longer necessary he went back for more water. He repeated this operation a number of times and it seemed to the therapist that Sol derived a different type of satisfaction than did the other boys. He was the only one to approach the therapist immediately after the flames were extinguished to ask if there would be any trouble resulting from the fire-setting. The therapist reassured Sol on this account. But the next session Sol did not turn up. This was the first time he was absent, a fact that he did not explain when he came to the session following the seventh.

While on the whole he steered clear of the therapist during this period he seemed to be a little less tense as the sessions wore on. For example, at the fifth session he offered to carry upstairs some of the refreshments the therapist was carrying. In the same session he approached the therapist to ask for a pointed instrument to mark out a design on a bracelet on which he was working. He accepted the instrument handed him with a slight nod and walked off quickly. The whining, baby-like intonation in his voice was quite marked.

As noted earlier, Sol did not come to the seventh session of the group. He did come to the following three. The first of these three sessions was held at the clubroom and the other two were trips away from the room. At the eighth session Sol again arrived early and seemed anxious to get to the clubroom first. He asked the therapist for the keys to the room, which were given him, and he ran ahead. In the group's locker there was plenty of material available of all kinds including belt makings and enough to go around, but Sol grabbed more than his share. He had materials for one belt to work on and enough for two others stuffed into his pockets. As if contented with his take, he sat quietly working on his belt. There was a spirit of sociability about him not present before. He chatted rather easily with the boys as he worked and once when he was stuck he called out to one of them for help, which was given him. A few minutes later, however, attracted by one of the boys breaking into another club's locker, he joined in and they came up with an unusual acquisition: two bottles of orange "pop," which they greedily drank.

As if activated by this "forbidden" act and the resultant anxiety, a restlessness set in on the group and a small fire was soon blazing. As the room filled with smoke Sol ran for water to empty over it. He was the only boy to do so; all the others ran to open the windows. Again Sol seemed to derive great pleasure out of pouring the water slowly and carefully in a stream over the flames. When later the fire was rekindled, Sol very excitedly, joined in arranging a kind of fuse out of lanyard. Again he was the prime mover in extinguishing the flames, enjoying watching the water spread. A little later he painted the walls, but without any real plan, more intent upon watching the paint slowly ooze down the walls. He then joined in rowdy play where some of the boys barricaded themselves in the clubroom, shutting some of the others out. Sol joined in making noise, hammering, and in the general excitement; in this he seemed to find relief for his pent-up tensions, leaving at the end of the session quietly as if in a satisfied mood.

The two trips that followed were to a penny arcade in midtown, this spot being chosen by majority vote of those who came to the trip. Sol seemed rather indifferent as to the choice of destination, waiting for the others to make the decision. While some of the boys whooped it up on the subway, Sol was rather quiet with occasional bursts of animation and interest. Sol accepted his share of the money and went off to the various machines in the arcade. There was no contact with any of the others.

As one viewed Sol from a distance one gained the impression of a busy, alert and self-sufficient boy. This impression quickly vanished, however, when one came closer to him. With his money gone, he came to ask how soon the group would be going home and the whine in his voice reflected tentativeness, fearfulness and uncertainty. On the subway ride home when fellow group members teased Sol by grabbing his hat and tossing it about, he sat disconsolate in a corner looking very unhappy. He made no effort to retrieve it and looked as though he was completely defeated. When he rode for a time with the therapist in the subway, being the last boy to alight, Sol seemed to shrink into himself, withdrawing completely from the therapist.

On the second trip he seemed a little more relaxed. Perhaps it was the change from the accustomed group atmosphere in the room that proved disconcerting to him at the previous excursion. He remained pretty much to himself, though he made an effort to win a prize, in which he did not succeed. At one point, seeing him standing near a mechanical hockey game, unable to play because his money was gone, the therapist approached and asked if he would like to play. He shook his head negatively and shrank away. When the therapist offered to pay for the game, Sol seemed pleased and silently played out the game with the therapist; then another. As if satisfied, after the games, he wandered off by himself. He was the only boy who did not ask the therapist for money out of the allowance set aside for refreshments. As a result he later got his full share of food. However, he did approach the therapist a little later and asked for a few extra pennies he needed to buy more food. These were given him.

As the group descended to the subway platform, Sol was missing. A search located him on the upper level where he was running around wildly and very frightened at having become separated from the group. On the platform Sol's hat was again tossed around and again he stood by helplessly. Another boy, on leaving, gave the therapist some packages of candy he had won as prizes, and Sol quickly, as if he could not control himself, asked the therapist for one. When the entire lot was offered him, he looked at the therapist for a moment in astonishment, not accepting it, as if unable to believe his ears. He asked whether the therapist was sure that he did not want the candy for himself. When offered again, he took it quickly, stuffed it in his pocket and looked away. A moment later as the train he had boarded at the transfer point moved away, leaving the therapist on the platform, Sol turned and waved in a friendly fashion.

Sol attended three of the following four sessions, again offering no explanation for the one absence. However the fact that it followed another daring effort on his part to act out may cast some light on it. At the session preceding the absence Sol had joined with another boy in painting the walls with long uneven strokes of dark paint seemingly enjoying it. He then painted some offensive words and laughed loudly and nervously as he did so. Later, at the refreshment table he listened avidly to some off-color jokes told by other boys which led to his reciting an off-color rhyme. Other than this, Sol's activity seemed to waver between working fairly consistently on some constructive project and his being attracted by the destructive activity initiated by fellow group members. He seemed to experiment with aggression and testing himself out. He would throw clay and small sticks out of the window at passing children, join in scuffles in the clubroom, throw around missiles, mark up the walls or play mischievous tricks with others during refreshments. The more constructive behavior consisted of playing ping-pong with one of the quieter boys and working on a block of wood with various instruments. He requested airplane models in a voice that seemed more confident and assertive and devoid of its whine. On one or two occasions he took the lead in some of the rowdy behavior, once seizing a broom and waving it aloft, another time leading an attack of a number of the boys on an opposing group within the therapy group.

Once when the group had refreshments in a restaurant he asked, without hesitation, for extra money to purchase candy. He had apparently taken courage to do so because some of the boys had done this for some time. After one of the sessions Sol accompanied to a bus stop one of the boys, though this took him out of the way from his own route and necessitated his retracing his steps. For Sol this represented a growing capacity for object relations as well as greater security.

Of the four remaining sessions before the summer recess, Sol attended three. This time he explained his absence, which was due to illness. It was the first time that he had offered such an explanation. He was now vocal and almost always near the center of whatever group activity was going on, though seldom as the leader or instigator. He seemed to enjoy the playful and sometimes boisterous activities, but his participation seemed to have less of the intensity and infantile frenzy that characterized it before. He also felt less guilty. He would grab a paint brush to smear up the walls and paint profane words. While he giggled as he painted, he did not paint over the words as he had done in the past. He participated in all the rough games much more freely, sometimes even upsetting his own glass of milk or that of another boy, as if by accident.

At the same time his relationship to the other boys was more direct and freer. He called upon boys for help in his projects and on occasion worked together with one or another of his fellow group members. He also assisted others when they encountered difficulties in assembling their planes. He became a sort of an expert in the latter activity, since it now was a hobby of his. When the group went to a nearby playground, Sol paired off with one of the boys. These two played together for most of the period.

Sol seemed anxious about a new experience he was facing at summer camp. He asked a number of boys about the camp and particularly about the physical examination. Noting his anxiety and also the fact that he was going to camp in August, while many of them were going in July, they teased Sol, telling him that the earlier period was preferable. Sol seemed to take this with a smile, but he actually was cast down partly from a feeling of anticipated loneliness, since there would be no one at camp whom he knew from the group. He turned to the therapist for reassurance, asking him about arrangements for going away. While by and large he continued in his withdrawal from the therapist, his shrinking away and obvious fear of him that had been so marked before was no longer in evidence. On one occasion he approached the therapist for advice and help. He also seemed to take the termination of the group sessions for the summer as a matter of fact, talking rather excitedly with the others about the ending of school and the prospective delights of the camp.

During this time, the periods of quiet and concentrated work were somewhat longer. Sol enjoyed the model airplanes in which he became very much interested. He would sit for fairly lengthy periods working on them as the group's general atmosphere had become more relaxed. There was now also greater socialization among the boys and as they worked quietly one could hear conversation about their projects. Sol seemed now on the road to becoming a part of this setting. His anxiety about being the first to arrive had greatly diminished by the end of five months to the extent that he came late on two occasions. He still rushed up the stairs and intensely surveyed the room when he entered it as though to ascertain whether there was anything he had missed. Apparently his basic expectation of being deprived was still present.

At the end of the five months of group treatment Sol was still curious about the locked cupboards, but this curiosity did not have the same intensity and impetuosity. When he wished to look into them he did not break them open and instead asked the therapist to unlock them and he would look at the contents with comparative indifference. As though afraid of being deceived, he once asked for a second look into the cupboards later in the same session.

There was a marked difference between Sol at the nineteenth session and when he first came to the group. He now moved about much more freely, his furtiveness all gone. He seemed very much aware of the presence of the other boys, reaching out to them and seemingly being accepted by them. He no longer shrank from contact with the therapist, though much was still desired toward real ease with the adult. His excessive neatness, diligence and politeness had given way to more childlike feelings and behavior. He acted and looked freer; he was now able to shout and laugh more easily as well as concentrate and work for longer periods with purpose and with a focused aim more appropriate to a twelve-year-old youngster.

That summer Sol was described as being very close to a model camper in that he was active, participated enthusiastically in all activities, excelling in most of them. Initially he was somewhat shy about joining in these with his bunk group, but in a short while became friendly with all of the members. Although not actually a leader in the group, his constant enthusiasm and good nature brought him the liking and respect of his bunkmates. In relation to the adults and counselors, he was initially reserved and seemed to show some resentment, but as he became more secure with them there was more spontaneity and friendliness on his part. He enjoyed talking with the counselors and revealed himself to be intelligent, and easily managed by a warm and friendly approach from adults.

Enuresis occurred almost every night but Sol apparently was not overly concerned about this. However, at times he attempted to avoid wetting by not having evening snacks. He took part in some sexual play with another boy who happened to be the only other bed wetter in the bunk. According to the camp report, there was some play by Sol with the other boy's penis. Occasionally they would walk hand in hand while they were bringing out their wet sheets to dry. Sol also appeared to spend some time with a much younger boy and once during a movie they were seen sitting with their arms around each other.

Although he was by far the best athlete in the bunk, Sol behaved overly concerned whenever he made an error. He did not appear to be so disturbed when the errors were made by others. Whenever a game was lost he would take the attitude that the fault was largely his. On one occasion when asked by another camper why he attended JBG, Sol stated he was not sure but he thought it was because he fought with his younger brother.

In the fall when Sol returned to activity group therapy, he was nearly twelve years of age. The group now had a different therapist.[1] Sol and Ray were in front of the building early for the first group session. The therapist indicated that he wanted to buy some refreshments for the "club" and asked if they cared to come along. Sol seemed pleased. He said later, speaking to Ray, "This year's refreshments are better than last year's." Ray said, "No, they're about the same." Sol asked for airplane models. He said that they had these last year and commented that he hoped none of the other members would come so that they could have all the refreshments for themselves. Sol asked the therapist to open some cupboards that did not belong to his group. When the therapist explained this to Sol, Sol complained in a whining somewhat angry tone.[2] He asked then if he could have all the model airplanes and when he was told that they belonged to the club as a whole, he took several. Ray reminded him to take his share only because others would be coming and Sol returned some of the models.

At about this point in the session Jules entered. Sol did not greet him. Jules commented: "Same room, but there's a new hockey board." He invited Ray to play a game of hockey. While the two were playing, he spoke about the things they did last year, how destructive they were, how they set fires, painted the walls, ran wild on the train. As Jules was talking, Sol picked up a saw, and cut at a workbench. With the drill, he began to drill holes in the wall. He

---

[1] Changing the therapist and group personnel is part of the therapeutic technique in activity group therapy. This gives each child an opportunity for making new adjustments and testing themselves in new relations.

[2] This was a test in "frustration tolerance" to which children in these groups are subjected as therapy progresses.

threw a piece of wood at the wall and as he did this, looked in the direction of the therapist out of the corner of his eye.

Sol then asked the therapist when they could eat. When he was told it was up to the "club" to decide, the three rushed to the refreshment table with a yell. At the table Jules again started a discussion about last year and "all the fun" they had had. Ray made some comment that "Murray [their previous therapist] got the can because of all our destructiveness." Sol began spilling a little of his soda. All laughed. He then stood up on a chair and threw small pellets of pretzels into his soda glass, yelling, "bombs away!" The other two joined him roaring with laughter.

Refreshments over, Sol picked up a hammer and said he was going to break in the walls. Jules said he better not and asked him to play hockey instead. In playing the game, Sol began to strike with the hockey stick aggressively at the table and wall.

When the session was over, the boys and therapist walked toward the train. Jules asked what kind of job the therapist had during the day and what kind of people did this type of work (group therapy). He laughed, answering his own question, "You must be a banker." Sol asked the therapist whether one had to graduate high school to do this work. Jules said this was a personal question and the therapist didn't have to answer. Sol asked if the therapist graduated public school yet. At this all the boys roared with laughter. Sol then talked about the previous therapist. He said that he was the kind of person who would sit around the table and a quiet smile would play on his face. The one thing that bothered Sol about him was "We never knew whether he planned to kill us or to love us." There was further discussion among the three about the kind of personality that was needed to do a job like this. Sol said that one had to be "a person of steel" in order to sit there and take their destructiveness. Jules said, "No, you don't have to be made of steel. All you need is to be able to sit quiet and not be upset as clay goes flying through the air." On leaving, Sol said good-by to the therapist in a friendly manner.

He came regularly and early for nearly all sessions thereafter. At first he messed with paint, splashing it over the table, the chairs and himself with no apparent guilt or anxiety. He painted his name on the walls saying, "This should be here forever," and initiated other aggressive and regressive activities of a similar nature. In one session he stopped up the water in the toilet bowl so that the water overflowed. At the refreshment table he often acted messily. One activity in which he took particular delight was to shake the soda bottle while holding his finger over it so that when released, the soda spurted out splashing over the room. At one session he shouted that this was his "wee-wee" as the soda spread over the room.

He continued to be interested in the cupboards of other groups and on occasion would pry them open. He would sometimes complain that other groups had more and better materials than his. In discussing the group with other members he repeated his preference for the present group (which consisted of five instead of eight members), because there were fewer members than the year before; and frequently argued this point with some of the others who preferred a larger group. Whenever he was alone with the therapist, he expressed pleasure because "now I can have more of the refreshments." He often checked to see that the new therapist gave the group exactly what the former had given. For example, he checked on the expenditure for refreshments and complained that the group did not go on as many trips. When the group did go on a trip, he carefully calculated the cost for each member and compared it with the costs of the previous year.

His characteristic distrust of and shyness with the therapist diminished. He made free contact and spoke in a spontaneous manner. Once he said, "I wish my mother and father could see how this club works." Sol's infantile speech mannerisms and whining disappeared. His conversations began to contain many sexual innuendos. He sang "It takes Two to Tango" and once when asked how old he was, he pointed to his pants zipper, saying, "Take a look at this and see how old I am."

He spent a good part of his time making useful objects and in the second year, he made a large book shelf, a boat, a number of airplane models and bookends. He took these objects home. Sol enjoyed the group. Not only was this evident in his attitude and manner but also in the fact that he attended twenty-one out of twenty-nine sessions. Throughout his experience in activity group therapy, Sol revealed sibling rivalry and a certain suspiciousness of the therapist. In the permissive atmosphere of the activity group, he found himself able to express these feelings freely in action and words. He felt free to regress to infantile wetting and smearing activities since he did not experience retaliation for his behavior. As a result, he had less inner hostility as well as less need to project these feelings. His trust in the therapist became markedly increased.

Encopresis completely disappeared. Only occasionally would enuresis occur in the face of anxiety-producing situations such as confirmation and in isolated instances after harshness by his parents. Both parents reported a new ease and friendliness with adults on Sol's part which contrasted sharply with his prior aloofness and distrust. The father described an increased frustration tolerance on Sol's part, noting that incidents which would have provoked temper tantrums before were now accepted by him calmly. Improved school adjustment was noted, with Sol having better relationships with teachers with whom he previously fought.

Two months before the end of the season, it was necessary to transfer the group to which Sol belonged to another therapist. Sol adapted well to this change with a new and strange adult. The third therapist described that from the beginning, Sol was at ease and got along well with him and with the other members of the group. He was cooperative with and friendly toward the therapist and did not seem at all disturbed. His behavior and personality, the therapist said, "would not attract attention in any group of children on the street or on a playground." He stressed the boy's friendliness and cooperativeness. Periodic follow-up interviews with Sol confirmed these changes in the boy: there was a spontaneity, a friendliness and relaxation which was in marked contrast to his original reactions characterized by passivity, reluctance, unresponsiveness to questions with an evident effort at being noncommital. He initiated talk about the group, how he liked it, his liking for the "leader," and discussed his free-time activities.

The impression Sol made during the follow-up interview two years after closing out of the group (three years after the parents' termination of group guidance) was reported on pp. 184-185. It is evident that he held the changes he had sustained in treatment, as the parents held theirs. As we review Sol's development, we find that while resisting his parents, Sol also submitted to and was afraid of them when he first came to us. This is clearly shown by the boy's attitude toward the therapist. He was first suspicious of the therapist, then challenged him by committing unacceptable acts and by acting out aggression. At the same time he was polite, well-dressed, well-mannered and seemingly submissive. This pattern he had lived out also in the family setting. He was disobedient to his parents in their presence, but discharged his responsibilities when they were not there. These two opposing trends in his personality had been resolved to a great extent, so that the more constructive of the two had taken precedence.

Sol began his career in the group by presenting a façade of maturity and constructiveness which soon gave way to his real self. He tentatively acted in an aggressive, provocative manner when he shot off his cap pistol during an early session. Later he was more definitely defiant when he set fires with the other boys and participated in various boisterous activities, finally reaching a point where he wrote profane words on the walls and used profane language. Although diffident and afraid of accustomed punishment, the therapist described the boy's elation and excitement when he took part in a clay battle at an early stage of treatment. We also see him growing less focused and less directed in his occupations as the sessions progress. Such aggressiveness when not punished becomes acceptable to the ego and produces several effects. One is decrease of anxiety which always accompanies guilt feelings and expectation of punishment as a result of aggression. The other is that the ego accepts this infantile behavior. Still another is that the chasm between the actual personality of the child and his "ego ideal" is reduced. The motivation derived from secondary gains (attention from and irritation by adults) is no longer available, since the group therapist and the group accept this negativism. Acceptance of behavior represents love to the child. Maturity therefore is an inevitable consequence in such a setting. The id, ego and superego become more harmonized.

In the past Sol responded to the pressure of his impulses chiefly because his ego was not strong enough to restrain them. At the same time, his guilt feelings resulting from superego demands and his fear of punishment caused anxiety. These destructive contending forces no longer existed and we can understand why the integration of his personality occurred.

We also observe very important changes in Sol's object relationships. His original distrust and fear of the therapist, which was a displacement from his parents, have gradually given way. This made it possible for him to relate more freely to the other children as well. He was tense and stiff when in the proximity of the therapist or when he found it necessary to speak to him. He even became frightened when the therapist attempted to praise his work. Having been accustomed to negative and punitive acts, the boy was unable to accept a positive approach from an adult. This took a considerable time to correct, and ease in relationships with an adult finally emerged.

When the therapist asked Sol to play a game with him on the second trip, Sol was visibly pleased by this attention, having been singled out by the therapist as a favorite child, as it were. When the therapist actually gave him the candy that another boy had presented to him, Sol felt sufficiently friendly and warm to smile and wave as the train was leaving the station. In a sense this may be considered the *critical event* in this boy's therapy. The working through of his basic distrust and fear of adults is the apex of the treatment process with such a patient, and fairly rapid improvement after this was noticeable. Sol became freer in his conversation with the boys, participated with them first in a quiet, constructive way, and even grew friendly enough to take a groupmate to the bus though it was out of his way. In the past the boy's ego energies were consumed with dealing with his aggressions, conflicts, and preoccupations with his problems and worries. Now this quantum of ego energies was freed for personality enhancement.

While on the trips he was disconsolate and helpless when his hat was being tossed about, but he was gradually accepted and no longer the object of ridicule. He became an expert in constructing airplane models and the boys turned to him for help, which changed his status, his growing sense of inner power, and corrected his *self-image* from a weak, inadequate, unloved person to a strong, desired and accepted individual. Another factor that operated in the improvement of this boy was that he was able to act out his urethral fixations. This was apparent by the way he poured water on the fire in a slow, steady stream, instead of splashing it as did the other boys, and in the delight he took in making paint ooze down the walls. These had a libidinal tinge and his preoccupation in this area was further revealed by his persistent, and what seems to be compulsive, investigation of the contents of the cupboards. This can be viewed as his need for sexual enlightenment and perhaps his fantasies concerning his parents' bedroom and bathroom activities.

The few episodes of sex play with another boy at camp were obviously of a passing significance, not uncommon for boys in early adolescence, though for a time it received our closest attention. We do know, however, that his sexual interest as revealed in the group by profanities and in the manner in which he played with the soda bottles suggested seminal emission more than urination. This acting out was also dropped, but we do not doubt that there remained in this boy a neurotic residue which he may or may not be able to deal with, and to function to his maximum potentials, Sol may need psychotherapy later. It is our feeling, however, that he will be able to function as adequately as the average person.

The point must be emphasized that improvement in this boy would not have been so rapid or as effective without the altering of the relationships in the family and without changes in the parents' attitudes toward Sol and their treatment of him.

Index

Abel (Bible), 194
Acting out, 69, 88, 157, 318, 328
Aggression, 71, 88, 127, 157, 250, 302, 314, 318, 323-324, 326; *see also* Anger, Hostility
Albert family, 174
Allen family
  Mrs. Allen, 238-243
  son, 238-242
  daughter, 238, 240
Anger, 80, 144, 206, 245, 272; *see also* Aggression, Hostility
Anxiety, 19, 24-25, 53, 66, 70-72, 78, 81, 85, 151, 162, 165, 167-168, 179, 191-192, 204, 206, 210, 212, 222-223, 226, 231, 245, 247, 255, 258, 269-270, 281, 300-302, 305, 312, 314, 316, 320, 323, 327
  avoidance, 58
  castration, 70, 255
  see also Fear
Arthur family
  Mr. Arthur, 91, 93
  Mrs. Arthur, 90-94, 228-229
  son, 90-93, 228-229
  daughter, 91, 228
Ash family
  Mr. Ash, 118-119, 150
  Mrs. Ash, 117-120, 134, 136, 142, 144-152, 214-215, 220-221
  son, Alfred, 117-120, 136, 144-146, 149-150, 221
  younger sons, 119, 215, 221

Barshay family, 244

Benson family, 224-225
Berk family, 204
Bernheim family
  Mrs. Bernheim, 85-90, 207-209
  son, Daniel, 85-90
Black family
  Mr. Black, 46-52, 54-56
  Mrs. Black, 51, 54, 55
  son, Sam, 49-51, 54
  daughter, 51
Brooklyn Bureau of Social Service, ix
Buckmueller, A. D., ix
Broom family, 107-108
Brown family, 97

Cain (Bible), 194
Castration, *see* Anxiety
Charles family
  Mr. Charles, 208
  Mrs. Charles, 208-210, 226-228
  daughter, 208-210
Childbirth pain, 40
Child Guidance League, ix
Child Study Association of America, ix
Children, Childhood
  crying in, 10, 33, 136
  development, 23-25, 135-136, 244
  eating difficulties of, 79-80, 158, 190, 199, 269-270, 273
  guidance with, *see* Guidance, child
  handicapped, 258-260
  psychotic, 260-262
  school difficulties of, 92-93, 98-101, 103, 107, 109-110, 123, 147, 153-154, 159, 165, 171, 239-241